MW00654167

GALATIANS

Brazos Theological Commentary on the Bible

GALATIANS

KATHRYN
GREENE-McCREIGHT

Brazos Press
a division of Baker Publishing Group
Grand Rapids, Michigan

© 2023 by Kathryn Greene-McCreight

Published by Brazos Press
a division of Baker Publishing Group
www.brazospress.com

Printed in the United States of America

Library of Congress Cataloging-in-Publication Data
Names: Greene-McCreight, Kathryn, 1961– author.
Title: Galatians / Kathryn Greene-McCreight.
Description: Grand Rapids, Michigan : Brazos Press, a division of Baker Publishing Group, [2023] | Series: Brazos theological commentary | Includes bibliographical references and index.
Identifiers: LCCN 2022035324 | ISBN 9781587431449 (cloth) | ISBN 9781493438471 (ebook) | ISBN 9781493438488 (pdf)
Subjects: LCSH: Bible. Galatians—Commentaries.
Classification: LCC BS2685.53 .G74 2023 | DDC 227/.407—dc23/eng/20220902
LC record available at https://lccn.loc.gov/2022035324

Baker Publishing Group publications use paper produced from sustainable forestry practices and post-consumer waste whenever possible.

23   24   25   26   27   28   29   7   6   5   4   3   2

With gratitude for my teachers

Brevard S. Childs (1923–2007)
Hans W. Frei (1922–1988)
George A. Lindbeck (1923–2018)
J. Louis Martyn (1925–2015)

May light perpetual shine upon them.

CONTENTS

ACKNOWLEDGMENTS

Thanks to all those who have shared exegetical insight, wise counsel, technical support, and friendship especially in these days of COVID-19 lockdown: Awet Andemichael, Phil Cary, Rick Elphick, Suzanne Estelle-Holmer, Karin Fransen, Gary Green, Matt Klemm, Michelle Knight, Cathie Lutter, Joe Mangina, Grace McCreight, Noah McCreight, Adam Michaele, Dave Nelson, the New Haven Theological Discussion group, Ephraim Radner, Rusty Reno, Peter Rodgers, Bill Rowley, the saints at St. John's Episcopal Church in New Haven, Eric Salo, Jamie Smith, Katherine Sonderegger, Kendall Soulen, Michael Tessman, and Ming Tseng.

My deepest thanks go to Matthew McCreight, whose love has sustained me in so many ways and through so very much.

All errors are my responsibility alone.

SERIES PREFACE

Near the beginning of his treatise against gnostic interpretations of the Bible, *Against Heresies*, Irenaeus observes that scripture is like a great mosaic depicting a handsome king. It is as if we were owners of a villa in Gaul who had ordered a mosaic from Rome. It arrives, and the beautifully colored tiles need to be taken out of their packaging and put into proper order according to the plan of the artist. The difficulty, of course, is that scripture provides us with the individual pieces, but the order and sequence of various elements are not obvious. The Bible does not come with instructions that would allow interpreters to simply place verses, episodes, images, and parables in order as a worker might follow a schematic drawing in assembling the pieces to depict the handsome king. The mosaic must be puzzled out. This is precisely the work of scriptural interpretation.

Origen has his own image to express the difficulty of working out the proper approach to reading the Bible. When preparing to offer a commentary on the Psalms he tells of a tradition handed down to him by his Hebrew teacher:

> The Hebrew said that the whole divinely inspired scripture may be likened, because of its obscurity, to many locked rooms in our house. By each room is placed a key, but not the one that corresponds to it, so that the keys are scattered about beside the rooms, none of them matching the room by which it is placed. It is a difficult task to find the keys and match them to the rooms that they can open. We therefore know the scriptures that are obscure only by taking the points of departure for understanding them from another place because they have their interpretive principle scattered among them.[1]

1. Fragment from the preface to *Commentary on Psalms 1–25*, preserved in the *Philokalia*, in *Origen*, trans. Joseph W. Trigg (London: Routledge, 1998), 70–71.

As is the case for Irenaeus, scriptural interpretation is not purely local. The key in Genesis may best fit the door of Isaiah, which in turn opens up the meaning of Matthew. The mosaic must be put together with an eye toward the overall plan.

Irenaeus, Origen, and the great cloud of premodern biblical interpreters assumed that puzzling out the mosaic of scripture must be a communal project. The Bible is vast, heterogeneous, full of confusing passages and obscure words, and difficult to understand. Only a fool would imagine that he or she could work out solutions alone. The way forward must rely upon a tradition of reading that Irenaeus reports has been passed on as the rule or canon of truth that functions as a confession of faith. "Anyone," he says, "who keeps unchangeable in himself the rule of truth received through baptism will recognize the names and sayings and parables of the scriptures."[2] Modern scholars debate the content of the rule on which Irenaeus relies and commends, not the least because the terms and formulations Irenaeus himself uses shift and slide. Nonetheless, Irenaeus assumes that there is a body of apostolic doctrine sustained by a tradition of teaching in the church. This doctrine provides the clarifying principles that guide exegetical judgment toward a coherent overall reading of scripture as a unified witness. Doctrine, then, is the schematic drawing that will allow the reader to organize the vast heterogeneity of the words, images, and stories of the Bible into a readable, coherent whole. It is the rule that guides us toward the proper matching of keys to doors.

If self-consciousness about the role of history in shaping human consciousness makes modern historical-critical study actually critical, then what makes modern study of the Bible actually modern is the consensus that classical Christian doctrine distorts interpretive understanding. Benjamin Jowett, the influential nineteenth-century English classical scholar, is representative. In his programmatic essay "On the Interpretation of Scripture," he exhorts the biblical reader to disengage from doctrine and break its hold over the interpretive imagination. "The simple words of that book," writes Jowett of the modern reader, "he tries to preserve absolutely pure from the refinements or distinctions of later times." The modern interpreter wishes to "clear away the remains of dogmas, systems, controversies, which are encrusted upon" the words of scripture. The disciplines of close philological analysis "would enable us to separate the elements of doctrine and tradition with which the meaning

2. *Against Heresies* 9.4.

of scripture is encumbered in our own day."[3] The lens of understanding must be wiped clear of the hazy and distorting film of doctrine.

Postmodernity, in turn, has encouraged us to criticize the critics. Jowett imagined that when he wiped away doctrine he would encounter the biblical text in its purity and uncover what he called "the original spirit and intention of the authors."[4] We are not now so sanguine, and the postmodern mind thinks interpretive frameworks inevitable. Nonetheless, we tend to remain modern in at least one sense. We read Athanasius and think of him stage-managing the diversity of scripture to support his positions against the Arians. We read Bernard of Clairvaux and assume that his monastic ideals structure his reading of the Song of Songs. In the wake of the Reformation, we can see how the doctrinal divisions of the time shaped biblical interpretation. Luther famously described the Epistle of James as an "epistle of straw," for, as he said, "it has nothing of the nature of the gospel about it."[5] In these and many other instances, often written in the heat of ecclesiastical controversy or out of the passion of ascetic commitment, we tend to think Jowett correct: doctrine is a distorting film on the lens of understanding.

However, is what we commonly think actually the case? Are readers naturally perceptive? Do we have an unblemished, reliable aptitude for the divine? Have we no need for disciplines of vision? Do our attention and judgment need to be trained, especially as we seek to read scripture as the living word of God? According to Augustine, we all struggle to journey toward God, who is our rest and peace. Yet our vision is darkened and the fetters of worldly habit corrupt our judgment. We need training and instruction in order to cleanse our minds so that we might find our way toward God.[6] To this end, "the whole temporal dispensation was made by divine Providence for our salvation."[7] The covenant with Israel, the coming of Christ, the gathering of the nations into the church—all these things are gathered up into the rule of faith, and they guide the vision and form of the soul toward the end of fellowship with God. In Augustine's view, the reading of scripture both contributes to and benefits from this divine pedagogy. With countless variations in both exegetical

---

3. Benjamin Jowett, "On the Interpretation of Scripture," in *Essays and Reviews* (London: Parker, 1860), 338–39.
4. Jowett, "On the Interpretation of Scripture," 340.
5. *Luther's Works*, vol. 35, ed. E. Theodore Bachmann (Philadelphia: Fortress, 1959), 362.
6. *On Christian Doctrine* 1.10.
7. *On Christian Doctrine* 1.35.

conclusions and theological frameworks, the same pedagogy of a doctrinally ruled reading of scripture characterizes the broad sweep of the Christian tradition from Gregory the Great through Bernard and Bonaventure, continuing across Reformation differences in both John Calvin and Cornelius à Lapide, Patrick Henry and Bishop Bossuet, and on to more recent figures such as Karl Barth and Hans Urs von Balthasar.

Is doctrine, then, not a moldering scrim of antique prejudice obscuring the Bible, but instead a clarifying agent, an enduring tradition of theological judgments that amplifies the living voice of scripture? And what of the scholarly dispassion advocated by Jowett? Is a noncommitted reading—an interpretation unprejudiced—the way toward objectivity, or does it simply invite the languid intellectual apathy that stands aside to make room for the false truism and easy answers of the age?

This series of biblical commentaries was born out of the conviction that dogma clarifies rather than obscures. The Brazos Theological Commentary on the Bible advances upon the assumption that the Nicene tradition, in all its diversity and controversy, provides the proper basis for the interpretation of the Bible as Christian scripture. God the Father Almighty, who sends his only begotten Son to die for us and for our salvation and who raises the crucified Son in the power of the Holy Spirit so that the baptized may be joined in one body—faith in *this* God with *this* vocation of love for the world is the lens through which to view the heterogeneity and particularity of the biblical texts. Doctrine, then, is not a moldering scrim of antique prejudice obscuring the meaning of the Bible. It is a crucial aspect of the divine pedagogy, a clarifying agent for our minds fogged by self-deceptions, a challenge to our languid intellectual apathy that will too often rest in false truisms and the easy spiritual nostrums of the present age rather than search more deeply and widely for the dispersed keys to the many doors of scripture.

For this reason, the commentators in this series have not been chosen because of their historical or philological expertise. In the main, they are not biblical scholars in the conventional, modern sense of the term. Instead, the commentators were chosen because of their knowledge of and expertise in using the Christian doctrinal tradition. They are qualified by virtue of the doctrinal formation of their mental habits, for it is the conceit of this series of biblical commentaries that theological training in the Nicene tradition prepares one for biblical interpretation, and thus it is to theologians and not biblical scholars that we have turned. "War is too important," it has been said, "to leave to the generals."

We do hope, however, that readers do not draw the wrong impression. The Nicene tradition does not provide a set formula for the solution of exegetical problems. The great tradition of Christian doctrine was not transcribed, bound in folio, and issued in an official, critical edition. We have the Niceno-Constantinopolitan Creed, used for centuries in many traditions of Christian worship. We have ancient baptismal affirmations of faith. The Chalcedonian Definition and the creeds and canons of other church councils have their places in official church documents. Yet the rule of faith cannot be limited to a specific set of words, sentences, and creeds. It is instead a pervasive habit of thought, the animating culture of the church in its intellectual aspect. As Augustine observed, commenting on Jeremiah 31:33, "The creed is learned by listening; it is written, not on stone tablets nor on any material, but on the heart."[8] This is why Irenaeus is able to appeal to the rule of faith more than a century before the first ecumenical council, and this is why we need not itemize the contents of the Nicene tradition in order to appeal to its potency and role in the work of interpretation.

Because doctrine is intrinsically fluid on the margins and most powerful as a habit of mind rather than a list of propositions, this commentary series cannot settle difficult questions of method and content at the outset. The editors of the series impose no particular method of doctrinal interpretation. We cannot say in advance how doctrine helps the Christian reader assemble the mosaic of scripture. We have no clear answer to the question of whether exegesis guided by doctrine is antithetical to or compatible with the now-old modern methods of historical-critical inquiry. Truth—historical, mathematical, or doctrinal—knows no contradiction. But method is a discipline of vision and judgment, and we cannot know in advance what aspects of historical-critical inquiry are functions of modernism that shape the soul to be at odds with Christian discipline. Still further, the editors do not hold the commentators to any particular hermeneutical theory that specifies how to define the plain sense of scripture—or the role this plain sense should play in interpretation. Here the commentary series is tentative and exploratory.

Can we proceed in any other way? European and North American intellectual culture has been de-Christianized. The effect has not been a cessation of Christian activity. Theological work continues. Sermons are preached. Biblical scholars produce monographs. Church leaders have meetings. But each dimension of a

---

8. *Sermon* 212.2.

formerly unified Christian practice now tends to function independently. It is as if a weakened army has been fragmented, and various corps have retreated to isolated fortresses in order to survive. Theology has lost its competence in exegesis. Scripture scholars function with minimal theological training. Each decade finds new theories of preaching to cover the nakedness of seminary training that provides theology without exegesis and exegesis without theology.

Not the least of the causes of the fragmentation of Christian intellectual practice has been the divisions of the church. Since the Reformation, the role of the rule of faith in interpretation has been obscured by polemics and counterpolemics about *sola scriptura* and the necessity of a magisterial teaching authority. The Brazos Theological Commentary on the Bible series is deliberately ecumenical in scope because the editors are convinced that early church fathers were correct: church doctrine does not compete with scripture in a limited economy of epistemic authority. We wish to encourage unashamedly dogmatic interpretation of scripture, confident that the concrete consequences of such a reading will cast far more light on the great divisive questions of the Reformation than either reengaging in old theological polemics or chasing the fantasy of a pure exegesis that will somehow adjudicate between competing theological positions. You shall know the truth of doctrine by its interpretive fruits, and therefore in hopes of contributing to the unity of the church, we have deliberately chosen a wide range of theologians whose commitment to doctrine will allow readers to see real interpretive consequences rather than the shadowboxing of theological concepts.

The Brazos Theological Commentary on the Bible endorses a textual ecumenism that parallels our diversity of ecclesial backgrounds. We do not impose the thankfully modest inclusive-language agenda of the New Revised Standard Version, nor do we insist upon the glories of the Authorized Version, nor do we require our commentators to create a new translation. In our communal worship, in our private devotions, and in our theological scholarship, we use a range of scriptural translations. Precisely as scripture—a living, functioning text in the present life of faith—the Bible is not semantically fixed. Only a modernist, literalist hermeneutic could imagine that this modest fluidity is a liability. Philological precision and stability is a consequence of, not a basis for, exegesis. Judgments about the meaning of a text fix its literal sense, not the other way around. As a result, readers should expect an eclectic use of biblical translations, both across the different volumes of the series and within individual commentaries.

We cannot speak for contemporary biblical scholars, but as theologians we know that we have long been trained to defend our fortresses of theological concepts and formulations. And we have forgotten the skills of interpretation. Like stroke victims, we must rehabilitate our exegetical imaginations, and there are likely to be different strategies of recovery. Readers should expect this reconstructive—not reactionary—series to provide them with experiments in postcritical doctrinal interpretation, not commentaries written according to the settled principles of a well-functioning tradition. Some commentators will follow classical typological and allegorical readings from the premodern tradition; others will draw on contemporary historical study. Some will comment verse by verse; others will highlight passages, even single words that trigger theological analysis of scripture. No reading strategies are proscribed, no interpretive methods foresworn. The central premise in this commentary series is that doctrine provides structure and cogency to scriptural interpretation. We trust in this premise with the hope that the Nicene tradition can guide us, however imperfectly, diversely, and haltingly, toward a reading of scripture in which the right keys open the right doors.

R. R. Reno

ABBREVIATIONS

General

→	indicates a cross-reference to within this commentary	MT	Masoretic Text
AT	author's translation	t.	Tosefta
LXX	Septuagint	VG	Vulgate
m.	Mishnah	y.	Jerusalem Talmud

Bible Translations

ASV	American Standard Version	KJV	King James Version
BBE	Bible in Basic English	NET	New English Translation
CJB	Complete Jewish Bible	NIV	New International Version
ESV	English Standard Version	RSV	Revised Standard Version
JANT	Jewish Annotated New Testament	WEB	World English Bible

Bibliographic

ANF   *The Ante-Nicene Fathers: Translations of the Writings of the Fathers Down to A.D. 325.* Edited by Alexander Roberts and James Donaldson. 10 vols. New York: Christian Literature, 1885–1887. Reprint, Peabody, MA: Hendrickson, 1994.

BDAG   Frederick W. Danker, Walter Bauer, William F. Arndt, and F. Wilbur Gingrich. *Greek-English Lexicon of the New Testament and Other Early Christian Literature*. 3rd ed. Chicago: University of Chicago Press, 2000.

CD   Karl Barth. *Church Dogmatics*. 4 vols. Edinburgh: T&T Clark, 1956–1975.

LW   Martin Luther. *Luther's Works*. American edition. Edited by Jaroslav Pelikan, Helmut Lehmann, Christopher Boyd Brown, and Benjamin T. G. Mayes. St. Louis: Concordia; Philadelphia: Fortress, 1955–1986; 2008–.

| NA²⁸ | *Novum Testamentum Graece.* 28th ed. Edited by Barbara Aland et al. Stuttgart: Deutsche Bibelgesellschaft, 2012. | PL | Patrologia Latina [Patrologiae Cursus Completus: Series Latina]. Edited by Jacques-Paul Migne. 217 vols. Paris, 1844–1864. |
| PG | Patrologia Graeca [Patrologiae Cursus Completus: Series Graeca]. Edited by Jacques-Paul Migne. 162 vols. Paris, 1857–1886. | *TDNT* | *Theological Dictionary of the New Testament.* Edited by Gerhard Kittel and Gerhard Friedrich. Translated by Geoffrey W. Bromiley. 10 vols. Grand Rapids: Eerdmans, 1964–1976. |

Old Testament

Gen.	Genesis	Song	Song of Songs
Exod.	Exodus	Isa.	Isaiah
Lev.	Leviticus	Jer.	Jeremiah
Num.	Numbers	Lam.	Lamentations
Deut.	Deuteronomy	Ezek.	Ezekiel
Josh.	Joshua	Dan.	Daniel
Judg.	Judges	Hos.	Hosea
Ruth	Ruth	Joel	Joel
1–2 Sam.	1–2 Samuel	Amos	Amos
1–2 Kgs.	1–2 Kings	Obad.	Obadiah
1–2 Chr.	1–2 Chronicles	Jonah	Jonah
Ezra	Ezra	Mic.	Micah
Neh.	Nehemiah	Nah.	Nahum
Esth.	Esther	Hab.	Habakkuk
Job	Job	Zeph.	Zephaniah
Ps. (Pss.)	Psalm (Psalms)	Hag.	Haggai
Prov.	Proverbs	Zech.	Zechariah
Eccl.	Ecclesiastes	Mal.	Malachi

New Testament

Matt.	Matthew	1–2 Thess.	1–2 Thessalonians
Mark	Mark	1–2 Tim.	1–2 Timothy
Luke	Luke	Titus	Titus
John	John	Phlm.	Philemon
Acts	Acts	Heb.	Hebrews
Rom.	Romans	Jas.	James
1–2 Cor.	1–2 Corinthians	1–2 Pet.	1–2 Peter
Gal.	Galatians	1–3 John	1–3 John
Eph.	Ephesians	Jude	Jude
Phil.	Philippians	Rev.	Revelation
Col.	Colossians		

INTRODUCTION

Paul's letter to the Galatians makes for challenging reading. Scenes open suddenly without introduction; conflicts end with seemingly little resolution; journeys begin without stated intent. Paul's voice changes suddenly: he moves from direct address to indirect discourse, addressing his Galatians and referring to still others. He exhorts, he scolds, he curses, he blesses. Grave disappointments mar relationships; loyalties are tested and crumble; trusted colleagues desert. Literary forms blend: narrative, illustration, virtue and vice lists, exegesis, sacred types. Even the content of Paul's message is hard to pin down.

Therefore, many ways of reading the letter have been suggested over the centuries. The position that has had the greatest staying power in the West is that the letter is about justification by faith, a claim made most forcefully by Martin Luther and his disciples.[1] Galatians has been embraced as a balm for the soul[2] and a proclamation of freedom in Christ.[3] It is seen as a declaration of the continued faithfulness of the God of Israel,[4] a New Testament example of apocalyptic thought,[5] and a voice representing Second Temple Judaism.[6]

---

1. The literature here is too vast to catalog. For a brief introduction to the modern reception, rejection, and defense of Lutheran interpretations of Galatians, see Westerholm, *Perspectives Old and New on Paul*.

2. "I do prefer this book of Martin Luther upon the Galatians (excepting the Holy Bible,) before all the Books that I have ever seen, as most fit for a wounded Conscience." Bunyan, *Grace Abounding to the Chief of Sinners*, in Riches, *Galatians through the Centuries*, 4.

3. See, e.g., Bruce, *Paul*; Harmon, *She Must and Shall Go Free*.

4. Wright, *Paul and the Faithfulness of God*.

5. Martyn, *Galatians*; Gaventa, "Maternity of St Paul."

6. Sanders, *Paul and Palestinian Judaism*; Dunn, *Jesus, the Law, and the Jewish People*; Dunn, *New Perspective on Paul*.

The letter has been read as one of the most anti-Semitic texts in the New Testament, thus an obstacle for post-Holocaust constructive theology[7] and for post-supersessionist Christian theology.[8] It has been read through the lenses of postcolonial theory[9] and gender criticism.[10] By now it is cliché to refer to Paul as the "founder of Christianity."[11] He is not a Christian.[12] He is a "radical Jew."[13]

As for me, two concrete experiences with the letter over the years have led me to read somewhat differently from the above. The first was reading the text closely in the context of a parish Bible study; the second was attempting a gender-neutral translation of the letter. These two experiences opened my eyes to elements I had missed even despite their being so obvious. The Bible study helped me notice the extent of the role that circumcision plays in the letter, and my translation clarified for me the gendered nature of election itself. Both of these elements point to the heart of the letter to the Galatians: covenant election in Christ.

First, my parish Bible study. The participants were intellectually curious and passionate in their study of scripture. Because the group initially seemed overly comfortable with reading Galatians through the lens of the doctrine of justification by faith, I invited a friend and former teacher of mine, Lou Martyn, to present his own approach: Paul's apocalyptic thought. The group's enthusiasm was meager. Instead of being challenged by the lens of apocalyptic, the group expressed their recurring discomfort at Paul's implicit as well as explicit references to circumcision. The only member of the study who did not share their squeamishness was a man who himself had been circumcised on the eighth day. But all of them, including him, were eager to know why Paul cared so much about Galatian foreskins, and what this had to do with the gospel of Jesus Christ.

Why indeed does Paul care so much about the Galatians' foreskins? The Galatians are Gentiles; their males would have retained their foreskins. But

---

7. Cohn-Sherbok, *Holocaust Theology*; Sweeney, *Reading the Hebrew Bible after the Shoah*; Williamson, *Guest in the House of Israel*; Klein, *Anti-Judaism in Christian Theology*; van Buren, *Theology of the Jewish-Christian Reality*.

8. Novak, "Supersessionism Hard and Soft"; Ruether, *Faith and Fratricide*; Soulen, *God of Israel*.

9. Kahl, *Galatians Re-imagined*; Harker, *Colonizers' Idols*.

10. Wiley, *Paul and the Gentile Women*.

11. Luedemann, *Paul, the Founder of Christianity*.

12. While it is obvious that Paul is not a Christian in the fuller ecclesiastical sense of the term, to suggest that Paul did not see himself as a witness to the cross and resurrection of Jesus Christ is a fundamental misreading of his letters.

13. Schoeps, *Paul*; Sandmel, *Jewish Understanding*; Boyarin, *Radical Jew*.

Paul's flock in Galatia has been misled into thinking they need to be circumcised to become Christians. The scriptural requirement for Gentiles who wanted to join the people of Israel stipulated that they submit to conversion rites, one of which was circumcision.[14] But in Galatians, Paul speaks not of conversion of Gentiles to the people of Israel, nor even of Jews to the Jewish Messiah, but only of Gentiles to the body of Christ. Circumcision, the mark of election of the people of Israel, is being imposed on the Galatian Christian converts in error by those whom I will refer to as the Third Party.[15]

Paul uses the noun "circumcision" or its verbal forms explicitly in Galatians at 2:3, 7, 12, again at 5:2–3, 6, 11–12, and again at 6:12–13, 15. However, as early as chapter 1, the controversy about the rite lies just under the surface of Paul's passionate address. Circumcision is the conceptual framework that organizes his descriptions of his mission journeys. The place names of the regions he visits are not simply geographical markers of the stages on his itinerary, but also serve as implicit indicators of the identity of the people to whom he preaches—that is, those who specifically do *not* observe the rite: the Gentiles. In chapter 1, Paul says that his first mission of the one gospel was to Arabia (uncircumcised peoples). In chapter 2, he describes a trip to Jerusalem to meet with the pillars of the church whose mission was to the Jews (circumcised). Yet Peter and James and John commend Paul's mission to the Gentiles (uncircumcised) as equal to Peter's own mission to the Jews (circumcised). In Antioch, Peter (a missionary to the circumcised) eats with Gentiles (uncircumcised). But when people falsely associated with James arrive (circumcised men who impose circumcision on Gentiles), Peter draws back from the Gentiles (uncircumcised).

In Gal. 3 and 4, Paul turns to the Genesis stories about Abraham. That Abraham was uncircumcised in Gen. 15 when the promise was given governs Paul's theological logic. The Galatian Gentiles (uncircumcised) are elect in the promise of Christ, as was Abraham himself, who trusted that promise. This is

---

14. E.g., Gen. 17:10–14; Exod. 12:43–45. In the second century, Rabbi Judah the Prince points to more than this one requirement. *Keritot* 9a (quoted in Novak, *Election of Israel*, 180n60): "Just as your ancestors did not enter the covenant (*nikhnesu la-berit*) except through circumcision, immersion, and being sprinkled with sacrificial blood, so they may not enter the covenant except through circumcision, immersion, and being sprinkled with sacrificial blood" (see also Rabbi Akiva, *Mekilta* Exod. 19:5; Schoeps, *Paul*, 66). There is evidence that Jewish baptism could substitute for circumcision in Gentile conversion (Rabbi Joshua, *Baraita Yebamoth* 46a, cited in Klausner, *From Jesus to Paul*). However, when Paul mentions baptism in Gal. 3:27, it is clearly a Christian rite.

15. Little is known about this faction apart from their activity of circumcising male Gentiles who convert to the messianic movement. See Gal. 1:7–9; 2:4, 13; 5:7, 12.

the "truth of the gospel" that Paul preaches and that is jeopardized in Galatia (2:5, 14)—namely, that election is in Christ apart from circumcision.

The letter's teaching on election follows an elaborate path through further readings from Genesis that focus on the mothers Hagar and Sarah and on their respective sons, Ishmael and Isaac. The Galatians, "born in the ordinary way," are children of the slave woman Hagar, but "as a result of the promise" they are like Isaac, the child of Abraham's wife Sarah.[16] The argument of the letter comes to its apex at 5:1 with Paul's injunction that his converts not submit to the yoke of the law (in Galatians, the word "law" refers to circumcision), after which he turns to the pastoral ramifications in Gal. 5 and 6.

The second observation about the letter should also have been obvious to me, but I stumbled on it only as I tried to render the Greek into gender-neutral English. Because one of the stated goals of the NRSV translation is to "avoid language that might inappropriately suggest limits of gender," I took it as my model.[17] But I found that in Galatians most of the nouns and pronouns associated specifically with the concept of election—son, father, mother, and so on—were stubbornly resistant to gender-neutral translation without sacrificing verbal sense. Because Paul uses these terms in a specifically christological way, my project of inclusivizing biblical language was jeopardized on a theological rather than lexical level. Gender is a nonnegotiable presence even in the famous declaration of Gal. 3:28, where Paul may seem to qualify it, but as I read he ultimately does not.

Then I encountered another unavoidable glitch in my plan to translate the (grammatically gendered) Greek into (nongendered) English: the correspondence between physical gender itself and election. Especially in the allegory of Hagar and Sarah in chapter 4, problems in interpretation arise not from the women's gender roles per se but from the fact that the plot is governed by body parts—namely, reproductive organs. Not only does circumcision as a sign of the covenant draw blood from the foreskins of the sons (here, Isaac and Ishmael), the promise itself comes through the blood and gestation of a specific womb (Sarah's, not Hagar's). While offering nongendered language certainly renders the letter to the Galatians more palatable to my feminist sensibilities, I found that it distorts the plot of Jewish election so central to the letter.

16. "Born in the ordinary way" is Rabbi Jonathan Sacks's rendering of *kata sarka* in Gal. 4:23, while "born as a result of the promise" is his rendering of *di' epangelias* there. Sacks, *Not in God's Name*, 95. See my comments at 4:21–31, where I use his translation.
17. *HarperCollins Study Bible*, xvii.

The specifically gendered focus of election has a corollary: Galatians is so much more about the human body than we are often willing to see— circumcised penises; Abraham's testes; an infertile uterus; a quickened womb; the wounds of Christ on Paul's own body. For a letter often accused of dualism, it in fact presents an anti-gnostic anthropology and thus opens the way for a Chalcedonian Christology. Indeed, the two natures of Christ are expressed most explicitly in the opening verses of chapter 4, the earliest (written) Christian reference to the birth of Jesus and to the mother who bore him. While the letter's focus on circumcision and other matters of gender may be off-putting to the Gentile ear, it insists on the physicality of election in Christ and mitigates any tendency to untether the body of Christ from the story and people of Israel.

This then forces us to see that the letter is ultimately not a theological tract about justification by faith, or any other doctrine for that matter, but is a pastoral response to a deeply fraught intracommunal controversy in which gendered elements of Jewish election are interpreted by Paul in a specifically messianic form. The key pastoral issue in Galatia that develops between the time of Paul's preaching among the Galatians and the subsequent disruption among his congregations is the confusion over the role of circumcision in Christian conversion. During the interval between Paul's leaving the Galatians and his learning of their having abandoned the gospel, the Galatians have been convinced by an unidentified group that in order to become Christians they first must become Jews by undergoing the rite of circumcision. But Peter and the Jerusalem church had agreed that Paul's Gentile mission was not to impose circumcision upon Gentiles converting to Christ. Because the Galatian churches are composed only of Gentiles, Paul turns to the Abraham stories in Genesis, where, as he sees it, Abraham is a Gentile before his covenant election. Paul points out that the scene where Abraham is commanded to circumcise the males in his house in Gen. 17:10–14 is *preceded* by the episode where Abraham trusts the messianic promise and is reckoned righteous (Gen. 15:5–6). Paul wants the Galatians to understand that in Christ they already share the election of Abraham through his promised seed, Jesus Christ, apart from circumcision. This is what Paul means when he speaks of justification by faith in Galatians: the gracious infrasession of the gospel of Jesus Christ to the Gentiles even within the promise to Abraham before the command of the covenant rite.[18]

---

18. For more on my use of the terms "infrasession," "typology," "type/antitype," "universal/particular covenants," and others, see the epilogue below.

GALATIANS 1

Paul's relationship with the Galatian churches had once been strong. He was their founding missionary, and they had welcomed him as a messenger of God.[1] He addresses them as brothers and even as little children with whom he is in childbirth.[2] Yet at times his anger overflows his affection: their former goodwill toward him has soured, and in deserting the gospel of Christ they have also deserted their friend and teacher (4:15). He is frustrated with them, even to the point of fearing that his work among them may have been undone by preachers of a "different gospel."[3] He refers in cursing tones to this Third Party: they are hypocrites (1:8–9; 2:13).

That his churches have caused him great pain is not unique to the Galatian community. Some of his other churches gravely disappoint as well, proclaiming a different Jesus (*allon Iēsoun*), calling on a different Spirit (*pneuma heteron*), preaching a different gospel (*euangelion heteron*).[4] But the conflicted pastoral situation among the Galatians is of a different order: they are a church composed entirely of pagan Gentiles who have been convinced of the error that they must first become Jews in order to become Christians.

Barely upon entering the letter, we hear of the exclusive truth claims of the gospel that Paul had first preached in Galatia. He illustrates his divine commission as apostle to the Gentiles: after encountering Jesus, Paul goes directly to the Gentile territory of Arabia. After three years of mission work among the Gentiles, he heads up to Jerusalem for his first meeting with Peter.

1. *Angelon theou*, 4:14.
2. *Adelphoi*, NRSV "friends," 4:12; 5:11; *tekna mou*, 4:19.
3. See Gal. 1:7–9; 3:4; 4:11; 5:7, 10; 6:12–13.
4. See also 2 Cor. 11:2–4; Phil. 1:15; 3:18; 2 Thess. 2:11.

1:1–2 Paul an apostle—Following his usual style, Paul adapts the stock forms of letter writing in antiquity. He opens with his name and identifies himself, "an apostle" (1:1). He mentions his colleagues, "and all the brothers and sisters who are with me."[5] Paul makes it clear that the letter is not from him alone, but at this point he does not name his companions. Later he will mention two of his coworkers: Barnabas and Titus (2:1). That he has some who are with him may have a corollary: there are some who are against him.

sent . . . through Jesus—Unlike the disciples who lived and traveled with Jesus during his earthly life, Paul first learned of the Lord through the preaching of the church in the gospel that he once found blasphemous and opposed fiercely (1:13, 23).[6] His own apostleship is the result of a direct call from the risen Jesus transforming him from a persecutor into a missionary of the church (1:1–16). Galatians and Acts agree on this.[7] The Lord's appearance to Paul and his commission from the risen Lord authorize his preaching (1:1, 12, 16).[8]

This revelation to Paul is described with great drama in Acts (chaps. 9, 22, and 26), but here in Galatians Paul gives us no details of the experience. Paul's commission is somewhat like Jacob's dream at Bethel: to both men, God appears completely unbidden (Gen. 28:10–22). Both Jacob and Paul are commissioned not as a reward for pious deeds nor in response to prayer but simply to a future vocation. Jacob is given the task of stewarding God's gifts of land and descendants for Israel; Paul is commissioned to preach to the Gentiles.[9]

God the Father—Paul refers to God the Father four times in the greeting of the letter. First, he identifies the Father as the one who raised Jesus from the dead and who sent Paul to the Galatians (1:1). Second, with the Son, the Father is the source of the grace and peace with which Paul greets the Galatians (1:3). Third, it is according to the will of the Father that Jesus gives himself for the sin of the world (1:4). Fourth, Jesus Christ and the Father are the single object (*hō*) of the church's praise forever (1:5) and are of one will in the single

5. This is my adaptation of the verse, adding "sisters" to "brothers" (*adelphoi*) for the sake of inclusivizing. But we should not be misled here; while other Pauline letters do indicate the presence of female coworkers, there is no such evidence in Galatians.
6. See also 1 Cor. 15:9; Phil. 3:5–6; Acts 9:4; 22:4, 7; 26:14.
7. Acts 9:1–19; 22:1–21; 26:2–23; see also 1 Cor. 9:1; 2 Cor. 12:1–10.
8. It is not clear whether Paul is referring multiple times to the same experience or to multiple encounters. See also Eph. 3:3.
9. Gal. 1:1, 12, 16; 2:9; see 1 Cor. 15:8–9.

event of the incarnation, crucifixion, and resurrection. That God is one, Paul knows from his religious heritage (3:20; Deut. 6:4). But he speaks of the God of Jesus Christ in the course of the letter as one God in three persons: Father, Son, and Spirit.[10]

Whereas Paul usually addresses his churches as "saints" (*hagioi*), sanctified in Jesus, and follows with a thanksgiving for them, the pattern changes in Galatians.[11] Here Paul omits the word "saints" and leaves out the conventional thanksgiving section. While he fears that his converts have let themselves be swayed from the truth, he does not hold them alone accountable.[12] The Galatians are simply "the churches" (*ekklēsiae*; literally, "those called out"). Because Galatia was a region, not a single city, there would have been a number of churches there. Even geographically speaking, they are not a unified community.

1:3 grace . . . and peace—The greeting "grace and peace" in Greek looks on the page somewhat like the conventional greeting from ancient Greek letter writing, and Paul attaches a Hebrew salutation. "Greetings" (*chairein*) resembles the word for "grace" (*charis*); Paul replaces the former with the latter, immediately adding a Greek translation of the conventional Hebrew greeting (*shalom*, "peace"): *eirēnē*.[13] While it is true that he greets his congregations with his Greek-plus-Hebrew blessing throughout his letters, the greeting does meet the specific irritant at the center of the pastoral disturbance among the Galatian churches: confusion of the Gentile and Jewish missions and the attendant question of whether converted Gentiles are required to observe the law.

1:4 gave himself for our sins—Jesus's death is on behalf of our sins, *hyper tōn hamartiōn hēmōn*.[14] Paul does not use the word "atonement" nor does he offer any description of the mechanics of the atoning death of Christ, but the detail here that Jesus gave himself for sin clearly points to the atonement.[15] Paul certainly could have made reference to the elaborate atoning sacrifices of the

---

10. Gal. 1:1, 3–4; 3:2, 5, 14; 4:1–7, 29; 5:5, 16, 22, 25; 6:1, 8.
11. See, e.g., Rom. 1:7–8; 1 Cor. 1:2, 4.
12. Gal. 1:6; 3:1, 4; 4:11, 17, 20; 5:2–4, 7.
13. This salutation is Paul's convention (Rom. 1:7; 1 Cor. 1:3; 2 Cor. 1:2; Phil. 1:2; 1 Thess. 1:1; Phlm. 1:3). See also the disputed letters (Eph. 1:2; Col. 1:2b; 2 Thess. 1:2; 1 Tim. 1:2b; 2 Tim. 1:2b; Titus 1:4).
14. Also Rom. 4:25; 5:8, 15–19; 8:3; 2 Cor. 5:21; Titus 2:14; 1 Pet. 2:24; 1 John 4:9.
15. Gal. 4:9, 31; 5:1, 13; see also Rom. 6:6; 8:21.

Hebrew Bible, particularly in Leviticus and Numbers. But here he simply asserts that Christ's death liberates us from our sins from the present evil age. This is the will of both the Father and the Son. The greeting ends with a doxology: we owe praise to "our God and Father," who dwells in glory to the ages of ages.

1:5 Amen—The final word of the greeting section, "amen," also finds its home within the language of Paul's religious upbringing.[16] The word "amen" closes prayers and doxologies throughout the Bible and across the ages for both Christians and Jews. The word is sprinkled throughout Paul's letters and here it turns his greeting into a prayer. The word "amen" will likewise close the entire letter (6:18), making it a long (to be sure, complex) prayer.[17] Paul's pastoral care for the Galatians is evident from the beginning.

In the salutation, Paul has laid out some of the subject matter of the letter: his divine commission; the single atoning act of the Father and the Son at the cross and the resurrection of Christ; the liberating power of Jesus's self-giving death; Paul's own love for and profound disappointment with the Galatians. Paul gives glory to God in doxology, prayer, and blessing before he moves into stern speech. Remarkably, we have not yet encountered the theme of justification by faith.

1:6–7 so quickly deserting—Normally in a letter from the ancient world, indeed in Paul's other letters, the writer details the reasons for his gratitude for the addressees. Such remarks serve the purpose of encouraging the recipients of the letter and strengthening their bond with the writer. The absence of the conventional thanksgiving section in Galatians is especially glaring at this point. Certainly Paul would have had reason to give thanks for the Galatians: when he was first among them, they welcomed him (4:14–15) and he nurtured them (4:19). But now they have strayed from his teaching (1:6) and have turned to following improperly catechized missionaries. He does not give thanks.

astonished—This stock epistolary "astonishment form" emphasizes the impact of the lack of thanksgiving.[18] Paul's reaction to the situation in Galatia tells us that he expected differently of his beloved flock: since his earlier visit,

---

16. Our word "amen" is the English transliteration of the Hebrew word, meaning something like "may it be confirmed."
17. See also Rom. 16:27.
18. On the "astonishment form," see Richards, *Paul and First-Century Letter Writing*, 130.

the Galatians have deserted the gospel. Having been led astray, they no longer obey the truth (5:7, 10). This has happened swiftly and unexpectedly. The sudden betrayal points to how the close relationship they once shared has been broken; the sting he expresses comes only from having been betrayed by those whom he once held dear. The Galatians' abandonment of Christ has transformed them so thoroughly that Paul barely recognizes them.[19] And yet he knows that this is not entirely their fault; he casts blame on the Third Party.[20] If the Galatians' desertion of the gospel were their fault alone, it would primarily be Paul's responsibility because he is the one who first called them in the grace of Christ, and they are his work in the Lord (4:16; 1:6).[21] His passion is that of a father in exhortation, a mother in nurture, a brother in admonition (6:1; 4:1, 9).

What began in the Spirit has ended in the flesh (3:3; 5:19–21). The Galatians have now become like the Israelites who committed apostasy at the foot of Sinai, handing over to Aaron their gold purloined from the Egyptians to be made into gods. While at Sinai it was those from within Moses's flock who sought out their own downfall; in Galatia it is those from without who seek Paul's flock to prey on them. Even though they have aligned with this Third Party, the Galatians still belong to the Lord (1:8–9; 3:27–28) and to him. Nowhere will Paul show himself to have given up on them. He continues to call them "brothers" (3:15; 4:12, 31). He will remind them that they are children of God (3:26); in their baptism they have been clothed with Christ (3:27) and belong to Christ (5:24). Even though they are no longer "running well," Paul has confidence in them in the Lord (5:7, 10).

1:7 another gospel—The noun "gospel" (*euangelion*, "good news") comes from the same root as the Greek verb *euangelizō*, which can be translated into English both as "to preach" and as "to evangelize." Of the thirteen occurrences of the root in Galatians, five appear in these four verses alone (1:6–9). This gospel is true not because it is Paul's but simply because it is the truth: it is eternal and fulfills prophecy (3:6–14; 4:21–31). There can in fact be no false gospel, because the gospel itself defines what is true. But the Third Party confuses the Galatians by proclaiming a message that even they themselves

19. The word translated in the NRSV as "deserting" can also be translated "changing," or "being transferred from one place to another" (BDAG 513).
20. See also 5:10: "Whoever it is that is confusing you will pay the penalty."
21. See also 1 Cor. 9:1.

are not willing to hear or obey. They are hypocrites; they do not even want to follow their own demands of circumcision (6:12; 4:17).

The word "gospel," *euangelion*, is not a Christian innovation but is inherited from the language of the Septuagint; it can be translated literally as "good message." In Isa. 52, the prophet runs over the mountaintop, shouting so the captives can hear the good news: it is not their oppressors who have ultimate power but the God of Israel who is victorious in battle.[22] Like this messenger's good news, the gospel about Christ is an oral, aural, and visual event, openly accessible to all. Even the practice among Paul's churches of reading his letters aloud in their gatherings is an instance of the oral and aural nature of the gospel (Col. 4:16; 1 Thess. 5:27; 2 Thess. 2:15). Not only have the Galatians heard the gospel announced by Paul's voice, they have also seen it publicly exhibited in Paul's wounds (Gal. 3:1, 5; 6:17; see also Rom. 10:17).

some who are confusing you—There are "some" (*tines*) whose goal, according to Paul, is to pervert the gospel of Christ and confuse the Galatians (*tarassontes*; see also 5:10). Apart from Paul's comment about their self-centered motives (4:17), we have no information as to why they engage the Galatians at all. The teaching of those who "confuse" results in spiritual and moral deformity in the Galatian churches (5:16–21; cf. 1 Tim. 6:3).

1:8–9 if anyone proclaims to you a gospel contrary to what you received, let that one be accursed!—This statement foreshadows Paul's rebuke of Peter at Antioch (2:14) and Sarah's sharp command to Abraham (4:20). Here at 1:8–9 Paul curses the Third Party for their interference in the spiritual health of the Galatians, casting an anathema on the false teachers, a pastoral judgment that functions both to exclude those in error and to embrace those who must be corrected.

While the Gospels themselves were not written documents in Paul's day, the traditions about Jesus that eventually found their way into the written texts of the Gospels would certainly have been in oral circulation during the immediate years after Jesus's death, during Paul's Gentile mission. We can safely assume that Paul would have been familiar with at least some of these Jesus traditions. One of these links between Paul's letters and the Jesus traditions is

---

22. "How beautiful upon the mountains are the feet of the messenger [LXX: *euangelizamenou*, "evangelist"] who announces peace, who brings good news [*euangelizamenos*], who announces salvation, who says to Zion, 'Your God reigns'" (Isa. 52:7).

found here in Gal. 1; we will encounter a similar correspondence to the same tradition in Gal. 2, and to others elsewhere.

In Matt. 18 Jesus gives directions on intracommunal disputes, teaching that if one person offends another, the offended individual must first seek redress directly from the one who has offended. If the offender does not attend to the complaint, the offended person is to repeat the communication in front of two or three others; if there is still no reconciliation, the offended party is to go to the church. If there is still no resolution, the church is to treat the offender as a Gentile and tax collector—that is, beyond the pale of the community (Matt. 18:15–17).

This procedure will be borne out in later church tradition. Just one example of this is the sixth-century Anathema I of the Second Council of Constantinople in which a negative statement about proper belief is followed by a positive declaration of doctrine. These sandwich the anathema: "If anyone does not confess that the Father and the Son and the Holy Spirit are one nature . . . let him be anathema . . . for there is one God and Father."[23] Anathema I of Constantinople II anathematizes heresy while embracing those who confess an orthodox doctrine of the Trinity. Paul's anathematizing of the Third Party functions similarly to this; there are boundaries to be maintained. In Matthew, the boundaries are pastoral; in Constantinople II they are doctrinal; for Paul they are both. His own concern for the truth of the gospel among the Galatian churches leads him, with churchly authority, to cut off those who confuse his flock with a false gospel. But a false gospel is by nature a spiritual oxymoron, an empirical impossibility. Anyone who accepts another gospel has already abandoned the Holy Spirit, cursed the Lord Jesus, and cut themselves off from the church.[24]

1:10 If I were still pleasing people, I would not be a servant of Christ— Here Paul turns to more direct reference to his own ministry, underscoring the authenticity of his teaching by its relation to its subject matter: Jesus's revelation to and in him. From this point to the end of chapter 2, Paul will use his own experience in ministry and mission to emphasize the severity of the problem the Galatians are creating for themselves: the falsification of the gospel of Christ and the rupture of his body, the church.

---

23. Leith, *Creeds of the Churches*, 46.
24. See also Gal. 3:3; 5:15; see 1 Cor. 12:3; 16:22.

A trend too broad to catalog has taken Paul's remarks in this section as a defense of his own apostolic authority in light of the threat from opponents.[25] Paul has been read throughout the centuries as motivated by self-defense from his opponents at least as early as Chrysostom.[26] It is clear that in Galatians Paul defends his authority as an evangelist of Jesus Christ. This is also true of the depictions of him in Acts 22–26 that portray him engaging in apologetics and self-defense. But if this is the extent of what we can learn from Paul's self-defense, we overlook the fact that he is motivated by pastoral care and catechesis. He is defending not only the gospel but also his Galatians.

seeking human approval—If Paul were trying to please others, he would be unfaithful in his vocation as pastoral catechist to the Galatians, putting an already fragile community in further jeopardy. But if he were indeed trying to please others, who might these people be? Possibly the Galatians, or the Third Party, or maybe even his former compatriots among the Pharisees. He points out that if he were trying to please them, he would still be instructing the Galatians to observe the rite of circumcision (5:11), but he does not. The "if" of the rhetorical questions in 1:10 are contrary to fact.

Instead, Paul says that his intent is to please Christ, of whom he is a slave (*doulos*; 1:10). Some English translations, the NRSV among them, translate *doulos* as "servant" rather than "slave." If Paul had meant to identify himself as a servant, he had other words he could have used to express this.[27] We lose the force of Paul's self-identification if we translate *doulos* as "servant" in Gal. 1:10 given that the trope of slavery is integral to the identity of the Galatians themselves. Paul identifies them theologically as children of Hagar the slave; the church fathers identified them as Celts who were slaveholders and slave traders (→3:1). Paul identifies himself as Christ's slave in 1:10, a specifically christological relationship (2:19–20; 5:24). Paul's identity in Christ is his pride and reason for boasting (6:13–14). Paul is Christ's slave.

1:11–12 the gospel that was proclaimed by me is not of human origin— Galatians 1:11 pivots the opening of the letter to Paul's teaching: its nature and his reception of the gospel. The two references to the divine nature of Paul's

---

25. See Gal. 2:11–14.
26. Chrysostom (PG 61:613–14). For Reformation and modern sources, see Gaventa, "Galatians 1 and 2," 310n2.
27. E.g., *oiketēs* (Rom. 14:4), *synergos* (1 Cor. 3:9), *hypēretēs* (1 Cor. 4:1), *diakonos* (Phil. 1:1).

teaching point to his having received it through a direct revelation of Jesus Christ (1:12, 16). He purposely avoids the phrase "my gospel," choosing instead a rather clumsy construction: "the gospel [*to euangelion*] which was proclaimed [*to euangelisthen*] by me."[28] His preaching is not "of human origin" (*ouk estin kata anthrōpon*); the singularity and truth of his proclamation are based on its having been divinely revealed. Elsewhere in his letters Paul also speaks of the divine revelation that authorizes his apostolic commission: "Am I not an apostle? Have I not seen [*heoraka*] Jesus our Lord?" (1 Cor. 9:1; cf. 11:23). His statement points to his passive witnessing of something being unfolded: Paul is not dreaming or composing; he is receiving. He is quite clear: the gospel is not his private possession. It is simply the one gospel that is preached by him to the Galatians.

1:12 received it through a revelation—Paul doubles back to his earlier statements about how to discern the authenticity of the gospel. There is no "Paul's gospel message" or "Peter's gospel message." While Paul's mission to the Gentiles is distinct from Peter's mission to the Jews, both proclaim the one gospel revealed by the risen Lord also to Paul. But his point here is that to him, it is revealed; to the Galatians, it is passed down. Paul says that he received the words of institution directly "from the Lord" and he hands this tradition on to the Corinthians (1 Cor. 11:23). This pattern and process of handing down tradition corresponds to both the content of what is passed along as well as the practice of doing so. The gospel is like the water of a bucket brigade, passed along carefully from bearer to bearer lest a precious drop be spilled. Paul has received his bucket of water directly from Jesus.

1:13–14 my earlier life in Judaism—The authorial first-person "I want you to know" of 1:11 now tips into a second-person address, "You have heard, no doubt": we learn something that others have told the Galatians about Paul or that Paul has told them about himself.[29] Paul assumes that the Galatians know about his former life of persecuting the church, and he reminds them that when he turned to Christ, he left behind his religious hostility toward the messianic movement.

---

28. While some letters use the term "my gospel" (Rom. 2:16; 16:25; 2 Tim. 2:8) or "our gospel" (2 Cor. 4:3; 1 Thess. 1:5), this is not the case here. His phrase "the gospel preached by me" is a roundabout way of distinguishing his ministry from the Third Party. See also Gal. 2:5, 14; 3:6–9; 4:27, 30.

29. Roetzel, *Letters of Paul*.

According to Acts, Paul's first reaction to the Jesus movement was a theologically driven violence directed at what he deemed to be a blasphemous threat to his own religious Pharisaic tradition. But from Paul himself we learn few details about the shape of his persecution of the church.[30] Acts paints vivid scenes of this former life, as he went from house to house dragging (Jewish) Christian believers off to prison.[31] Paul is said to have been present at, and consenting to, the stoning of Stephen, the first Christian martyr (Acts 7:54–8:1). In each of the Acts accounts of Paul's conversion, the risen Jesus questions Paul, signaling that Paul's violence toward the church is equal to violence against Jesus himself: "Saul, Saul, why are you persecuting *me*?" (Acts 9:1–19; 22:1–21; 26:2–23).

While in Acts the depiction of the development of the Gentile mission is more complex than in Paul's letters, it is clear from Galatians that Paul understands the Gentile mission as his sole vocation. While Paul's church in Rome is composed of Jews *and* Gentiles, there are in fact no Jews at all among the Galatian churches.[32] Paul was the only Jew among them, and even he is absent as he writes the letter. While there are other Jews whom Paul mentions in the letter, they play no role in the Galatian communities. Barnabas (a Jewish Christian) is present in the scenes at Jerusalem and Antioch in chapter 2, but he has no role in Galatia. Paul also tells of two substantive exchanges with Jewish Christians in chapter 2, again in Jerusalem and Antioch: first with the three pillars and later with Peter alone. But according to the letter, none of them is actually present among the Galatian churches. Key to these scenes is the fact that they are initiated by controversies surrounding Gentile circumcision, the pastoral occasion of the letter.

What is this "Judaism" to which Paul refers here in 1:13–14? Research on Second Temple Judaism has shown that translating the word "Judaism" (*Ioudaismos*) is more complicated than previously assumed.[33] There were many streams of Judaism in Paul's day, and his messianic mission to the Gentiles was one among them.[34] The word *Ioudaismos* occurs only twice in the New

---

30. In addition to Gal. 1:13, see 1 Cor. 15:9; Phil. 3:6; 1 Tim. 1:13.

31. Acts 8:3; 9:1–19; 22:3–21; 26:9–20.

32. Martyn, *Galatians*, 16n11, 40n70. Martyn suggests that the phrase "works of the law" in Galatians (2:16; 3:2, 5, 10, 12) refers to the practice of Gentile circumcision.

33. Other translations proposed for the term *Ioudaismos* are "Jewishness" (Cohen, *Beginnings of Jewishness*, 31), "occupation," "pattern of activity," or even "Judaization" (Novenson, "Paul's Former Occupation," 25, 35).

34. The classic texts on Second Temple Judaism and the New Testament are Dunn, *Jesus, the Law, and the Jewish People*; Sanders, *Paul and Palestinian Judaism*; Sanders, *Paul, the Law, and the Jewish People*.

Testament, and both are found here in 1:13–14. It appears in Second Temple literature in reference to the kind of behavior that Paul describes here, before his encounter with the risen Christ.[35] While the term *Ioudaismos* may not refer to any single religious expression, and no matter how diverse Judaism was in his day, Paul nevertheless assumes that the word points to a sufficiently identifiable form that defines his earlier religious life. To this reality Paul himself gives the name "Judaism" (*Ioudaismos*).[36] For Paul this is a cogent phenomenon of his former religious behavior in which he once excelled but which he now has left behind for Christ. This "Judaism" will be shown in chapter 2 to be a phenomenon commonly acknowledged by both Paul and Peter to such an extent that they can have a heated disagreement about it, specifically with regard to the Gentile mission and its relation to "Judaism." Paul's understanding of his former religious tradition has a coherent integrity and shape, even if it does not overlap entirely with the Judaisms of the first century, as well as the twenty-first century. This poses an important question that cannot be fully addressed by simply comparing Paul's thought against the backdrop of the many and various sects of Judaism of his day.

Our modern terms "Christianity," "Jew," and "Christian" are, like the term "Judaism," difficult to use in translating Paul's letters.[37] To contemporary ears, the terms "Jew" and "Christian" point to distinct forms of religious belief and life, but the fact that the earliest Christian communities were composed of Jews alone complicates this further.[38] In Paul's day, the church had not become the largely Gentile phenomenon it is today (there had been as of yet no "parting of the ways"), and there was no Christian church in the full ecclesial sense of the term.[39] However, Paul clearly sees the gospel as a coherent message that shapes individuals and communities in a Christ-centered identity that can be reasonably called "Christian."

Even while they may be somewhat anachronistic here, the terms "Gentile Christian" and "Jewish Christian" are helpful for a close reading of the letter

35. See 2 Macc. 2:21; 8:1–7; 14:38; 4 Macc. 4:26 and in a late Roman inscription (Barclay, *Paul and the Gift*, 357n20). Paul's zeal may fall into the category represented by the behavior of Judas Maccabeus (Novenson, "Paul's Former Occupation," 37).

36. See Schwartz, "How Many Judaisms Were There?"; Novenson, "Paul's Former Occupation," 28.

37. Paula Fredriksen suggests, but ultimately rejects, the terms "Christian movement" or "nascent Christianity" to refer to gospel communities in general. Fredriksen, "Judaism," 236n248, 248n48, 255.

38. Thiessen, *Paul and the Gentile Problem*, 14.

39. See Dunn, *Jews and Christians*; Robinson, *Ignatius of Antioch*; Becker and Reed, *Ways That Never Parted*.

to the Galatians. I use these terms to distinguish those to whom Paul preaches (Gentile Christians) from those to whom Peter preaches (Jewish Christians).[40] This distinction is integral to the subject matter of Galatians. Paul writes about the relationship between his own mission to the Gentiles and Peter's mission to the Jews explicitly in chapter 2 and implicitly throughout the letter. They are identifiably distinct Christian missions, and yet there is one single economy of God: grace in Christ to the elect (Jews) and to the non-elect (Gentiles) alike.

Paul's move from what he calls "Judaism" to what we call "Christianity" could be described as a move from one of the various streams of Judaism associated with covenantal nomism to another. This is the view offered by much of the new perspective.[41] However, it is clear that Paul did not see it this way. His new religious life according to his letters and Acts involves a fundamental break with whatever he saw to be his former life "in Judaism." Thus he can say that, while he was "advancing in Judaism," even his significant progress did not bring him to any dawning realization that the promise to Abraham was Christ. According to Paul, there was no development of doctrine, no step-by-step "coming around" to another branch of Judaism. There was only a self-manifestation of Christ to him and in him.

The discourse now moves into a fuller narrative that leads the reader forward by means of temporal and coordinating conjunctions that direct the episodic accounts toward chapter 2.[42]

---

40. Alternatives have been suggested. E.g., Martyn uses the term "Christian Jew" since the earliest Christian communities were Jewish sects ("Law-Observant Mission," 350n6; *Galatians*, 125n120). But as I see it, Paul understands his own religious identity to be grounded solely in Christ, and therefore the emphasis falls on the noun "Christian." The adjectives are "Jewish" and "Gentile"; they thus precede and modify the noun "Christian."

41. The term "new perspective" originates with James D. G. Dunn's remark about E. P. Sanders's groundbreaking work on Second Temple Judaism. Dunn's comment is itself anticipated by Krister Stendahl (*Paul among Jews and Gentiles*, 126–33), who himself noted the theological import of the research. Sanders's term "covenantal nomism" describes what he sees to be the core concepts of Palestinian Judaism in Paul's day: "(1) God has chosen Israel and (2) given the law. The law implies both (3) God's promise to maintain the election and (4) the requirement to obey. (5) God rewards obedience and punishes transgression. (6) The law provides for the means of atonement, and atonement results in (7) maintenance or re-establishment of the covenantal relationship. (8) All those who are maintained in the covenant by obedience, atonement, and God's mercy belong to the groups which will be saved. An important interpretation of the first and last points is that election and ultimately salvation are considered to be by God's mercy rather than human achievement." Sanders, *Paul and Palestinian Judaism*, 422.

42. Gal. 1:15, 18, 21; 2:1, 7, 9, 11, 14.

1:15 set me apart before I was born—Paul presents his own call in the imagery of the prophetic calling of Isaiah and Jeremiah. Like these prophets, Paul has been set apart for this vocation before he was born.[43] He understands his own mission as witnessing to Jesus among the Gentiles, the form of prophetic task assigned to him under the providence of God even before his birth.

1:16 to reveal his Son to me—Before his conversion, Paul must have had more than meager contact with the fledgling messianic movement: he was familiar enough with it to find it so troublesome that he wanted to destroy it. Even so, Paul is not converted by the preaching of the apostles; rather, he turned to Christ as the result of a revelation (1:12, 16). We do not hear what the content of the revelation is; Paul makes clear only that the revelation was Jesus himself.

any human being—After God revealed his Son to and in Paul with the commission to preach among the Gentiles, Paul "did not confer with any human being"—literally, "flesh and blood" (*sarki kai haimati*). He uses this same phrase in 1 Cor. 15:50 and Eph. 6:12 to refer to humankind in general. It is also found in Jesus's response to Peter's confession at Caesarea Philippi: "Blessed are you, Simon son of Jonah! For flesh and blood has not revealed this to you [*hoti sarx kai haima ouk apekalypsen soi*], but my Father in heaven" (Matt. 16:16–17). Just as Peter's confession was not elicited through catechesis (it seems to have caught even Jesus off guard) but by a revelation, Peter's confession and Paul's conversion lead to their respective vocations: Peter preaches to the Jews, and Paul to the Gentiles. Paul may have heard the story of Peter's confession in the Jesus traditions, or Peter may have shared the story himself with Paul during their two weeks together in Jerusalem (Gal. 1:18–20). The church has seen these two events—Peter's confession and Paul's conversion—as a set of parentheses of sorts around the unity of the mission of the one gospel. The conviction of this fundamental unity is illustrated in the discernment implicit in the twentieth-century decision to sandwich the Week of Prayer for Christian Unity between the Feast of the Confession of St. Peter (January 18) and the Feast of the Conversion of St. Paul (January 25; →2:11–15).

43. "Before I formed you in the womb [*en koilia*] I knew you, / and before you were born [*ek mētras*] I consecrated you; / I appointed you a prophet to the nations [Gentiles]" (Jer. 1:5); "I will give you as a light to the nations [Gentiles], / that my salvation may reach to the end of the earth" (Isa. 49:6).

1:17 Arabia—After his commission by Jesus, Paul does not first go to "those who were already apostles before me" (*tous pro emou apostolous*). He acknowledges that there are other apostles with greater authority than his. While in Gal. 1:15 he describes himself as commissioned from before his birth, in 1 Cor. 15:8 he says that he is the least of the apostles and that he brings up the rear of the line.[44] While Paul admits that he knows that the other apostles are associated with the Jerusalem church, he gives no reason as to why he does not go up to meet with them before going to Arabia to preach there (1:17–18; 2:1).

This itinerary seems curious: Why Arabia? Later in Galatians, Paul will mention Arabia in his description of Sarah's Gentile slave, Hagar (4:25). Jerome points out the significance of the link between the place-name Arabia here in chapter 1 and Paul's later use of the character Hagar in chapter 4: "[Paul] teaches that the Old Testament, that is, the son of the bondwoman, was established in Arabia. And so, as soon as Paul believed, he turned to the Law, the Prophets, and the symbols of the Old Testament that were then lying in obscurity and sought in them the Christ whom he was commanded to preach to the Gentiles."[45] This is an interesting observation, but Jerome disregards the fact that, for Paul, Hagar represents *neither* covenant. As will become clear in the allegory of Sarah and Hagar in chapter 4, Hagar represents the gospel to the Gentiles, not the "Old Testament." Rather, she is the church of Gentile Christians—that is, the Galatians.

Why then does Paul go to Arabia? If we look to the Old Testament and to Jewish sources, we find that Arabia is the place-name used to refer to the general region of the Nabatean Kingdom. This area was inhabited by ethnic groups who, according to the genealogies in Gen. 25, were most closely related to the people of Israel among any of its Gentile neighbors.[46] Abraham was the grandfather of its namesake, Nabaioth, the firstborn of Ishmael (Gen. 25:13); Arab tribes traced their religious lineage to Abraham through Ishmael (Hagar's son). And while Ishmael himself is not specifically named in the New Testament, his role in Gal. 4 will be determinative in the allegory.

Another significant point about Paul's trip to Arabia is that the inhabitants of Nabatea were among the least hellenized peoples in the ancient Near East,

---

44. *Eschaton*, "the last after which there is no other." BDAG 314.

45. Jerome, *Epistle to the Galatians* 1.1.17 (PL 26:328c–329a), translation in Edwards, *Galatians, Ephesians, Philippians*, 13.

46. See Josephus, *Jewish Antiquities* 1.221, 239; Bauckham, *Jewish World*, 260. I am indebted to this masterful study.

the province of Nabatea not having been annexed by the Roman Empire until the early second century.[47] In "Arabia," the use of Greek is not significantly attested; the common secular and religious language of the day would have been Nabatean.[48] Like the Nabateans, the Galatians are unhellenized; unlike the Nabateans, the Galatians have no Abrahamic heritage at all apart from Christ. But both the Galatians and the Nabateans of Arabia share the identity of "Ishmael": both groups are Gentiles in need of the good news of Christ. Paul's mission to those in Arabia thus sets the stage for his ministry among the Galatians.

The itinerary itself continues to highlight the prophetic nature of Paul's mission to the Gentiles.[49] The prophecies in Isa. 60 and 66 name the Gentile tribes of northwestern Arabia as among those who will bring eschatological blessings to Zion: "The wealth of the nations shall come to you" (Isa. 60:5–7; cf. 66:12). In the last days the "outcasts of Israel" from among these tribes in the diaspora will stream in eschatological return to the Holy City (Isa. 11:11–12; 60:4–9; 66:18–20). Among the first of those nations ascending to Zion mentioned in Isa. 60:6–7 are the tribes of northwestern Arabia, children of Abraham through his wife Keturah (Gen. 25:1), including Midian (Exod. 2:15), Ephah (Gen. 25:4), and Sheba (Gen. 10:7; 25:3). Isaiah mentions also the tribes of southern Arabia, Kedar and Nabaioth (Isa. 21:13–17).[50] Paul's own Isaianic mission to the Gentiles begins specifically here in Arabia.[51]

1:18–19 up to Jerusalem—"Then" (*epeita*) occurs here at 1:18 and again at 2:1, marking Paul's first and second journeys to Jerusalem. These each bookend a "then" at 1:21 that marks another mission in Syria and Cilicia. The resulting pattern is a back-and-forth journeying between Gentile mission and the Jerusalem church that will eventually lead us to Antioch in chapter 2. This is significant: the itinerary beginning in Arabia in 1:17 prepares us for its goal in Antioch with the controversy specifically over the circumcision of Gentile converts to Christianity.

The use of the verb "to go up" (*anēlthon*) to Jerusalem in 1:18 and again in 2:1 evokes the Jerusalem pilgrimage festivals of Pesach (Passover), Shavuot

---

47. Bauckham, *Jewish World*, 261.
48. Bauckham, *Jewish World*, 261, citing Millar, *Roman New East*, 401–7.
49. See also Isa. 49:1–6.
50. See also Jer. 49:28–29; Gen. 25:13. Bauckham, *Jewish World*, 261.
51. Matt. 4:16; Luke 2:32; John 1:4; 3:19; 8:12; 9:5; 12:46.

(Pentecost), and Succoth (Booths) with the singing of the joyful Psalms of
Ascent (Pss. 120–134). Pilgrims go "up" to Jerusalem; even if they come from
the north, there is no "descending" to Jerusalem. The holy city is the theological and spiritual crown of the land, the pinnacle to which pilgrims ascend.
But pilgrims are not to come empty-handed; they bring an offering (Deut.
16:16–17; see also Isa. 66:20). Paul's journey "up to Jerusalem" is itself such
a pilgrimage. His own goal, though, is not the temple but the Jewish church
in Jerusalem, the temple's antitype.[52]

After his conversion and commission but before his proclamation of the
gospel to the Gentiles, Paul had no pilgrimage offering to bring up to Jerusalem
to lay at the feet of the pillars there. But, after his three years of preaching in
Arabia and Damascus, he now bears such a gift: abundant Gentile praise.[53] The
Gentiles' participation in the joy of the gospel is itself Paul's own pilgrimage
offering. He has not neglected his religious duties to "the present Jerusalem"
(*tē nyn Ierusalēm*; 4:25), the type and sacrament of "the heavenly Jerusalem"
(*hē anō Ierusalēm*; 4:26).

to visit Cephas—The verb "to visit" (*historēsai*) derives from the same root
as does our noun "history" and bears the connotation of inquiring information
in order to learn something. While Paul says that he has received the gospel
directly from Jesus Christ ("through a revelation," 1:12), he does not disregard
Peter. Despite Paul's remark that he did not go immediately to Jerusalem to
visit Peter after his conversion (1:17), and his later statement that the Jerusalem
leaders contributed nothing to him (2:6), he does not claim independence
from Peter and the Jerusalem pillars. While he was not taught by the disciples
but instead received the gospel directly from Jesus, Paul clearly respects those
who were apostles and eyewitnesses before him for their certification of his
own mission (2:1–2). While Acts places Barnabas in this role, Galatians depicts
Peter as Paul's first apostolic superior and colleague. In fact, Peter may have
been Paul's link between the first disciples of Jesus and the church at Corinth.[54]

Paul refers to Peter by his Aramaic name, Cephas (*Kēphas*), a word that
corresponds to the Aramaic word for "rock" (*kēphas*).[55] The Greek equivalent,

52. On types and antitypes, see the epilogue.
53. Bauckham, *Jewish World*, 257–68.
54. Bauckham, *Jesus and the Eyewitnesses*, 37.
55. Gal. 1:18; 2:11; 1 Cor. 1:12; 15:5. The only exception to this will be in Gal. 2:7–8, where Paul
uses the Greek name Petros, but in Gal. 2:9 the Aramaic name Cephas returns. In the Gospel according

Petros, also corresponds to the Greek word for "rock" (*petra*). At Peter's confession at Caesarea Philippi, Jesus puns on the name, saying, "I tell you, you are Peter [*Petros*], and on this rock [*petra*] I will build my church" (Matt. 16:18). Cephas or Peter, Peter or Cephas, this is the man Paul visits in Jerusalem after his mission in Arabia. I will refer to this Jerusalem leader by his Greek name Peter, in part because the Jesus traditions and the Gospels prefer the name, but more importantly because of Paul's key reference to him in Gal. 2 at Jerusalem: he is Peter, "apostle to the circumcised" (2:8).

Here we have another example of Paul's familiarity with the Jesus traditions. In the Gospels, despite Peter's general lack of perception of Christ's identity, at Caesarea Philippi he confesses Jesus as Messiah. Jesus asks the disciples who they think he is.[56] Peter answers on behalf of all: Jesus is the Christ, the Son of the living God. Jesus then turns directly to Peter and addresses him alone, granting him the authority to forgive and to discipline.[57] In the Gospel according to John we also find Peter's leadership role: even while the apostle John is the first to reach the empty tomb, Peter is the first to enter it (John 20:3–8). Given Peter's primary apostolic role throughout the Jesus traditions, and Paul's former persecution of the community that held these traditions sacred, it would have been odd if Paul had known absolutely nothing about Peter and if, once converted, Paul would have remained aloof from him.[58] Paul went to Jerusalem not to meet with a figure completely unknown to him but to inquire of the one he recognized as the chief representative among those who had known the earthly Jesus. Here is the link between Paul and the Jesus traditions: a two-week crash course from Peter himself.[59]

The visit poses an interesting question as to the relationship between Peter's teaching (1:18) and Paul's reception of the gospel (1:1, 12, 16). The length of stay became a matter of comment in the history of interpretation. For Marius Victorinus, the fact that the visit lasted only two weeks shows that Paul could

---

to John, the Greek translation of the Aramaic name is given in the narrator's editorial comment, "'You are Simon son of John. You are to be called Cephas' (which is translated Peter)" (John 1:42).

56. *Hymeis*, "you all"; Matt. 16:15; Mark 8:29; see also Luke 9:20.

57. *Su ei Petros*, "but you, Peter" (Matt. 16:18–19).

58. Dunn, *Epistle to the Galatians*, 80.

59. "When Paul claims his own apostleship despite its anomalous character [1 Cor. 15:9–11], he asserts the unanimity between himself and the other apostles on the key matters he has just rehearsed [1 Cor. 15:11]. This unanimity existed *because* he had received the tradition in question from the Jerusalem apostles." Bauckham, *Jesus and the Eyewitnesses*, 266, citing Hengel and Schwemer, *Paul between Damascus and Antioch*, 147.

not have learned anything of substance from Peter.[60] In his 1519 lectures on Galatians, Luther comments that Paul could not have been fully catechized in such a short time.[61] However, they must have spoken of at least some matters of substance, for they could not have spent all the time "talking about the weather."[62] In telling us that he sought out Peter and stayed with him for two weeks in Jerusalem, Paul forces us to revisit his earlier claim in 1:11–12 where he asserts independence from a human source other than direct encounter with the Lord. How do we understand the relationship between these claims? We might conclude either that the later verses contradict the earlier or that in 1:18 Paul is simply giving a different interpretation of 1:11–12. Neither of these solutions satisfies. The inner tension points to the nature of divinely revealed truth. Located in the person of Jesus, revelation is also tied to the authoritative teaching of the earliest eyewitnesses, those who first confessed Jesus as Lord. For Paul these manifestations of revealed truth are neither contradictory nor complementary. They form a unity.

James the Lord's brother—The fact that Paul identifies this James as Jesus's brother poses another difficulty for early interpreters. The question can be approached from two standpoints. First, it can be seen as a chronological question. There are a number of Jameses among the apostles, at least two of whom could be possible candidates. James the son of Zebedee and brother of John, an early leader in Jerusalem, was martyred ca. AD 44 under Herod Agrippa. James the Just, the brother of the Lord, was martyred ca. AD 62 under Ananus ben Ananus. Determining the identity of the James of 1:19 and 2:9 could possibly affect our dating of the letter: if the James of 1:19 is not the brother of the Lord but rather the son of Zebedee, the letter could reflect a very early first visit in Jerusalem.

Second, and more importantly, Paul's identification of James at 1:19 can be approached as a theological problem: If James is the brother of Jesus, how can his mother Mary be ever-virgin? This belief holds that Mary "remained a virgin in conceiving her Son, a virgin in giving birth to him, a virgin in carrying him, a virgin in nursing him at her breast, always a virgin."[63] This ran

60. Marius Victorinus, *Epistle to the Galatians* 1.1.18.
61. Luther, *LW* 27:194.
62. Dodd, *Apostolic Preaching*, 16, 66.
63. Augustine, *Sermon* 186 (PL 38:999), translation in *Catechism of the Catholic Church*, #510; see also 487–511. The dogma is linked traditionally to Mary's faith rather than to her sexuality.

at crosshairs not only with Gal. 1:19 but also with the other New Testament texts that mention Jesus's siblings.[64] Declared dogma at the Fifth Ecumenical Council of Constantinople (553), the belief that Mary was ever-virgin has roots far deeper than the sixth century. Jerome's late fourth-century *Against Helvidius* is an example, but the idea is found even as early as the second-century noncanonical infancy gospel, the *Protevangelium of James*. The dogma is still held today across Christian communions, even though the Protestant churches give it little attention. The concern over the identity of James is a Mariological question, and as such it is fundamentally christological. For this reason, it occupied much interpretation in the patristic era as the fathers tried to address the discrepancy between devotion and text.

Jerome takes up the question and suggests that Paul must have used the term "brother" colloquially: James is simply a cousin of Jesus. Or maybe, wonders Jerome, Paul refers to James as "the Lord's brother" in an honorific way: "on account of [James's] outstanding character, incomparable faith, and superior wisdom."[65] Ambrosiaster suggests that James was the son of Joseph by a previous marriage.[66] Theodoret prefers the explanation that James was a cousin of Jesus. Paul's confusion in misidentifying the James in 1:19 must come from the fact, claims Theodoret, that the cousins' mothers were sisters and that the boys shared the same name and the same home.[67] Another stock proposal looks to a detail from the Gospel according to John: James cannot be the blood brother of the Lord because, from the cross, Jesus entrusts Mary to John. If James were Jesus's blood brother, he would certainly have entrusted Mary's well-being from the cross not to John but to his own brother, James.[68] Among the early Latin patristic commentators, Marius Victorinus was the only one who took Paul at face value: the James of 1:19 was indeed Jesus's blood brother.[69] He is James the brother of the Lord, not James the disciple and brother of John, son of Zebedee.[70]

But for Paul, it is less important who James is in relation to Jesus than who James is in relation to Peter, and in turn Peter to Paul himself. When Paul

64. Mark 3:31–32; 6:3; John 2:12; 7:3, 5, 10; Acts 1:14; 1 Cor. 9:5.
65. Jerome, *Commentary on Galatians*, 91.
66. Ambrosiaster, *Epistle to the Galatians* 1.19 (CSEL 81.3:15–16), translated in Edwards, *Galatians, Ephesians, Philippians*, 15n10, 15n13.
67. Theodoret, *Epistle to the Galatians* 1.19 (CPE 1.333) (trans. Hill, 2:10).
68. Reflected in Pitre, *Jesus and the Jewish Roots of Mary*, 123.
69. Cooper, *Victorinus's Commentary*, 266n76, 275n114.
70. Eusebius, *Ecclesiastical History* 3.5.2 and 3.7.5; Bockmuehl, *Jewish Law in Gentile Churches*, 77.

tells of visiting Peter in Jerusalem, he mentions James only in passing. While James is the leader of the Jerusalem church (2:9), Paul seeks out Peter as the authoritative one among the original circle of the disciples. This highlights the theological role that Paul's relationship with Peter plays in the letter, as it represents the relationship between the Jewish and Gentile missions that the Galatians have misconstrued. The christological question posed by the identification of James in 1:19 therefore points to the two missions of the one gospel. Even the Mariological issue is about that same dual mission of the one gospel. In 4:4, Paul identifies Mary simply as the woman who bore Jesus "under the law." That is, Paul does not locate Mary's role in the incarnation in her sexual status. His sole claim about her is that she was a female Jew. This itself also points to the fact underlying the key pastoral problem in Galatia: the Lord of the gospel even to the Gentiles is a Jew.

1:21–24 Syria and Cilicia—Syria and Cilicia together formed a Gentile area (Jdt. 1:12; 4 Macc. 4:2). Tarsus, Paul's native city, was in that same area, and according to Acts Paul's work took him there (Acts 15:23, 41). Antioch in Syria has a missional relation to Paul's home city: Barnabas fetched Paul from Tarsus to introduce him to the church at Antioch. There is also a missional connection between Antioch and the Jerusalem church (Acts 11:19–30). Barnabas and Paul are sent to the Gentile believers in that area to hand on the Jerusalem church's apostolic decree regarding the status of law observance for Gentile Christians (Acts 15:22–29). This decree instituted relaxed dietary and sexual purity codes, giving Gentile Christians a minimal degree of Torah observance as they lived among Jews.[71] After visiting Peter in Jerusalem, Paul heads back into Gentile territory. While he gives no concrete reason as to why he travels specifically there, it makes intuitive sense: as missionary to the Gentiles, he continues his earlier evangelization of Arabia among the Gentiles in Syria and Cilicia.

unknown by sight . . . they only heard it said—While the Gentiles in Arabia have met Paul, the churches of Judea still have only heard of his pre-conversion reputation: he was "the one who formerly was persecuting [the church]."[72]

---

71. The decree reflects an implicit understanding of the relationship of Jews and Gentiles basic to the rabbinic Noahide commands. These will become important in my discussion of 2:10.

72. Gal. 1:23, 13; Acts 9:1–2, 21; 8:1–3.

glorified God because of me—The chapter closes with a statement that news of Paul's conversion brings glory to God even throughout the churches of Judea. This circles us back to the letter's salutation with its doxology (1:5). Glory to God bookends the chapter, and we now turn again toward Jerusalem.

GALATIANS 2

Chapter 2 brings Paul to Jerusalem for a second time, but for a different reason and with different colleagues. Paul, Barnabas, and Titus, apostles to the Gentiles, seek out the pillars of the Jerusalem church: Peter, James, and John, apostles to the Jews. Paul's description of this meeting in Gal. 2 corresponds on various levels to a similar account in Acts 15.[1] Both meetings address the problem of Gentile conversion to the Jewish church. That the two accounts overlap in subject matter is clear.[2]

The account of the Jerusalem meeting in Gal. 2 concludes abruptly at 2:10. The Gentile mission has been recognized: Paul will evangelize the uncircumcised, while the Jerusalem church (Peter at the helm) will evangelize the circumcised. These two separate missions share equally in the one gospel. Even so, as will become clear at 2:10, the relationship of the Gentile Christians to the Jewish Christians is asymmetrical. The apparently conflict-free meeting in Jerusalem is followed immediately by a painful exchange between Paul and Peter at Antioch that centers on church ethics, or more precisely, halakah.

2:1–5 up again to Jerusalem with Barnabas, taking Titus along with me—
The episode of Paul's second trip to Jerusalem (2:1–10) is immediately followed by a tense interaction between him and Peter in Antioch (2:11–14). These two episodes in chapter 2 are linked verbally by the double occurrence of the phrase "the truth of the gospel" (2:5, 14). The phrase reflects the urgency of Paul's pastoral care to the Galatians, who themselves risk deserting the truth

---

1. For a richly argued view of how the accounts in Acts 15 and Gal. 2 relate, see Bauckham, "James, Peter, and the Gentiles."
2. While I read Gal. 2 as reflecting the basic logic of the apostolic decree of Acts 15, I am agnostic as to how they relate chronologically and whether they refer to the same meeting.

of the gospel in their having been drawn away from circumcision-free conversion (3:3; 4:9; 5:7).

The purpose of the earlier trip was tersely described: of his own accord, Paul goes to visit Cephas (1:18). But in Galatians 2, Paul was not summoned by the leaders in Jerusalem as depicted in Acts 15:2; here in Galatians, his second Jerusalem trip is a response to a revelation. On this second trip, Paul (a circumcised Jew) goes up with his leader Barnabas (a circumcised Jew). They take along Titus (an uncircumcised Gentile). Titus will play a brief but crucial role in the meeting in Jerusalem, literally embodying the key issue in the letter.

2:2 revelation—In Acts 9, 22, and 26, Jesus's self-revelation to Paul is vividly described as though with a *son et lumière* show: a bright light blinds Paul, and he hears the voice of Christ. The scene in Acts has drawn the attention of artists throughout the centuries. One of the most famous embellishments on the story that has shaped popular imagination is the early seventeenth-century painting by Caravaggio. His striking interpretation of the story inserts the detail of Paul's being cast to the ground *from a horse*. Caravaggio's painting captures the contrast of light and dark that alludes to Paul's self-described prophetic vocation of bearing Christ's light to the Gentiles.

In Galatians, however, Paul gives us no details as to the event of his conversion and commission. There is no description of Jesus's revelation to him. Paul simply refers to its function: the revelation sends him. Analogously, the Gospels do not describe Jesus's resurrection; they simply pass along the reports of the eyewitnesses at the empty tomb and the resurrection appearances. The function of the resurrection appearance stories becomes clearest in the risen Jesus's sending them to teach and baptize in Matt. 28:18–20. The Gospel stories are fundamentally ecclesial, as are Paul's minimal mentions of the Lord's appearances to him.

In the first mention of a revelation in 1:11–12, Paul's focus is not on his experience but on his receiving (*parelabon*) the gospel directly from Christ; in 2:2 the revelation sends him to Jerusalem to lay before the pillars the gospel that he preaches among the Gentiles. This harks back to 1:17 and his mission to the Gentile territory in Arabia: Paul is now bringing this teaching to the Jerusalem leaders. They will acknowledge its integrity. The apostolic approval of his mission to the Gentiles ensures that there is only one degree of separation for Paul's converts from the Jerusalem church: the link between Jewish and Gentile mission begins with the church at Jerusalem.

Over the next few decades after Paul, this language of giving and receiving the gospel came to coalesce into the rule of faith (→6:16). This norming hermeneutical guide began to develop from the second century through the fourth century as a teaching tool for catechesis and biblical interpretation. The rule of faith was essentially a trinitarian lens for interpretation that proscribed (rather than prescribed) readings.[3] That is, it allowed for a broad array of interpretations, provided they did not violate the integrity of the gospel as taught by the church; likewise it set boundaries on exegesis beyond which were only nonvalid interpretations. Paul's bringing his revelation before the Jerusalem pillars already reflects this traditioning impulse for passing along the fullness of the gospel in its integrity.

The second time he speaks of the encounter with Jesus (1:16), Paul says that God "was pleased to reveal his Son to me" (literally, "in me," *en emoi*) with the explicit purpose of preaching to the Gentiles. Jesus's revelation to Paul generates his mission to the Gentiles. In his third reference to the revelation (2:2), we read that Christ sends Paul to Jerusalem specifically to meet with the Jerusalem church leaders to make sure that his Gentile mission is not "in vain." Again, there is no mention of his being summoned by the pillars.

The role of Barnabas and Titus in connection with the trip is important; Barnabas is a Jewish Christian and Titus is a Gentile Christian. Their presence in the story frames the Jerusalem pillars' decision over Paul's law-free Gentile mission and the subsequent account of the controversy in Antioch between Paul and Peter over Gentile ministry and missional integrity. Both of these inform Paul's pastoral message to the Galatians as exemplars.

We meet Barnabas in Acts 9:26–27, where he introduces Paul to the Jerusalem church leaders and vouches for his trustworthiness despite his reputation for persecuting the church. In Acts, Barnabas is described as a man righteous in word and deed; as a Levite he would have been strictly law observant, possibly with halakic practices similar to those of Saul the Pharisee. As a native of Cyprus, Barnabas also would have had contact with Gentiles. At the time when believers still held all things in common, Barnabas fulfills his obligation to the

---

3. The rule is most often associated with, but is not limited to, the figure of Irenaeus of Lyon. The faith received "always by the Spirit of God, renewing its youth, as if it were some precious deposit in an excellent vessel, causes the vessel itself containing it to renew its youth also. For this gift of God has been entrusted to the Church, as breath was to the first created man." *Against Heresies* 3.24.1 (*ANF* 1:458). The role of Irenaeus in biblical interpretation alone is decisive: "In the early church, all roads lead not to Rome but to Irenaeus and the last quarter of the second century." Kugel and Greer, *Early Biblical Interpretation*, 155.

church, giving his proceeds to the apostles (Acts 4:32; see 2:44). He is portrayed in Acts as the spiritual inverse of Ananias and Sapphira; the righteousness of Barnabas's own behavior contrasts with their infidelity (Acts 5:1–11). The couple sells a piece of their property and, unlike the faithful Barnabas, they deceitfully withhold some of the proceeds. Peter confronts Ananias in the lie, and both Ananias and Sapphira meet a dire end. Barnabas's faithful generosity foregrounds Peter's request of Paul that the Gentile mission care for the poor (Gal. 2:10).

Barnabas and Paul split over the company of a younger colleague, John Mark (Acts 15:36–39). When Paul suggests a pastoral visit to the churches they had founded earlier, Barnabas wants to bring John Mark; he is willing to overlook the young man's desertion during a prior mission. But Paul refuses. The disagreement becomes so sharp that the two senior colleagues separate, Barnabas taking John Mark and Paul taking Silas. Barnabas drops out of the story in Acts at this point. In the episode at Antioch in Gal. 2, Barnabas joins in Peter's hypocrisy, betraying his mentor and colleague (2:13), then disappears from the remaining exposition in the letter.

2:3 Titus . . . was not compelled to be circumcised—Paul mentions Titus now for the second time. His role has been minimal up to this point: "taking Titus along" (2:1), "who was with me" (2:3). But Titus is in fact important to the depiction of the larger problem in Galatia. Being a Gentile ("a Greek"), he is uncircumcised; with Paul's support he successfully resists the rite. Titus thus embodies the response Paul expects of the Galatians: they, Gentile Christians like Titus, are not to receive circumcision. Titus himself now drops out of the letter, having served his function in the narrative.

2:4 false believers—Paul refers to those who have taught a distorted gospel. These people confuse the Galatians (1:7; 5:10); they pervert the gospel (1:8); they make a fuss over the Galatians yet want to exclude them (4:17); they prevent the Galatians from obeying the truth (5:7); they unsettle them (5:12); they want to boast in the Galatians' circumcised flesh (6:12–13). In teaching that Gentiles must be circumcised upon conversion, these teachers bear a resemblance to the people (falsely said to be) from James whom we will meet in Antioch (2:12). But Paul does not tell us who the "false believers" of 2:4 are, where they are from, or to whom they are related. Their single identifying feature is that they have infiltrated the community to assess the freedom of

Gentile Christians who remain uncircumcised. These false Christians create a fracas that will be mirrored in Paul's dispute with Peter in Antioch (2:11–14).

2:5 the truth of the gospel—Here Paul turns from speaking about his visit with the Jerusalem church and addresses the Galatians directly, drawing them also into the scene. This phrase, "the truth of the gospel," brackets two episodes: Paul's agreement with the leaders in Jerusalem (2:5) and his opposition to Peter in Antioch (2:14). Among the Jerusalem leaders, there is agreement about this truth of the gospel, but in Antioch the concord breaks down, and along with it goes Paul's concord with Peter. A subversion of the truth has caused an analogous breach in Paul's formerly peaceful relationship with the Galatian churches.[4] Concord within the body of Christ depends on this truth of the gospel.

2:6 those leaders contributed nothing to me—Paul lays before the acknowledged "pillars" (RSV; *styloi*) the gospel he has been preaching among the Gentiles (2:2, 6). Seeming to qualify their status ("what they were makes no difference to me"), Paul does not thereby minimize his acknowledgment of the pillars' authority. If he had not held them in high apostolic regard, he would not have sought them out in order to lay before them his gospel for their recognition. He is simply saying that it is neither their personal charisma nor affection nor their virtue that draws him but rather their office as leaders of the church. At this meeting the pillars approve Paul's mission to the uncircumcised as a parallel track to Peter's mission to the circumcised, one gospel in a biethnic mission. Paul says that the pillars added nothing to his office (i.e., apostolicity) or to the content of his teaching (i.e., doctrine). While the pillars may have "contributed nothing," they give to him and Barnabas the right hand of fellowship (2:9) and an additional request (2:10).

2:7–9 gospel for the uncircumcised . . . gospel for the circumcised—In Acts 15 we find an account of a similar meeting where the Jerusalem church approves of the Gentile mission. Because the accounts describe the meeting differently, questions arise as to whether they refer to the same event. What is clear, however, is that both accounts take up the question of how Gentiles

---

4. See Gal. 1:6; 3:1–4; 4:16; 5:7.

are to convert to the Jewish messianic sect: Do Gentiles have to become Jews before converting to Christ? And after converting, what is their responsibility regarding law observance?

While Paul's account of his first Jerusalem trip offers no details about either its purpose or its results, the outcome of the second trip is clear. Paul receives what he went to find: apostolic recognition of his Gentile mission. James, Peter, and John agree with Paul and Barnabas: there is one gospel in two missions, one to the circumcised and one to the uncircumcised. This scene illustrates the complexity of, and accounts for, the creative tensions within earliest Christianity in its coequal Jewish and Gentile forms.[5]

One extended thought is expressed over the course of these three long verses (2:7–9). The Jerusalem leaders "recognized the grace that had been given" to Paul (2:9), and a division of labor along ethnoreligious lines results (3:9, 14, 18, 29). Gentiles are elect in Christ as Gentiles, apart from the law; this is "the gospel for the uncircumcised," or, literally, "the good news of the foreskin" (*to euangelion tēs akrobystias*; 2:7).[6] This phrase and its implications would offend any law-observant Jew, in part because it implicitly claims that election is not tied to the covenant of circumcision. It is perhaps difficult for contemporary Gentiles to sense the force of this statement.[7] The phrase "gospel of the foreskin" itself serves as a cipher for Paul's theological construct of "justification of the ungodly."[8] To claim that those of the circumcision (*peritomēs*) and those of the uncircumcision (*akrobystias*) are equally elect in Christ may seem a contradiction in terms; yet that is exactly what Paul is saying.

At 2:9, Paul shifts from cultic terms (circumcised/uncircumcised; *peritomē/ akrobystia*) to ethnic terms (circumcised/Gentile; *peritomē/ethnē*). Earlier, in 1:15–17, Paul used the ethnic term *ta ethnē* to speak of his own prophetic calling to bring the Gentiles into the people of Israel (Isa. 49:1–6; 66:18–20; Zech. 8:23). The cultic term *akrobystia* (uncircumcised) will return in the later pastoral contexts of 5:6 and 6:15, where Paul again explicitly takes up the subject.

Paul describes his mission to the Gentiles and Peter's mission to the Jews with terms that do not translate easily into English. In Greek and in Hebrew, the words do not form a binary as our English translation: "circumcised"

---

5. Schoeps, *Paul*, 66n1.
6. See Kahl, *Galatians Re-imagined*, 275.
7. Barclay, *Paul and the Gift*, 362.
8. Rom. 4:5. Barclay, *Paul and the Gift*, 362n32.

and "uncircumcised."[9] In English these nouns share the same root; the term "uncircumcised" is created simply by adding the prefix "un-" to the term "circumcised." But in the overwhelming number of occurrences of this (seeming) binary in both the Septuagint and the Greek New Testament, there is no lexical negative. That is, the opposite of circumcision, *peritomē*, is the etymologically unrelated term *akrobystia*.[10]

The male Gentile retains what the male Jew has had cultically removed (the foreskin). The word "circumcised" indicates that something has literally been "cut around." The word "uncircumcised" describing the Gentile penis might be translated "retaining foreskin." But Paul's concern is not simply about what the penis either retains or does not retain (its appearance), but about the specifically cultic (religious) meaning of the rite. For Paul, the Gentile is not the cultic opposite of the Jew; the Gentile is simply the cultic "other."[11] At the heart of the pastoral problem that Paul addresses in Galatians is how a misunderstanding of the relationship of cult and ethnicity in the body of Christ can compromise the "truth of the gospel."

The cultic distinction manifest in the observance or nonobservance of the rite of circumcision not only threatens the "truth of the gospel," but it also confounds the Galatians and ruptures their communities. The confounding is caused by "false believers" (2:4) who are apparently wary of the Jewish Christian mission's allowing Gentiles the freedom to convert without circumcision. Whoever these false believers are, they are clearly outsiders to the Jewish church at Jerusalem, where the pillars have already agreed to accept what these false believers reject: the Gentile circumcision-free mission. They foreshadow those said to be "from James" (2:12) in Antioch, who will test the resolve of both Peter (the Jewish mission) and Barnabas (the Gentile mission). Both Peter and Barnabas will resort to hypocrisy (2:13), dishonoring the integrity of the two distinct missions and the truth of the gospel (2:5, 14). The truth of the gospel is God's grace that justifies by faith.[12] Here we come full circle to Paul's main concern: the integrity of the Galatian churches as they face the threat of the circumcising Third Party.[13]

9. In Hebrew the nouns are *himmol/arel*. Because Paul reads the LXX, I focus on the Greek terms here (→3:28; 5:6).

10. There are some notable exceptions in the LXX, but none in the New Testament. This will be important for how I will read Paul's discussion of baptismal identity in 3:28 (→5:6).

11. Thanks to Michelle Knight for helping me clarify my thoughts on this.

12. Ephesians emphasizes grace by placing it first: "By grace you have been saved through faith" (Eph. 2:8).

13. Gal. 1:6; 3:1; 5:7; 6:12.

2:9 James—The James of 2:9 is the same brother of the Lord whom we met in 1:19.[14] On his first Jerusalem trip, Paul intentionally seeks out Peter but has only a passing encounter with James (1:19). In 2:9, James is mentioned first among the three pillars, and Peter is only second. While Peter is clearly one of the "pillars," James the brother of the Lord is depicted as the authority figure in the Jerusalem church.

2:10 that we remember the poor—The leaders who "contributed nothing" (neither apostolicity nor doctrine) to Paul's ministry did, however, give to him and Barnabas the right hand of fellowship, recognizing that the same God who worked through Peter among the Jews also worked through Paul among the Gentiles (2:7–8). James, Peter, and John (in that order) give to Barnabas and Paul (in that order) the "right hand of fellowship" (2:9) and shake on the agreement: while there is one God and one gospel, there are two missions to two peoples. Jews will remain Jews as they convert to Christ; Gentiles will remain Gentiles as they convert to the one gospel, without taking on the rite of circumcision. While the pillars do not add the requirement of circumcision to the Gentile mission (2:6), they do add a single request: to remember the poor. This is odd; Peter's request has no explicit counterpart for the Jewish mission. Are they already caring for the poor and we have not heard? Or are the Gentiles the only ones to care for the poor? And who are these poor?

The question has been addressed in various ways.[15] Jerome suggests, following the words of Jesus, that these are the poor in spirit who are blessed in the Sermon on the Mount (Matt. 5:3 // Luke 6:20).[16] Another possibility is that they are poor people in general. After all, throughout the Bible, care for the poor and needy is required, especially in Leviticus; Jesus's summary of the law is drawn in part from Lev. 19:18 (Mark 12:31). Galatians 2 reflects the tradition of charity to the poor commanded throughout the Torah and Talmud, as well as in the New Testament. It would follow, then, that Peter's request of Paul, and Paul's subsequent passing this request on to the Galatians in his letter, point to the care for the needy linked to the law's demands (Gal. 5:14; cf. Rom. 13:9).[17] But the matter is more complex and has a specifically christological form.

14. See my comments at 1:19 for the doctrinal implications posed by the relationship between Jesus and James for the early church.
15. Betz offers some of these; see *Galatians*, 102n422–23.
16. Jerome, *Commentary on Galatians*, 103–4.
17. Longenecker, *Remember the Poor*.

The story of Mary's anointing Jesus's feet at Bethany in John 12:1–8 offers us a christological interpretation of what poverty means among Jesus's disciples. The episode at Bethany immediately follows the scene of Jesus's raising Mary's brother Lazarus in John 11: both stories foreshadow Jesus's death and resurrection. When Mary anoints Jesus's feet, Judas feigns objection at her waste of resources: the money could have gone to care for the poor. But Jesus cuts through Judas's ruse: "You always have the poor with you, but you do not always have me" (John 12:8). These words are an implicit interpretation of Deut. 15:11: "Since there will never cease to be some in need on the earth, I therefore command you, 'Open your hand to the poor and needy neighbor in your land.'" That the poor are an ever-present reality is, according to Deuteronomy, not a reason to neglect them but to be generous to them. In responding to Judas, Jesus follows Deuteronomy: care for the poor is never entirely fulfilled, because they are always among us. Jesus does not release the disciples from responsibility to the poor. Rather, care for the poor is linked specifically to his own death and resurrection ("You do not always have me"), thus to Christian identity and vocation. For Paul's mission, Gentile care for the poor is care for the Lord's body.

But the question is not closed here. At the Jerusalem meeting where the head of the Jewish mission makes the request of the head of the Gentile mission, the poor to whom Peter refers and whom the Gentiles are to "remember" are Jewish Christians.[18] There is historical as well as theological evidence for this claim. In Acts the early Christian prophet Agabus predicts a famine that will come under the reign of Claudius (AD 42–54; Acts 11:28). Josephus himself refers to a famine that hit Judea about AD 45–48.[19] Eusebius says that Jesus himself predicted the famine, citing the Lord's prophecy about the destruction of Jerusalem (Luke 21:20–24). Relying on Josephus's account, Eusebius details the extreme suffering of the Jews during the famine, when over one million people died of hunger. He reports that almost one hundred thousand youths were sold into slavery, and there were accounts of mothers

18. "Paul does not mean the poor in general, and surely not the spiritually poor (for how would taking up a collection improve that condition?), but rather the poverty-stricken among the saints in the Jerusalem church." Witherington, *Grace in Galatia*, 144–45.

19. Josephus, *Jewish Antiquities* 20.51–53, 101. The famine had long-term consequences: even as late as the second century, there were still rabbis who were traveling to Antioch to request support for Jewish scholars impoverished by the famine. Bockmuehl, *Jewish Law in Gentile Churches*, 55n25, noting Rabbis Eliezer, Joshua, and Akiva: *y. Horayot* 3.7, 48a; par. *Leviticus Rabbah* 5.4; *Deuteronomy Rabbah* 4.8; and pointing to Acts 11:27–30.

who cooked and ate their infants.[20] The residents of Jerusalem who would have been unable to flee would certainly have included Jewish Christians, those who lost family, friends, and material security on their conversion to Christ, and those who had given their wealth for the common good of the church (Acts 4:34–35).[21]

The suffering caused by the famine demands a response. Acts 11:29–30 reports that the disciples organized a relief effort. Barnabas and Paul bring the collection for the Jerusalem church to the elders in Judea (1 Cor. 16:1–3). Paul prays that his "ministry to Jerusalem may be acceptable to the saints" (Rom. 15:31). He instructs the church to gather the collection for the poor: on the first day of the week, the day of resurrection, they are to "put aside and save whatever extra [they] earn," so that when Paul arrives, the logistics of the collection will not distract from his visit (1 Cor. 16:2). The Galatians themselves are mentioned as an example of this pattern of generosity (1 Cor. 16:1). The Gentile church in Macedonia, even despite their own poverty, has also participated generously in the relief (2 Cor. 8:1–4). They are like the widow in Jesus's parable who gives to the temple even out of her poverty (Mark 12:41–44; Luke 21:1–4). The charism of sharing is one of the defining marks of the early church, as the unhappy fate of Ananias and Sapphira illustrates in counterexample (Acts 5:1).

The collection from the Gentile Christians for the famine-struck Jewish church flows from a debt of gratitude. While the gospel is one and the missions are equal in blessing, their mutual responsibility to and gratitude for each other is asymmetrical. Gentile Christians are grafted into the rootstock of Israel (Rom. 11:17–24). Gentile Christians who participate in the collection are "giving back" to the Lord, to his body present as the Jewish church in Jerusalem. They share in spiritual blessings from the Jewish church; they are to share their material blessings with the Jerusalem church (Rom. 15:27). Paul's mission to the Gentiles has a unique responsibility to the Jerusalem church that both sides assume is not reciprocal. Peter's request that the Gentile mission remember the poor in Gal. 2:10 emphasizes the unity, even in asymmetry, of the Jewish mission and the Gentile mission. The motivation is not simply generosity; it expresses the christological unity of the two missions of the single church of Jews and Gentiles.

---

20. See Eusebius, *Ecclesiastical History* 3.4.3–3.7.9 (trans. Lake, 203–19).
21. These are among the solutions of Luther and Calvin. See Luther, *LW* 27:210; Calvin, *Epistles of Paul*, 33.

Galatians 2, Acts 15, and the Noahide Laws

Whereas the Jerusalem meeting in Gal. 2 concludes with the simple request
to remember the poor, the Acts 15 account of the meeting ends with a short
list of purity codes for the Gentile Christians (Acts 15:20, 28–29; cf. 21:25).[22]
The list of observances that James delivers in Acts corresponds formally, and
to some extent even materially, to the Noahide commandments.[23] Why, then,
does Paul not mention these laws in the chapter 2 account of the Jerusalem
meeting in Galatians? After all, these codes themselves represent Paul's and
Peter's missions insofar as they negotiate a religious coexistence between Jews
and Gentiles. They provide a relaxed code of ritual purity for Gentiles while
freeing them from full Torah observance.[24] In other words, the Noahide laws
govern the boundaries within which Gentiles may live halakicly among Jews.

They occupy, then, the same theological intersection as does Paul's Gentile
mission with Peter's Jewish mission.[25] They are as follows: "Seven commandments were the sons of Noah commanded: (1) concerning adjudication (*dinim*),
(2) and concerning idolatry (*avodah zarah*), (3) and concerning blasphemy
(*qilelat Ha-Shem*), (4) and concerning sexual immorality (*giluy arayot*), (5) and
concerning bloodshed (*shefikhut damim*), (6) and concerning robbery (*ha-gezel*),
(7) and concerning a limb torn from a living animal (*ever min ha-hy*)."[26] While
most of them are prohibitions, only one is a positive command: to establish
courts of justice.

At the Jerusalem meeting in Acts 15, the requirements for the Gentile mission include only prohibitions ("to abstain from," Acts 15:20), with no positive commandments. In Galatians, the pillars lay down no prohibitions at all,
giving just one prescription or "request": to remember the poor (Gal. 2:10).

22. Dating to the late second century AD, the Noahide commandments are commonly understood
to have roots much earlier in the Torah, and fruit in the Talmud Exod. 12:48–49; Lev. 24:16, 22;
Num. 9:14; 15:14–16, 26, 29–30. See also Exod. 20:10; Lev. 16:29; Num. 19:10; 35:15; Deut. 5:14;
16:11, 14; 26:11; Josh. 20:9. It is highly probable that the laws date from the first half of the second
century. Bockmuehl (*Jewish Law in Gentile Churches*, 159n61) points to Müller, *Tora für die Völker*,
47 and Millard, "Die rabbinischen noachidischen Gebote," 80–81, 84, who confirm.

23. Among those who think that the Jerusalem meeting in Acts 15 may reflect to an extent the
Noahide laws are Nanos, *Galatians Debate*, 438; Bockmuehl, *Jewish Law in Gentile Churches*, 150;
Schoeps, *Paul*, 66–67; Simon, "Apostolic Decree." For the opposite conclusion, see Fitzmyer, *Acts of
the Apostles*, 555. For an accessible account of the historical and halakic development of the Noahide
laws, see Novak, *Image of the Non-Jew in Judaism*, 11–35.

24. Simon, "Apostolic Decree," 445, 450.

25. All of the commandments address the original (Gentile) crime, the violence of blood spilled
in Cain's murder of his brother. Novak, *Election of Israel*, 119n29; Novak, *Image of the Non-Jew*, 2.

26. t. *Avodah Zarah* 8.4. Novak, *Image of the Non-Jew in Judaism*, 11.

The single positive command among the Noahide laws (to establish courts of justice) can be seen, I suggest, as the analogue of the single positive request that Peter adds to Paul's mission (to remember the poor). Peter's request itself has to do with the relationship of the Gentile mission to the Jewish mission. Abiding by Peter's request, the Gentile Christians will address the suffering of the Jewish Christian poor; Gentile Christian aid to the poor among the Jewish Christian mission will effectively serve as their own law court judging the righteousness of their deeds before God.[27]

But Jewish Christians are today not the only poor among us, and 2:10 corresponds to Jesus's own command to care for the poor, as I showed earlier. The Gospels reflect this deep concern for the plight of the suffering and needy that is set before us in each generation. Jesus's preaching points to ethical problems such as the distribution and use of wealth (Mark 10:22; Luke 18:25).[28] In his parable of the good Samaritan (Luke 10:25–37), Jesus narrates his summary of the law with an illustration of inheriting eternal life: our life to come is linked to deeds of mercy toward the vulnerable. In the parable of the judgment of the Gentiles (Matt. 25:31–45), Jesus teaches that we are judged according to our acts of generosity to the poor in specifically christological terms. Peter's request of Paul comes to the church as a current issue judging us today. Our own response to the poor, either charity or contempt, is a court of justice where we are either convicted or acquitted. The poor are our own Noahide law court: they are our witnesses, our defense lawyers, and our prosecutors.

2:11–14 the incident at Antioch—The conflict at Antioch depicted in Gal. 2:11–14 is possibly the most theologically significant episode in the development of early Christianity. It reflects the problem that Paul encounters among his congregations in Galatia and sheds light on the boundaries of Jewish Christianity as it incorporates Gentile Christians while releasing them from Jewish Christian Torah observance.[29] On the surface, the controversy at Antioch appears to be halakic table fellowship: who can eat with whom. However, the extent to which Torah observance in Second Temple Judaism varied covered an array of halakic practice regarding dietary laws that affected

27. It does not follow from this interpretation that Peter is proposing "works righteousness." See Anderson, *Charity*.

28. For a study on this important topic, see Wheeler, *Wealth as Peril and Obligation*.

29. Dunn, "Incident at Antioch," 234; Froehlich, "Fallibility Instead of Infallibility?," 259–69, 351–57.

table fellowship.[30] These may have ranged from the refusal of all contact with Gentiles to the allowing of shared meals between Jews and Gentiles, as long as the foods were halakicly permissible for the Jewish guests.[31] But if we read closely, table fellowship is in fact not the issue in Antioch.[32] The controversy at Antioch is said specifically to be introduced by the arrival of those who impose *circumcision* on Gentile converts (2:12); table fellowship is merely an incidental extension of circumcision/uncircumcision. As in Galatia, so in Antioch, taking on the rite of circumcision ruptures the community, as will become clear in Paul's words to Cephas.

In the previous scene, Paul went to Jerusalem with two travel companions: Barnabas and Titus. There he defended Titus from circumcision. Now he suddenly finds himself alone in Antioch, again defending Gentile Christians from circumcision. Barnabas, Paul's senior, has deserted. But the focus at Antioch is not Barnabas's desertion but Peter's hypocrisy. He has violated the earlier agreement in Jerusalem that exempted Gentile Christians from all Torah observances, most importantly circumcision. When some of the circumcision faction arrives, claiming to be from the Jerusalem church ("from James," 2:12), Peter withdraws from the Gentiles. The text does not tell us precisely why Peter has separated himself from the Gentiles, apart from the mention of the circumcision faction's arrival. Paul upbraids Peter, accusing him of abandoning the truth of the gospel, the phrase appearing again in the context of Gentile circumcision. Peter is weak; he stands self-condemned; he has engaged in hypocrisy; he lacks apostolic integrity. Even this chief disciple who, unlike Paul, had known Jesus in the flesh, has folded in hypocrisy.

Paul had accepted Peter's authority and his request to care for the poor, but now chastises him for breaking his earlier accord of releasing Gentiles from Torah observance. Paul had held Peter to a higher standard from which his senior has now slipped.[33] He describes Peter in terms that are consistent with the Gospel portrayals of his character. Despite his confession of Jesus as Messiah at Caesarea Philippi, Peter is unfaithful at the scene of Jesus's arrest.[34] All four Gospels relate Peter's denial of Jesus, and all narrate his hypocrisy

30. Bockmuehl, *Simon Peter*, 94.

31. Bockmuehl, *Jewish Law in Gentile Churches*, 57–58.

32. "The problem was not the food but the company." Bockmuehl, *Jewish Law in Gentile Churches*, 73.

33. Many Reformation interpreters (e.g., Erasmus Sarcerius, John Calvin, Georg Major) came to the opposite conclusion, finding in this passage proof for their criticism of the pope. Bray, *Galatians, Ephesians*, 64–65.

34. Matt. 16:16 // Mark 8:29 // Luke 9:20.

under pressure.[35] Peter's behavior at Antioch is predictable: he draws back and separates himself out of fear.

2:11 Cephas came to Antioch—The scene suddenly shifts from Jerusalem with its approval of the Gentile mission to Antioch and the threat to the mission by a circumcision faction. The account begins with Peter's self-condemnation (2:11) and closes with his condemnation by Paul (2:14). Between these bookends, we learn of the arrival of a circumcision faction. The opening scene, "But when Cephas came to Antioch" (2:11), marks Peter's betrayal of Paul's Gentile mission, in contrast to the earlier scene when they had shared the "right hand of fellowship" (2:9). Discrete scenes within this section are linked by a series of chronological markers. "Until" (*pro*) and "but after" (*hote de*) sandwich the arrival of the so-called people from James (2:12) that initiates Peter's hypocrisy.

"Other Jews" (unnamed) join Peter in his hypocrisy. Barnabas himself succumbs to peer pressure and is "led astray by their hypocrisy" (2:13). The choppy narrative reaches its high point at 2:11–13, where Paul publicly chastises Peter "before them all" (*emprosthen pantōn*): "If you, though a Jew, live like a Gentile and not like a Jew, how can you compel the Gentiles to live like Jews?" (2:14). The conflict is not Christian against Jew; the argument between Paul and Peter is specifically intra-Christian—more precisely, intra-Jewish-Christian. The subject matter is the extent of the demands of Torah observance for Gentile Christians.

I opposed him to his face—The incident at Antioch between Paul and Peter received much attention in the early church, most famously in the correspondence between Augustine and Jerome.[36] The argument between the two church fathers, complicated as it was by their respective personalities, their hermeneutical approaches, and the unreliability of the ancient Roman post, is far more convoluted than even the narrative of Gal. 2 itself. Jerome embroiders the scene in Antioch, refusing to acknowledge that Paul could have rebuked Peter. For Jerome, this would have tarnished the reputation of both men, but

35. Matt. 26 // Mark 14 // Luke 22 // John 18. This is one of the details consistently depicted in each of the four Gospels.

36. For a translation of their letters, see White, *Correspondence*. Marius Victorinus influenced both Augustine and Jerome. Later interpreters took up the argument itself between Jerome and Augustine as an integral piece of the commentary tradition on Gal. 2:11–14. See, e.g., Levy, *Letter to the Galatians*, 185–206.

most problematically Peter's.[37] Jerome suggests that Peter's hypocrisy and Paul's scolding were staged for pedagogical purposes: Peter the bishop of Rome cannot have been in error, so he must have only pretended to engage in hypocrisy. This would have given Paul the opportunity to feign rebuke in turn. According to Jerome, the argument between the men provides an apostolic example for how churchly conflicts should be managed; each apostle was able to instruct their respective mission field (Gentiles, entrusted to Paul; Jews, entrusted to Peter). Because it was all playacting, Peter and Paul were not actually at odds. In Jerome's view, the authority of the church is at stake. If there was no argument, apostolic concord is maintained and church unity is preserved.[38]

Augustine was horrified at Jerome's suggestion that the scene was a pretense. The claim that they were making up an argument would lead to the conclusion that Scripture lies, thus jeopardizing Scripture's authority. One underlying contributor to the friction between the two church fathers was that Augustine did not approve of Jerome's text-critical work on the Old Testament and his Latin translation. Augustine's objection to Jerome's biblical work was likewise grounded in his concern for preserving ecclesial liturgy and worship. In Augustine's view, Peter and Paul had an honest disagreement, an authentic quarrel. Scriptural authority is maintained.

The argument between Paul and Peter depicted in 2:11–14 can also be read as Paul's implicit awareness of the Jesus traditions, specifically with regard to resolving disputes within the church: "If another member of the church sins against you, go and point out the fault when the two of you are alone" (Matt. 18:15).[39] Following Jesus's instructions, Paul opposes Peter to his face. Not succeeding at winning him over, Paul then continues with Jesus's teaching, "If the member refuses to listen to them, tell it to the church" (Matt. 18:17). Paul rebukes Peter "before them all" (Gal. 2:14).

However, Paul does not follow Jesus's instruction to its exact conclusion in the same verse: "If the offender refuses to listen even to the church, let such

37. "Paul would not speak with such offensive aggression of the head of the church, nor did Peter deserve to be held to blame for disturbing the church. Therefore it must be supposed that he is speaking of someone else who had either been with the apostles, or was from Judea, or was one of the believing Pharisees, or at any rate was reckoned important among the Galatians." Jerome, *Epistle to the Galatians* 3.5.10 (PL 26:403C–D), translation in Edwards, *Galatians, Ephesians, Philippians*, 78.
38. Jerome may have come to this interpretation because of his complete chagrin at Porphyry's use of the apostolic argument to discredit the church. Plumer, *Augustine's Commentary on Galatians*, 44–45.
39. Jerome links Gal. 2 and Matt. 18. Jerome, *Galatians, Titus, and Philemon*, 99.

a one be to you as a Gentile and a tax collector" (Matt. 18:17). There is no indication in the text that Paul treats Peter as a "Gentile or tax collector," but we do hear that he scolds the chief apostle for his behavior specifically as a Jewish Christian among Gentile Christians. This is significant: even apostolic disagreement does not permit mutual separation.

2:12 used to eat with the Gentiles—These people "from James" never could have represented James himself since he along with the other pillars had already approved of Paul's circumcision-free mission to the Gentiles in 2:9.[40] Wherever they come from and whoever they are, they are clearly not from James. But they are associated with a circumcision faction whose arrival in Antioch leads Peter to draw back from his established practice of eating with the uncircumcised. Peter's hypocrisy indicates that the Jerusalem accord over the circumcision-free Gentile mission has disintegrated. By including this scene, Paul illustrates for the Galatians what can result when Gentiles are left to the wiles of missionaries who require circumcision: ecclesial discord and breakdown. Paul will address the ethics of this discord in chapter 5.

2:13 even Barnabas was led astray by their hypocrisy—Hypocrisy is neither a concept, nor a quality, nor an emotion; it is an act. In the case of Peter and Barnabas at Antioch, this act takes the form of physical separation from Gentiles. For Paul, this is both the cause and the result of falsifying the truth of the gospel that is at the core of the Galatians' own pastoral difficulty.

2:14 consistently—Earlier Peter upheld the truth of the gospel of the circumcision-free Gentile mission, but now he draws back out of fear of those who would circumcise the Gentile Christians. The truth of the gospel is threatened by figures external to the scene from both cities: "false believers" in Jerusalem (2:4) and "people from James" in Antioch (2:12). But here in 2:14, the actual offense is caused by internal apostolic figures: Peter and Barnabas. We are not told what the circumcision faction actually said or did. We only hear that Peter fears them because of what they do: they circumcise Gentile Christians, a practice that Peter has already publicly committed himself to reject. Peter in effect says "here they are; I'm leaving now," abandoning the Gentile Christians to the circumcision faction.

40. See Bockmuehl, *Jewish Law in Gentile Churches*, 72.

If you, though a Jew, live like a Gentile and not like a Jew, how can you compel the Gentiles to live like Jews?—While Peter has falsified the gospel in implicitly siding with those who require circumcision of Gentile Christians, Paul now turns to an interaction that illustrates the truth of the gospel.

Readers throughout the centuries have taken Peter's "Judaizing" to be imposing law observance in order to gain righteousness ($\rightarrow$1:13–14). But the verb *Ioudaizō*, "to Judaize," takes no direct object; that is, "living like a Jew" is not something one does to others. It is something that non-Jews take on themselves: Jewish customs and law observances.[41] In the scene at Antioch, Peter is not instructing the Gentiles in Jewish practices; in retreating, he plays only a passive role. He is simply separating from the Gentiles on the basis of a perceived threat from the circumcision faction. What exactly, then, is Paul accusing Peter of doing?

In chapter 1, as Paul describes his own religious life prior to his encounter with the risen Christ, he uses a cognate noun, *Ioudaismos*. In my comments at 1:13–14, I suggested that this word may refer to the traditions of Paul's Pharisee elders regarding law observance, traditions that Paul had relinquished for the sake of spreading the gospel among the Gentiles for whom they would be irrelevant. Peter, along with James and John, had given approval to this law-free gospel to the Gentiles (2:9). Peter, although he was a Jew, "lived like a Gentile" (that is, he did not require circumcision for Gentiles who converted to the Messiah). But by separating from the Gentiles, Peter now implicitly permits the Gentile Christians in Antioch to think that they must "live like Jews" and take on law observance. It is as if Paul said to Peter, "Look, you yourself don't require Gentile circumcision, so how will you now let the Gentiles assume that they should take it on themselves?" In Antioch, Peter's key offense is not "Judaizing"; rather, it is his hypocrisy, his inconsistency, and his dishonesty about the Jerusalem church's stated commitment to the circumcision-free mission to the Gentiles. Again, the question of Gentile Christian circumcision is at the forefront of the scene.[42] Paul's words to Peter are not an attack on so-called

41. Novenson, "Paul's Former Occupation," 29.
42. The problem is not Jewish Christian law observance per se. That itself is not an issue in Galatians, because there are no Jews in Galatia. In fact, we find no evidence in his letters that Paul assumes that Jewish Christians have abandoned law observance. In 1 Corinthians, there may be Jewish Christians who are law observant even in the company of Gentile Christians who are not (1 Cor. 9:19–23). Whether this is descriptive or normative is not clear. In Romans, Paul indicates that table fellowship between Gentile Christians and Jewish Christians should allow for Jewish Christians to abstain from meat and wine, thus not violating dietary laws (Rom. 14:1–15:6). Bockmuehl, *Jewish Law in Gentile Churches*, 172.

works righteousness nor on Torah observance; they are a condemnation of Peter's hypocrisy at having deserted his earlier ecclesial agreement regarding Gentile Christian circumcision. In other words, Peter's hypocrisy is not a matter of a faulty doctrine of justification, but of a betrayal of ecclesiology. With this scene from Antioch, Paul again illustrates the presenting problem in Galatia: Gentile Christian circumcision.[43]

The question arises as to whether the sharp break between Paul and Peter narrated in Gal. 2 has severed their apostolic relationship. Paul mentions Peter no further in Galatians, but he does speak of him elsewhere. Paul easily could have dropped the brief mention of Peter from the list of the resurrection appearances he passes along to the Corinthians (1 Cor. 15:3-10). But he retains the reference to Peter. Paul upholds the continued importance of Peter's mission to the Jews even as he writes to his Gentile converts (Gal. 2:7–8; 3:28; 5:6; 1 Cor. 12:13). It is significant in the later tradition that the two apostles are not presented as having founded distinct sects. This easily could have been the conclusion. But both apostles are understood to have preached the same, and the only, gospel (Gal. 1:6–9; Acts 15:11). Paul's mission to the Gentiles is authorized on the basis of the primacy of Peter's mission to the Jews (Gal. 2:7–10).

Both Galatians and Acts agree: Paul and Peter each evangelize a distinct mission of a biethnic church, preaching the single gospel. Even the end of Acts presents the two apostles as though the rupture between them at Antioch had been healed: both are portrayed as evangelists at Rome. In placing Acts as the crown of the Gospels and the introduction to the epistles, the canon depicts both Paul and Peter as interpreters of the one gospel for the life of the church.[44] Even the literature deemed heretical by the later church regards Peter as the chief defender of the faith, acknowledging that Paul does not displace Peter's authority.[45]

The tradition understands the two apostles as a pair; they are not rival evangelists to two separate churches. In ancient Christian art and iconography, the two men were venerated in the classic pagan motif of *concordia*

---

43. Bockmuehl makes an advisedly minimalist though important distinction between halakah and theology among the players in Antioch, pointing out that their understanding of the saving work of Jesus is the same, but how that is actually lived out in the church may differ. Bockmuehl, *Jewish Law in Gentile Churches*, 80.

44. Trobisch, "Council of Jerusalem," 338.

45. Bockmuehl, *Simon Peter*, 95.

(like-mindedness); they were understood to be a team. In the case of these two missionaries, *concordia* indicates their shared witness to the one gospel and to apostolic truth.[46] Paul enters early Christian art at Peter's side.[47] And their images are each easily recognizable as *them*, not stock figures. There is no mistaking one for the other, or for anyone else in early Christian art. Peter is traditionally depicted with white hair and a rounded, curly beard; Paul is balding with a dark, pointed beard and a crooked nose. This tradition comes from early Christian literature: in the *Acts of Paul and Thecla*, Paul is described as a "man small in size, bald headed, bandy-legged, well-built, with eyebrows meeting, rather long-nosed, full of grace."[48] This depiction is one of the most stable images in the entire history of early Christian art, uniquely Paul.

Images in frescoes and funerary art also present the two apostles together, sometimes even in embrace. In the fourth-century frescoes in the Domitilla and the Via Latina catacombs in Rome, Peter and Paul flank Christ, present as co-witnesses to the Lord's glory.[49] The apostles' authority is thus depicted as equal under the lordship of Christ, even when their vocations are represented with different motifs. Peter is sometimes portrayed as holding keys, indicating his authority to bind and loose (Matt. 16:19). Paul often holds a scroll, symbolizing the authority of his writings. They are not set in juxtaposition; they do not compete; they do not vie for supremacy one over the other.

The fathers share this assessment. According to Clement, it is the martyrdom of the two apostles in Rome that unites them as a team.[50] According to the *Deposito martyrum* and the *Martyrologium*, their feast was celebrated in Rome as early as 258 on the same day: June 29.[51] Augustine refers to this early tradition:

> There is one day for the passion of two apostles. But these two also were as one; although they suffered on different days, they were as one. Peter went first, Paul followed. We are celebrating a feast day, consecrated for us by the blood of the

46. Cooper, *Victorinus's Commentary*, 51.
47. Cooper, *Victorinus's Commentary*, 58.
48. *Acts of Paul and Thecla* (ANF 8:487). See also Cooper, *Victorinus's Commentary*, 57n76.
49. I rely here on Sullivan, "Saints Peter and Paul."
50. "To these men [Peter and Paul] who spent their lives in the practice of holiness, there is to be added a great multitude of the elect, who, having through envy endured many indignities and tortures, furnished us with a most excellent example." *1 Clement* 6.1 (ANF 1:6). The dating has been assigned to the early second century, but this has been revised downward with the suggested date as early as AD 70. See Herron, *Clement and the Early Church of Rome*.
51. Sullivan, "Saints Peter and Paul," 78n27.

apostles. Let us love their faith, their lives, their labors, their sufferings, their confession of faith, their preaching.[52]

Tertullian ranks Paul's martyrdom to be as significant for the church as Peter's and John's, the implication being that Paul effectively takes the place of James in the triumvirate. This is all the more striking in light of the fact that Paul did not know the earthly Jesus, but James did. Paul is embraced as though a Jerusalem "pillar," filling in for James and elevated to the status of the inner circle around Jesus. Tertullian sees the unity of Peter and Paul's testimony specifically in their united testimony in martyrdom.[53]

Gregory the Great later split the celebration of their single feast day (June 29) into two separate ones: Paul's on the day following Peter's. That there was a *change* in the celebration of the feast days shows that the church intentionally chose to honor each apostle on his own; that is, the shift was from an early assumption of their apostolic unity to a later acceptance of their apostolic independence.[54]

According to Irenaeus, Peter founded the church at Rome together with Paul.[55] Ignatius of Antioch mentions their common work as an example for his own preaching and witness.[56] Two generations after Paul, Papias hands down a tradition that had already coalesced before him that both apostles had authoritative roles in the shaping of the written Gospels: Mark preserves Peter, and Luke preserves Paul. The underlying assumption is that Paul provided equally important and reliable source material for the Gospel according to Luke as Peter did for the Gospel according to Mark, and that Paul's writings themselves were considered authoritative at this early date even at Rome.[57] This again is all the more remarkable since Paul was, as he says, "untimely born"

52. Augustine, *Sermon* 295.1–2, 4, 7–8 (PL 38:1348–52), translation at https://www.crossroads initiative.com/media/articles/peter-and-paul-st-augustine. See Augustine, *Sermons*, 197–202. See also Cooper, *Victorinus's Commentary*, 50.

53. Tertullian, *Prescription against Heretics* 36 (*ANF* 3:260).

54. In 1970 Pope Paul VI restored the ancient celebration in the *Missale Romanum* to a single feast day of June 29. Farmer and Kereszty, *Peter and Paul*, 84. See Sullivan, "Saints Peter and Paul," 77n20. In the Anglican Communion, a Week of Prayer for Christian Unity opens with the celebration of the feast of the Confession of St. Peter on January 18, and closes with the feast of the Conversion of St. Paul on January 25.

55. Irenaeus, *Against Heresies* 3.3.3 (*ANF* 1:416).

56. "Not like Peter and Paul do I issue any orders to you. They were Apostles, I am a convict; they were free, I am even until now a slave." Ignatius, *Letter to the Romans* 4.3 (trans. Lake, 231); see also Eusebius, *Ecclesiastical History* 3.1–3.

57. See Eusebius, *Ecclesiastical History* 3–4.

(1 Cor. 15:8); he was not in the earliest circle of disciples, for he had not lived among the disciples and with them known the earthly Jesus. The argument at Antioch in Gal. 2, from the earliest New Testament writers through the sixth century, is not understood ultimately to pit the two apostles in opposition to each other or to sever their apostolic work into different sects.

2:15 We ourselves are Jews by birth—Paul's speech to Peter begins clearly ("I said to Cephas") in the middle of Gal. 2:14. But where it ends is not as clear. Even the manuscript tradition does not help us. Because ancient Greek manuscripts did not provide punctuation or paragraph breaks, later editors and translators are left to make their own interpretive decisions. For example, the NA[28] Greek text puts a soft tab break after 2:14, indicating a potential continuation of Paul's speech into 2:15 with the words, "We ourselves are Jews by birth." But the NRSV gives a sharp full-paragraph break, indicating that Paul's speech ends at "How can you compel the Gentiles to live like Jews?" If we follow the NA[28] with its soft break, Paul's address to Peter would continue from Gal. 2:14 ("if you though a Jew") potentially all the way to 2:21 ("If justification came through the law, then Christ died for nothing"). The next unit would begin at 3:1, when Paul turns his address again directly to the Galatians: "You foolish Galatians!" I find that the NRSV with its hard break after 2:14 reads more logically. Paul now leaves aside his confrontation with Peter, and a new unit of thought begins: "We ourselves are Jews by birth and not Gentile sinners."

The NRSV and RSV translate *physei* in Gal. 2:15 as "by birth," while the KJV gives "by nature."[58] However, given Paul's statements about Jewish identity and election, a better translation of *physei* would simply be "physically." Both circumcision and dietary laws are observances that fundamentally distinguish the body of the Jew from the Gentile—physically.

2:16 Yet we know that a person is justified not by the works of the law but through faith in Jesus Christ—This verse marks the letter's first opposition between justification by faith in Christ and justification by works of the law. However, the sentence structure as a whole forces us to see more broadly; these two couplets (justification by faith/justification by works) appear three times

---

58. At Rom. 2:27 the NRSV translates the word as "physically," while in Rom. 11:21, 24 it gives us "natural/by nature."

in this single verse, each in slightly different constructs. Paul does not actually address at this point the dichotomy between justification by faith in Christ and justification by law observance. But in English the words "faith" and "belief" both translate the same Greek noun *pistis,* and its verbal form *pisteuō* can mean either "to believe" or "to trust." Likewise, the English nouns "justification" and "righteousness" both translate the same Greek noun *dikaiosunē,* and its verbal form *dikaioō* can mean either "to pronounce righteous" or "to justify."

The construct "by the works of the law" (*ex ergōn nomou*) and its mirror twin "through faith in Jesus Christ" (*dia pisteōs Iēsou Christou*) in 2:16 compete for grammatical and theological attention. The construct "faith in Jesus Christ" and its variants appear three times, each sandwiched between three occurrences of the phrase "works of the law." The first occurrence is at the beginning of the verse; the second and third occurrences close the verse. The phrase "works of the law" is negated in all three of its occurrences ("*not* by works of the law"), while the phrase "faith in Jesus Christ" appears only in the affirmative and, significantly, at the center of the sentence.

This gives us a 1-3-2 pattern: the phrase "not by the works of the law" occurs once; then comes a threefold "through faith in Jesus Christ," then twice more the phrase "not by works of the law." This syntactical knot vividly expresses the tangle within which the Galatian churches find themselves trapped. Paul has illustrated this ensnaring in a number of contexts: the Third Party (1:6–9; 3:1); the challenge of the "false believers" (2:4; cf. Acts 15:1); the threat of the so-called representatives from James (2:12); and the tug-of-war between Paul and Peter (and Barnabas; 2:11–14). As the syntax points to the confusion in Galatia, it makes all the more astounding the fact that the meeting in 2:7–10 was initially pain-free.

While unwieldy in English, a literal translation allows us to hear Paul's sense: "*for by works of the law will not be justified all flesh.*" The position of the words "all flesh" at the end of the sentence takes some of the emphasis off the verb "to justify," placing the weight on the phrase "all flesh" (*pasa sarx*). These two words echo throughout scripture from a specific context; Paul's concern is not primarily justification by faith per se, but more specifically Gentile sin. By noting the structure of the verse, we find that Paul is focusing on the pre-Abrahamic universal covenant (Gen. 15) in contradistinction to Abraham's covenant of circumcision (Gen. 17).

The first time we hear the phrase "all flesh" in the canon is in the story of Noah, a Gentile who is reckoned righteous by God even before Abraham enters

the scene; indeed, like Abraham, Noah himself finds "grace in the eyes of the
LORD" (Gen. 6:8 KJV) even before he has done anything praiseworthy. The
words "all flesh" appear in the account of the flood story in Gen. 6–9, the locus
classicus for the Hebrew Bible's understanding of Gentile sin.[59] "And God said
to Noah, 'I have determined to make an end of all flesh, for the earth is filled
with violence because of them; now I am going to destroy them along with
the earth'" (Gen. 6:13; cf. 6:17; 8:17). There *pasa sarx* includes both humans
and animals. Because of the evil perpetrated by humanity beginning in the
garden of Eden, God sends a cataclysm to destroy Gentile corruption, human
and animals alike.

If we miss the phrase "all flesh" (Gal. 2:16) with its echo of the poison of
Gentile sin, the contrast between justification by faith and justification by
works overwhelms our attention. But behind Paul's discussion of justification
by faith is precisely the larger problem in 2:15: "We ourselves are Jews by birth
and not Gentile sinners." At this point in Galatians, Paul is not opposing faith
in Christ and Jewish law; he is opposing faith in Christ and Gentile sin, the
sin of those of the universal covenant.

Paul knows—and assumes that his fellow Jewish Christians of the Jerusalem
church would understand—that law observance is not a rival to the gospel.
Everyone knows (2:16) that there is only one means of being right before God.
Law observance was never a means to address sin; the election of Abraham
preceded the covenant of circumcision and the law. For Paul, covenant election never depended on observing the law; Abraham himself was elect in the
specific promise of the Messiah, the inner content and goal of the law. But this
does not leave Gentile Christians entirely without law, for all are to observe
the law of Christ (5:14; 6:2).

The late twentieth century has witnessed a debate over an element of Paul's
syntax and the English translation of the phrase "by faith in Christ." Paul's
genitive construct *dia pisteōs Iēsou Christou* (or *ek pisteōs Christou*) of 2:16 will
return in fuller form in his discussion at 2:20 and again in chapter 3.[60] Here
is the engine of the problem: syntactically, the proper noun "Jesus Christ"

59. The LXX phrase *pasa sarx* translates the Hebrew (MT) *kol basar*.
60. See also Gal. 3:2–5 ("by a report of faith," AT), 3:11 ("will live by faith"), 3:22 ("through
faith in Jesus Christ"), 3:24 ("justified by faith"); Rom. 3:22 ("through faith in Jesus Christ"), 3:24
("by his grace"), 3:26 ("faith in Jesus"), 5:1 ("justified by faith"); Eph. 2:8 ("by grace you have been
saved through faith"); Phil. 3:9 ("by faith in Christ"). The locus classicus of the scholarly discussion
is Hays, *Faith of Jesus Christ*.

(*Iēsou Christou*; or in its other form, simply *Christou*) is in the genitive case and thus can be read as either an object or subject of the prepositional clause that precedes it, "by faith" (*dia pisteōs, ek pisteōs*). Taken as an objective genitive, the proper noun with its title "Jesus Christ" is syntactically the object of faith and can be translated "faith *in* Jesus Christ." Our justifying faith is in the man Jesus Christ. However, the genitive can also be translated as a subjective genitive, in which the proper noun with its title "Jesus Christ" (*Iēsou Christou*) is grammatically the subject of its noun "faith," Jesus's own faith or even his own faithfulness. Our justifying faith is the faithfulness of the man Jesus Christ. Read in this way, the construct does not take Jesus Christ to be, properly speaking, the object of Christian faith.[61]

The latter construal has gained popularity in the late twentieth and early twenty-first centuries in part because of its correspondence to similar genitival constructs in Gal. 3 and Rom. 3.[62] The subjective genitive gives the sense that Jesus is faithful to God on behalf of the world and that his faith is exemplified in his obedience to God unto death on the cross. It is not our faith in him but his faith or faithfulness to God that justifies us.[63] However, interpreting the genitive in its objective sense has been the church's classic interpretation: faith in Jesus Christ justifies sinners.

Both the subjective and objective readings of the genitive are acceptable because of the multivalent nature of the genitive case itself. This is simply a syntactical observation. One of the positive theological contributions of the subjective interpretation is its potential for blunting a purely individualistic and cognitive emphasis on faith that can plague evangelical pieties. Justification before God is not dependent on a personal "decision" for Christ ("When

61. "In the case of Gal. 2:16, the sentence is so compact that it is difficult to decide what *dia pisteōs Iesou Christou* and *ek pisteōs Christou* might mean. . . . It is justifiable to maintain that the text means '. . . we place our trust in Christ Jesus in order that we might be justified on the basis of Christ's faithfulness.' This way of reading 2:16 should be taken seriously as an interpretive option, especially since the parallels in Gal. 3:22 and Rom. 3:22, 26 seem clearly to favor such an interpretation." Hays, *Faith of Jesus Christ*, 162.

62. Proponents include Richard Hays, N. T. Wright, J. Louis Martyn, Richard Longenecker, Douglas A. Campbell, Martinus de Boer, and many others. See Downs and Lappenga, *Faithfulness of the Risen Christ*, 11–12. Some theologians have also enthusiastically taken this on: e.g., Harink, *Paul among the Postliberals*.

63. I find the labeling of the objective genitive as "anthropological" and the subjective as "christological" (so Hays) to be inverted. It is the objective genitive (again, the more traditional reading) that is christological, because faith is in Jesus Christ. This is true especially if we understand, as Paul says, that the content of the promise to Abraham is specifically Christ the seed. *Sed contra*, see Hays, *Faith of Jesus Christ*, 293–94.

were you saved?"). The subjective genitive interpretation, therefore, allows for a more appropriately passive understanding of justification by faith than the objective genitive might.[64]

But interpreting the genitive construct "of/in Jesus Christ" as a subjective genitive can also reduce Jesus to a theological exemplar. This gives room for the conclusion that Jewish election and law are disposable at the advent of Jesus's lived faithfulness.[65] While Hebrews presents Jesus as paradigm (Heb. 2:10; 12:2), this is grounded firmly in his identity as the one who suffered on the cross. The most vexing theological problem with the subjective genitive interpretation for any reading of Paul is that it renders inexplicable his own remarks about the value of his suffering in Christ. After all, who would suffer, much less go to martyrdom, for a mentor, a teacher, an exemplar of faith?

The christological assumptions implicit in the claims to the subjective genitive interpretation of "Jesus Christ" are significant: in this debate, traditional claims to Jesus's atoning work on the cross are sometimes bracketed. An often unacknowledged reshaping of the classical web of Christian confession emerges. For example, the Chalcedonian confession of Jesus's two natures is weakened: Jesus may be fully human, but the fullness of his divinity seems to have gone missing.

But the most problematic aspect of the current debate over the genitive construct *pistis Iēsou Christou* is that it owes so much more to Enlightenment apologetics, with all of its internal contradictions, than to New Testament scholarship.[66] The debate is more properly theological than it is historical-critical. Its indebtedness to modern Christology runs far deeper than can be remedied by observations, no matter how interesting, that hang on grammar and syntax.[67]

64. "It should be said clearly that for Paul, *pistis Christou* refers to Jesus's obedience to death on the cross: in other words, the meaning of the phrase is focused on the kerygma's narration of his self-giving death, not on the whole ministry of Jesus of Nazareth. This narrower, punctiliar sense—focused on the cross—is the only meaning supported by Paul's usage" (Hays, *Faith of Jesus Christ*, 297n58).

65. One example of this view of Jewish law is this: "Torah was given for a good but temporary purpose. Once the Abrahamic promise is fulfilled, in the Messiah and his worldwide people, that purpose is accomplished. . . . The illustration I have sometimes used is that of a space rocket. You need a particular kind of booster to get the rocket up through Earth's atmosphere. But once it's out in space, someone presses a button and the booster drops away. That is not because it was a bad thing and you wish you'd never had it in the first place. You jettison the booster because it was *a good thing whose job is now done.* That is what Paul is saying about Torah." Wright, *Galatians*, 231.

66. See Hays, *Faith of Jesus Christ*, appendixes 1 and 2.

67. George Hunsinger points to the underlying assumptions about Pauline soteriology held by the proponents: "The faith-*of*-Christ interpreters . . . as a rule . . . lack any robust conceptions of expiation, substitution, transfer, and exchange" (*Philippians*, 208–9). For an attempt (unsuccessful, to my mind) of reading the subjective genitive while maintaining a more classical Christology, see Downs and Lappenga, *Faithfulness of the Risen Christ*, esp. 3.

To risk oversimplification, I will illustrate the internal contradictions by pointing briefly to the example of eighteenth-century philosopher G. E. Lessing. Son of a Lutheran pastor, Lessing came to be known in part for what he observed to be an unbridgeable chasm (he called this an "ugly ditch") between the "religion of Christ" and the "Christian religion."[68] For Lessing, the "religion of Christ" is the religion that Jesus embodied and practiced, Jesus's own religion. In many ways this category is formally akin to the logic behind the implicit Christology of the subjective genitive interpretation. But the "Christian religion" is the faith of the church with its doctrines and creeds; this is formally similar to the logic of the objective genitive interpretation.

Lessing anonymously published the fragments of deist H. S. Reimarus (1694–1768), effectively sparking the movement known as the quest for the historical Jesus. This was a generations-long theological project that included many New Testament scholars, among them notably Albert Schweitzer (1875–1965). The questers sought Jesus's identity through what they assumed they could determine him "actually" to have said and done; the assumption was that this project was possible. Like Lessing, many distinguished, whether implicitly or explicitly, the religion of Christ from the religion about Christ; while they were not uniform in method or in goal, they shared the idea that the church's doctrinal claims could be stripped away from the data of the New Testament like a husk from its kernel. The subjective is the kernel; the objective is the husk.

Instead, I suggest that the relationship between the objective and subjective genitives might be seen as a theological analogue to the relationship between justification and sanctification. Each pair (objective/subjective and justification/sanctification) speaks of a way in which the believer is related to Christ's benefits, the first from the standpoint of the identity of Christ himself, and the second from the standpoint of the believer's own identity in Christ. Looking to the second pairing, justification and sanctification, may be more theologically fruitful than limiting a discussion to syntax, especially as we listen for Paul's deep pastoral concern for moral formation among his Galatian churches.[69]

In his commentary on Galatians, the late-sixteenth-century Puritan theologian William Perkins offers a beautiful illustration of the link between

68. Lessing, *Lessing's Theological Writings*, 53.
69. Paul works with the concept of sanctification throughout his letters. See Rom. 6:19, 22; 12:2; 1 Cor. 1:30; 2 Cor. 3:18; 1 Thess. 4:3, 7; 2 Thess. 2:13; 1 Tim. 2:15; see also Phil. 3:21. In Galatians, Paul does not use the word "sanctification" (*hagiasmos*), but he emphasizes it in Gal. 5 and 6.

justification by faith and sanctification of the faithful. Even though Perkins does not explicitly use the word "sanctification" in the sample I have chosen from his commentary, he clearly operates with both theological concepts. He makes an analogy of the unity of the two: they are intimately bound to the eschatological horizon of the Christian faith. It is well worth a short detour.

Perkins considers justification through the function of the theological virtues: faith, love, and hope (in that order).[70] He describes faith as a hand that opens itself to receive the gift of justification. While justification is a gift, one must act in order to receive it by opening the hand. Love itself is also a hand, opening the heart.

Paul expresses this dual receiving and giving in Galatians as the summing up of "the whole law" (Gal. 5:14; Matt. 22:40). The single gift of justification and sanctification issues in the mutual bearing of burdens (6:2). Justifying faith is inseparable from sanctifying love. In linking justification and sanctification, Perkins follows Paul in the underlying logic of the two classic ecclesial rules for reading scripture: the rule of faith and the rule of love.[71] For Perkins, we take hold of "Christ and his benefits" through the theological virtues of faith and love.[72] While justifying faith has a passive element, sanctifying love is active. But they are not separate movements. The two work together in the justification and sanctification of the Christian.

While the rules of faith and love do not include the concept of hope, Paul's triad in 1 Corinthians does. Perkins adds hope to his own illustration of the function of justification and sanctification. Hope, says Perkins, is the eye that looks toward God's goodness, in which justifying faith trusts. "I wait for the LORD, my soul waits, / and in his word I hope" (Ps. 130:5). In receiving and giving, the two hands of faith and love work together with the eye of hope that looks to the future redemption in Christ's return. These are Christ's benefits; while inseparable, they remain distinct. And they engender the eschatological hope of resurrection life. Here is Perkins:

> A sinner is justified by meere faith: that is, that nothing within us concurres
> as a cause of our justification, but faith; and that nothing apprehends Christ's

70. Note his inversion of Paul's ordering of the triad: in 1 Cor. 13:13 it is "faith, hope, love."

71. On the rule of faith, see Tertullian, *Prescription Against Heretics* 15; on the rule of love, see Augustine, *Christian Instruction* 1.36.40; Luther, *LW* 27:159; Blowers, "Regula Fidei"; Jovanović, "St. Irenaeus." →2:2, 5; 5:6; 6:16.

72. Perkins adapts (possibly self-consciously) the phrase of sixteenth-century Lutheran theologian Philipp Melanchthon in his *Loci communes*: "To know Christ is to know his benefits" (trans. Pauck, 21).

obedience for our justification, but faith. This will more easily appeare, if we compare faith, hope and love. Faith is like an hand, that opens it selfe to receive a gift, and so is neither love, nor hope. Love is also an hand, but yet an hand that gives out, communicates, and distributes. For as faith receives Christ into our hearts, so love opens the heart, and powres out praise and thanks to God, and all manner of goodnesse to men. Hope is no hand, but an eye that willfully looketh and waiteth for the good things which faith beleeveth. Therefore it is the onely propertie of faith to claspe and lay hold of Christ and his benefits.[73]

For Perkins, justification and sanctification are ultimately not in opposition precisely because Christ is the object of faith. If Christ were the subject of faith, this single movement of justification and sanctification would no longer pertain. The benefits of Christ are precisely his gift of himself to us in grace, our justification in him who is the object of our faith. Justification is inseparable from sanctification, the gift of love that transforms us into Christ's own image. "And all of us, with unveiled faces, seeing the glory of the Lord as though reflected in a mirror, are being transformed into the same image from one degree of glory to another; for this comes from the Lord, the Spirit" (2 Cor. 3:18; →5:6).

2:19–20 crucified with Christ—We have a string of prepositions that make translating here a bit awkward. The tangle they create, however, makes clear the connection between Paul's being crucified with Christ through the law to the law and Christ's resurrected life. In other words, this is primarily a statement about Christ, not about the law nor about Paul. While he has been crucified with Christ (*Christō synestaurōmai*; see also 6:14, 17) such that Christ now lives in him (*en emoi*; 2:20) and he in Christ, Paul now lives not in the flesh (*en sarki*) but by faith (*en pistei*) in the Son of God (*tou huiou tou theou*). Dying in Christ releases Paul from observance of Mosaic law and brings him into the realm of its substance, the law of Christ (6:2; 5:14). Having been crucified with Christ, Paul belongs no longer to himself but to Christ (6:14). Because of this, and only because of this, Paul is willing to be subject to persecution in Christ's name (5:11), as the Third Party is not (6:12). The mutual indwelling of Christ and Paul is not an ex post facto add-on but is the eternal will of God. All of this is affirmation primarily about Christ, not about Paul.

73. Perkins, *Commentary on Galatians*, 113–14.

Dying through the law to the law comes from and issues in participation in Christ's suffering and life. We will encounter this again at 3:10–13, where Paul says that Jesus died as a cursed criminal under the law to redeem and bless.[74] His statement that he has been co-crucified with Christ anticipates his later report that the crucifixion of Christ was "publicly" exhibited to the Galatians (1) in his own preaching and (2) in the wounds of Christ that he bears on his own body (6:17; see Matt. 16:24). As we will see in chapter 3, through his preaching both oral (his message) and visual (his wounds), Paul announces the cross as the content of his preaching. The cross is the fulcrum of Christ's identity and life, and therefore also of Paul's own identity and vocation. Living in the death of Christ is the content and goal of dying to the law, not its opposite.

It is no longer I who live, but it is Christ who lives in me—Here is a mutual indwelling: Christ lives in Paul, and Paul lives in Christ. Paul has been crucified with Christ, and yet Christ lives in Paul. The life that Paul lives is a "no longer I"; nevertheless, it is Paul himself who truly lives it: "the life I now live in the flesh" (2:20). Paul thus lives into the eschatological new creation, in the fullness of time (6:14–15; 4:4). The mutual relationship of Paul and Christ is the intimacy of sacramental life in Christ: "Those who eat my flesh and drink my blood abide in me, and I in them" (John 6:56). The statement in Gal. 2:19–20 presents in compact form the doctrine of justification, placing it exactly where the doctrine belongs: in the sacramental life of the church.[75] The closing words of the Prayer of Humble Access express this mutual indwelling of communicant and Christ in the sacrament: "that we may evermore dwell in him and he in us."[76]

Crucified with Christ, Paul knows that his missionary work has not been wasted (Gal. 2:2). This forms the apostolic typology initiated by Christ: "Those who love their life lose it, and those who hate their life in this world will keep it for eternal life" (John 12:25). Paul lives as dying and dies as living. The sacramental identification with Christ will be mirrored in Paul's later implicit claim that in his preaching his life in Christ is a type of Christ's crucifixion

74. This is similar to his statement in Phil. 3:10 that he is conformed to the death of Christ.

75. See also 2 Cor. 5:14–15. The claim to Paul's "mysticism" comes in part from an interpretation of this verse; to my mind it seems a modern Protestant attempt to relocate the sacramental from the ecclesial context to the inner experience of the individual. See especially Schweitzer, *Mysticism of Paul the Apostle*.

76. *Book of Common Prayer*, 337. Sonderegger, "Doctrine of Justification."

(3:1; 6:17). And this mutual relation with Christ is not restricted to Paul's work as an apostle but is inherent in the Christian life and is shared by all believers (5:24). Death in Christ is already resurrected life in foretaste. "There lives that living bread which comes from heaven, there lives wisdom, there lives righteousness, there lives the resurrection."[77] Christ's atoning death melds the objective identity of Christ with the subjective identity of the believer. A new creation is formed; life is gathered up into the death of Christ. Both Abraham's faith in Christ the seed and the faithfulness of that seed on the cross bring life.

who loved me and gave himself for me—This draws us again to the opening of the letter, where Paul identified Jesus as the one "who gave himself for our sins to set us free" (1:4). But whereas there Jesus's death is described with the ordinary verb "to give" (*didōmi*), here at 2:20 the verb is "gave himself" (*paradidōmi*), a verb that can also be translated "to hand over" or even "betray" in the sense used in the Gospels to refer to Judas's role at Gethsemane.[78] Jerome makes clear the link between Paul's words in Gal. 2:20 and the Gospel story of the betrayal of Jesus: "Judas and the priests, with the princes, handed him over, and Pilate, to whom he was finally handed over, handed him over again. But the Father handed him over that he might save the abandoned world. Jesus gave himself, that he might do the Father's will. But Judas and the priests and elders of the people and Pilate unwittingly handed over their lives to death."[79]

Jerome points out that Jesus's cross is not simply an imposition or punishment by a tyrant Father but that Jesus's free self-giving is of his own will, at one with the Father's will. Jesus's self-sacrificing love, the extended hand that gives, defines the meaning of his atoning death, a free sacrifice and gift of love. While no single atonement theory has been defined throughout the history of Christian theology, Paul's confession that Christ's death is "for me" is at the foundation of all of them.[80] While the formulation of the doctrine of atonement is flexible, the confession itself is not. That Christ gave himself, and indeed went willingly to the cross specifically for us, *pro nobis*, is integral

---

77. Ambrose, *On Paradise* 76 (CSEL 32.1:335), translation in Edwards, *Galatians, Ephesians, Philippians*, 32. See also John 11:25.

78. It is also used in other contexts, as in Matt. 26; Mark 14; Luke 22; John 6, 12, 13.

79. Jerome, *Epistle to the Galatians* 1.2.20 (PL 26:346B), translation in Edwards, *Galatians*, 33. In a sense, Jerome anticipates feminist objections to the cross as an instrument of child abuse. See, e.g., Brock, *Journeys by Heart*, 56.

80. And "for us," *hyper hēmōn* (3:13). See also Matt. 20:28; Rom. 5:8; 14:15; 1 Cor. 8:11; 1 Thess. 5:10; 1 Tim. 2:6; Titus 2:14.

to classic Christian confession. The church's reticence to insist on uniformity of doctrinal statement here corresponds theologically to the canon's embrace of the fourfold account of the crucifixion and the multiple depictions of Jesus's death in scripture. *Pace* Lessing, the doctrine of the atonement is not an accretion of the church concocted long after the resurrection. Jesus's atoning death is linked specifically to his love (3:10–13) and is prophetically announced in the Torah and prophets.[81] In Gal. 5, Paul will include this love as the first on his list of the fruit of the Spirit (5:22). In this sense, to know Christ who gave himself for us is to know his benefits (5:6, 13–14, 22; →1:4; 4:20).

2:21 Christ died for nothing—Paul restates here what he said at the beginning of the letter, that the gospel by definition cannot be rendered null and void, nor broken apart into different manifestations or versions (1:6–9). Likewise, Christ's death by definition does not fit the category of "nothing." The significance of Christ's death precedes even that of his earthly life in the logic of Christian confession (4:4). The one gospel is in essence a passion narrative to which the earthly ministry of Jesus is the introduction.[82] Paul's mission journeys and apostolic witness are narrated as a participation in the cross and death of Jesus. Justification comes primarily neither through Jesus's teachings nor his ethics nor his miracles but through his death and resurrection.

---

81. Deut. 21:23; 27:15–26; 28:58; Hab. 2:4.
82. This dovetails with Martin Kähler's observation that the Gospels are essentially passion narratives with extended introductions. *So-Called Historical Jesus*, 80n11.

GALATIANS 3

Chapter 3 marks a sudden change in Paul's tone and focus. He scolds the Galatians for their behavior, turning to the Abraham cycle in Genesis at Gal. 3:6. He uses scripture as well as secular examples to illustrate the typological relationship between Christ and the law. He includes a reading of Deuteronomy to show how the law itself is specifically christological. Belonging to Christ, the Galatians themselves (Paul's mission) share with Jewish Christians (Peter's mission) the promise to Abraham apart from circumcision. The christological reality Paul explores in chapter 3 will be clarified further in terms of election in chapter 4 and in its corresponding ecclesial reality and moral formation in chapters 5 and 6.

3:1 You foolish Galatians! Who has bewitched you? It was before your eyes that Jesus Christ was publicly exhibited as crucified!—Paul leaves the interaction with Peter at Antioch in chapter 2 and returns to his sharp direct address to the Galatians such as at the beginning of chapter 1. His frustration with the Galatians in 3:1 echoes both his dismay that aborted his thanksgiving (1:6–9) and his opposition to Peter at Antioch (2:14). In upbraiding the Galatians, Paul uses the same adjective as does the risen Christ who chides his disciples at Emmaus. Just as the disciples are "foolish" (*anoētoi*, Luke 24:25), for they do not accept the report of the witnesses to the resurrection, so the Galatians are foolish for allowing themselves to be swayed from Christ. But while in the Gospel story Jesus describes the disciples as "slow of heart," Paul wants to know who has "bewitched" the Galatians; they have been caught up in pagan superstition.[1] In the ancient world, the Galatians were described as

1. The verb *baskainō* carries the connotation of bewitching "as with the 'evil eye.'" BDAG 137.

Celts whose pagan behaviors included war-mongering, deceit, sexual excesses, and even cannibalism.[2] If the Galatians' behavior followed this pattern, their pre-conversion practices may also have included Celtic devotion to pagan gods.[3] It may be this sort of behavior to which the Galatians had regressed during Paul's absence. His charge that they have been ensnared by others corresponds to his remark in Gal. 5:8, where he says that their behavior does not come from Christ's call. Paul will link this pagan trickery with the Third Party's demands for Gentile Christian circumcision (Gal. 3:8–10).

Paul had vividly taught the Galatians the saving significance of the crucified Christ. The verb translated in the NRSV as "publicly exhibited as crucified" (*proegraphē estaurōmenos*; 3:1) can refer to an announcement or a placarded public notice.[4] Paul describes his preaching as this kind of public event. Just as crowds would have gathered at the crucifixion to gawk at Jesus, so the Galatians gathered around Paul to hear the apostolic preaching about the crucified one. None of these events were preached "in a corner" (Acts 26:26); they were publicly declared and widely heard. As the content of Paul's public preaching, the word of the cross poses an offense (*skandalon*) to the Galatians as it did to the Christians in Corinth (1 Cor. 1:23–25; 2:2; Gal. 5:11; 6:12).

The Galatians have beheld with their eyes the scars that identify Paul as a slave of the crucified Jesus, the wounds that preach the gospel in an open and public way (6:17). Paul's "marks" are types of Jesus's wounds that marred even the Lord's resurrected body (John 20:26–27). This is one example where types and antitypes function intratestamentally; while types often precede their antitypes, this is not the case here. Paul's marks chronologically come after their antitype, which are Jesus's wounds.[5] Christ is never a type of something else; he is the ultimate antitype.[6] The wounds of Christ on Paul's body exhibit the gospel publicly and are evidence of his sacramental identification with Christ (2:20). In beholding Paul, the Galatians witness Christ.

At his conversion, Paul heard the voice of Jesus (Acts 9:2–4; 22:7–8; 26:14) and beheld the light of the world (see also John 1:9; 8:12; 9:5). This light temporarily blinded Paul's eyes (Acts 9:8; 22:11) and sent him to open the

---

2. See Diodorus of Sicily, "Galatian Excursus," in *Library of History* 5.24.32.
3. Kahl, *Galatians Re-imagined*, 45–50.
4. BDAG 704.
5. On types and antitypes, see the epilogue below.
6. This is the underlying difficulty with the concept of a Christ figure, in which Christ functions precisely as a type of a subsequent or more substantive human or historical reality. On Christ figures and their conceptual incoherence, see Frei, *Identity of Jesus Christ*, 62–83.

eyes of the Gentiles to the light of Christ (Acts 26:16–18; Isa. 42:6–7). The Galatians' love for Paul was so deep that they would have given even their own sense of sight, the physical means of their own sacramental beholding of the Lord (Gal. 4:15). Paul does not say that his intent was to exhibit Christ crucified; the verb is passive ("was publicly exhibited as crucified") and its subject is Christ, not Paul. It is Christ's work through Paul and not Paul's work apart from Christ that is exhibited.

In ancient theories of cognition, sight is sometimes understood to be the most important of all the senses.[7] The visible nature of the gospel is more important in Paul's preaching than we might otherwise think. This is another aspect in which Paul's letters conform to the Gospels, in this case especially the Synoptic Gospels, where verbs of seeing and beholding refer to christological witnessing. This is true especially of the accounts of the women at the cross and the tomb. The women see (*theōrousai*, Matt. 27:55; Mark 15:40; *horōsai*, Luke 23:49) Jesus die on the cross; they see (*etheasanto*, Mark 15:47; Luke 23:55) where he was laid in the tomb; they go on the first day of the week to see (*theōrēsai*, Matt. 28:1) the tomb; they see (*anablepsasai theōrousin*, Mark 16:4) that the stone has been rolled away; they see (*eidon*, Mark 16:5) the youth sitting on the right side; the angel invites them to see (*idete/ide*, Matt. 28:6; Mark 16:6) where Jesus had lain.[8] Paul's words in Gal. 3:1 likewise reflect the importance of visual witness, as he reminds the Galatians of their having beheld the Lord Jesus in him and on him (6:17).

Sight as a guarantee of the promise is also key in one of the Genesis stories of promise, a cycle foundational to Paul's teaching in Galatians. God commands Abram to look upon the land that God will give him: "The LORD said to Abram, after Lot had separated from him, 'Raise your eyes now, and *look* from the place where you are, northward and southward and eastward and westward'" (Gen. 13:14–15). In another episode of the promise important to Paul, Abram is told to "*look* toward heaven and count the stars, if you are able to count them" (Gen. 15:5).[9] Sight is a reliable witness to the promise of Christ for the Galatians, just as it was for Abram, and the Galatians have looked on the sacramental presence of the promise of Christ in Paul's own preaching and bodily witness.

---

7. According to Heraclitus, the sense of sight surpasses even hearing. Bauckham, *Jesus and the Eyewitnesses*, 48, citing Byrskog, *Story as History*, 52–53, 64–65.

8. Bauckham, *Jesus and the Eyewitnesses*, 48. See my comments at Gal. 2:20 for other formal coherence between Paul and the Gospels on the atonement.

9. Paul uses Gen. 15:6 in Gal. 3:6. See also Gen. 16:13.

3:2 Did you receive the Spirit by doing the works of the law or by believing what you heard?—Their receiving the publicly announced gospel is linked to the publicly manifested Spirit (4:6; 5:16–18, 22, 25; 6:1). In being duped by the Third Party, the Galatians are foolish: they have not discerned the Spirit's work. Paul will return to a fuller discussion of the Spirit's presence and activity in the church in chapter 5.

The NRSV translation of 3:2 suggests an echo of the juxtaposition at 2:16: "works of the law" (*ex ergōn nomou*) and "faith in Jesus Christ" (*dia pisteōs Iēsou Christou*). But here at Gal. 3:2 Paul's concern is not justification but the reception of the Spirit. The phrase "works of the law" (*ex ergōn nomou*) is juxtaposed not with "faith in Jesus Christ" but with "by believing what you heard" (*ex akoēs pisteōs*). Better translated as "a report of faith," this phrase echoes Isa. 52:7 (LXX), where the messenger announces the report about peace after a battle has been won.[10]

As we saw in Gal. 2:16, the inherent ambiguity of the genitive case allows for an array of possible translations.[11] We could take the phrase to mean any number of the following: "by hearing with belief (or faith),"[12] "by hearing the faith (or the gospel),"[13] "from a report that generates faith,"[14] or even "from the gospel message."[15] The *akoē pisteōs* presents the concrete content of the gospel: the Galatians have heard the report about the crucified Jesus (3:1). The content of the *akoē pisteōs* is the cross of Christ manifest in oral, aural, and visual form and in the Spirit's presence. The report forms faith and is the content of faith. Only in hearing about the cross of Christ through Paul's preaching and seeing it publicly displayed on his body do the Galatians come to believe this report of the good news. Through this experience of receiving the report, they also receive the Spirit.

3:3 Having started with the Spirit, are you now ending with the flesh?—The Pauline opposition of spirit and flesh has been caricatured in both the history of the tradition and in popular culture as opposition between the spiritual and the material. For Paul, the biblical word *sarx*, translated "flesh," is a far more complex concept than flattening caricatures would imply.

---

10. "How beautiful upon the mountains are the feet of the messenger who announces peace [*euangelizomenou akoēn eirēnēs*]" (Isa. 52:7).
11. Hays, *Faith of Jesus Christ*, 124–32.
12. Lightfoot, *Epistle of St. Paul*, 134.
13. Calvin, *Epistles of Paul*, 48.
14. Bultmann, "*Pistis, Pisteuō*," *TDNT* 6:213.
15. Betz, *Galatians*, 128n3.

Classic Christian confession has rejected the idea that the creator of the material world is a distinct being from the creator of the spiritual realm. The Nicene Creed (325) confesses the Father to be "maker of heaven and earth, of all that is, seen and unseen." The Christian tradition neither invents this conviction nor bases it solely on the New Testament, but instead inherits it first from the Hebrew Bible: created reality is good because God is its maker. In the creation narrative, the voice of God blesses material reality, repeatedly declaring it "good" (Gen. 1:4, 10, 12, 18, 21, 25, 31). Adam was created out of the fertile soil, and Eve out of his side: "bone of my bones and flesh of my flesh [*sarx*, LXX]" (Gen. 2:23). Flesh at its created order is good.

But as the narrative progresses, fallen order comes to be distinct from created order. Adam and Eve, who were once a team, side by side, rib to rib, now independently disobey God (Gen. 3:1–7). Their relationship with God, with each other, and with all creation becomes distorted, and a hierarchy results. In this now-cursed relationship, Adam will rule over Eve (Gen. 3:16). Patriarchy as dominance enters with the fall, and the blessing they share with all creation in the command to multiply is now experienced as multiplying Eve's agony in her bearing of children.[16] Eve's procreative role now brings her pain, but it does not extinguish her desire for her husband. While human flesh suffers from the fall, it retains the blessing of increase.

The good earth itself that once brought forth life (Gen. 2:15), giving seed for sowing and bread for eating (Isa. 55:10), now yields thorns and thistles (Gen. 3:18). Working the land will now be hard labor (Gen. 3:17–19). The first pair is cast out of the garden (Gen. 3:23–24); they are separated from the tree of life, itself a type of the cross of Christ (Deut. 21:23; Gal. 3:13). Their ultimate separation from God's presence will be death (Gen. 2:17). Although created good, flesh is now subject to decay and corruption as a result of the ancestral sentencing.

Yet in the fullness of time Jesus, human flesh of that same created order, comes like us in every way except sin.[17] In his coming, he restores our human flesh to health. But in Gal. 3:3 Paul mocks the Galatians for their foolishness,

---

16. In the MT, the verb *rabah* (to make great, multiply) is used for the multiplying of Eve's birth pangs (Gen. 3:16), as it was for the blessing of procreation, "Be fruitful and *multiply* [*rabah*]" (Gen. 1:28). Pitre, *Jesus and the Jewish Roots of Mary*, 203n8. The LXX uses the verb *plēthunō*, thus obscuring the echo. The linguistic link is pregnant (pun intended).

17. "For we do not have a high priest who is unable to sympathize with our weaknesses, but we have one who in every respect has been tested as we are, yet without sin" (Heb. 4:15).

manifest in their betrayal of the gospel promise. Having begun their life in the Lord through Paul's public preaching in the Spirit, do they really now think they can bring it to perfection through the flesh, either as the foreskin (circumcision) or as the stomach (dietary laws)?[18] They have experienced the Spirit for nothing.

3:5 Well then, does God supply you with the Spirit and work miracles among you by your doing the works of the law, or by your believing what you heard?—The word "miracles" can also be translated "powers," and Paul says these are wrought by the Spirit. Miracles are proof of the apostle's true identity and point to the Spirit in the life of the church.[19] Here the working of power (*energōn dynameis*) sits in opposition to the works of the law (*ergōn nomou*) and in apposition to the report of faith (*akoēs pisteōs*). Paul's emphasis here is on sanctification in the Spirit rather than on observance of the law.

At 3:5 the NRSV indicates in a note that the word "God" is supplied to translate the pronoun "he." But this misleads, precisely because the word "God" in the translation fills in not for the pronoun "he" but for a masculine article with a gerund. The translation thus hides a reference to Jesus Christ, who was the implicit subject of the verb at 3:1, "was publicly exhibited as crucified." And it is Jesus publicly exhibited who supplies the Spirit. At stake here is the dislocating of the cross of Jesus from the Spirit, something Paul is precisely eager not to do.

The Greek text can be read to indicate that the Spirit proceeds from the Son. The Christian West's eventual unilateral decision to include the *filioque* clause in the creed was the final precipitant of the Great Schism of the eleventh century, dividing Eastern from Western Christianity. The idea is attested long prior to that, as early as the fifth century Council of Toledo. The doctrine that the Spirit proceeds from both the Father and the Son may be *in nuce* here in Gal. 3:5. However, we do not hear this doctrinal embryo in Gal. 3:5 without looking to Paul's own Greek.

3:6 Just as Abraham "believed God, and it was reckoned to him as righteousness"—At this point, Abraham enters the letter and will occupy much of Paul's discussion in chapters 3 and 4. It is fair to assume that Paul speaks

18. The verb "to end," *epiteleō*, can also be translated as "to accomplish or to fulfill an objective" (BDAG 383).
19. Gal. 5:22–26; 1 Cor. 12:4–11; 14:26–33; 2 Cor. 12:12.

to those who have a prior familiarity with the story of Israel; he peppers his exposition with references to and quotations from scripture. Even though he preaches the gospel to pagans, he cannot avoid teaching the stories of Israel, for they are the foundation of the gospel. But this is curious: the Galatians lived in a non-hellenized, heavily pagan area and would have had little if any contact with Jews. How do they know the stories of Abraham? Paul himself would have introduced them to the covenant stories of election: even if he had given them texts when he left for his other mission fields, itself not unimaginable, it is unlikely that they would have been able to read them.[20] How then would they know the stories to which Paul so readily refers? The technique of memorization in the ancient world stabilized the passing of tradition, as remains the case among contemporary nonliterate cultures; the Galatians may have committed to memory the stories that Paul taught them.[21] Whatever the case, he is not speaking into a vacuum.

Paul takes up the figure of Abraham not to correct false teaching but to catechize the Gentile Galatian Christians.[22] He interprets Israel's scripture for them in messianic terms: Abraham has all along been the recipient of the messianic promise; Paul uses the figure of Abraham not to "retell" the story of Israel under a new messianic lens so much as to show how the promised Messiah has been "within" the story all along.[23] Among the other patriarchs, Abraham plays a key role in Galatians precisely because of his placement in the order of the Torah narrative. For Paul, the fact that the messianic promise to Abraham precedes the rite of circumcision makes Abraham the key interpretive figure for the Galatians' misunderstanding of their need for Gentile circumcision.

The figure of Abraham functions within Galatians' overall typological argument from scripture to show that God's eternal will has been to include the Gentiles within the covenant with Israel specifically through the Messiah, Jesus Christ. Before being called by God, Abraham was an alien, a foreigner, a Gentile, a "wandering Aramean."[24] The ordering of the episodes of Abraham's

20. See Abasciano, "Diamonds in the Rough."

21. See Bauckham, *Jesus and the Eyewitnesses*; Gerhardsson and Sharpe, *Memory and Manuscript*; Byrskog, *Story as History*; Bockmuehl, *Simon Peter*.

22. Martyn suggests that Paul introduces the Abraham stories chiefly to counter his opponents. *Galatians*, 300–306.

23. The idea that Christ dwells even within the story of Abraham is "infrasession." See the epilogue. *Pace* Wright, *Pauline Perspectives*, 572.

24. "A wandering Aramean was my father" (Deut. 26:5 RSV); see also Deut. 6:20–24; Josh. 24:2–13. Gerhard von Rad identified this formula of Abrahamic tradition as the organizing principle for what he called the Hexateuch, the first six books of the Hebrew Bible. See his landmark 1938

promises is therefore key for Paul: Abraham trusts and is "reckoned righteous" even before he is given the statute of circumcision. Abraham believes in the promise of the seed before God gives him the command to circumcise; he is a type of the Gentile Galatians who believe in that same messianic promise, Jesus.

God's promises to the first patriarch are key to the identity not only of Jewish Christians but also of Gentile Christians. The stories of Abraham will become increasingly important as we move through Gal. 3 and into Gal. 4, where Paul begins his own midrashic interpretation of the stories of God's promises in Gen. 12–21. He reads these chapters as distinguishing between Abram the Gentile, father of the *ethnoi* (the universal covenant) in Gen. 15, and Abraham the Jew, father of Israel (the particular covenant) in Gen. 17.

3:7 those who believe are the descendants of Abraham—There is a correspondence at this point between Paul's use of the Genesis stories and one of the Gospel traditions (→3:1). In the Gospel according to John, Jesus makes a typological link between Abraham and himself; Jesus existed before Abraham. "'Your ancestor Abraham rejoiced that he would see my day; he saw it and was glad.' Then the Jews said to him, 'You are not yet fifty years old, and have you seen Abraham?' Jesus said to them, 'Very truly, I tell you, before Abraham was, I am'" (John 8:56–58). The patriarchs and prophets knew Christ in a mystical sense.[25] The saints of old dwell as one body in asynchronic presence with the saints of the church, sharing the same faith in Christ. Much like in Jesus's statement in John 8, Paul shows that Abraham has seen Christ in this mystical sense. The patriarch Abraham reaches forward in the chronological ordering of the plot and grasps the promise of the seed in faith. That seed is the typological reality: Abraham's son through Sarah is Isaac, and yet is Christ.

The temporal ordering in 3:6–7 is key for Paul. Abraham first trusts the promise, then God declares him righteous. This in turn sets up Paul's observation about the ordering of promise and law. Those who believe in Christ

---

essay, "The Form-Critical Problem of the Hexateuch," later included in his *Old Testament Theology*, 1:129–306. We do not need to agree with von Rad's entire argument to appreciate his conclusion that the literary evidence within the Hebrew Bible itself shows that the exodus-conquest tradition and the Sinai tradition were originally independent from each other. His argument is formally similar to Paul's understanding of the relationship of the episodes of the messianic promise and the covenant.

25. A similar mystical knowledge of those who did not know the earthly Christ but knew him "from a distance" is described in Hebrews: "All of these died in faith without having received the promises, but from a distance they saw and greeted them. They confessed that they were strangers and foreigners on the earth" (Heb. 11:13).

share Abraham's faith, which itself is not based on law observance because it precedes the law. The Abraham of Gen. 15 that Paul refers to in Gal. 3 is at this point still upstream of the command to circumcise, as are the Galatians. Biologically they are strangers to the people of Abraham, but according to the promise they are Abraham's children.[26]

3:8 And the scripture, foreseeing that God would justify the Gentiles by faith, declared the gospel beforehand to Abraham, saying, "All the Gentiles shall be blessed in you"—For Paul, Abraham was a Gentile before God chose him out from Ur of the Chaldeans, long before the rite of circumcision and even longer before the law of Sinai (Gen. 12:1; 17:11; Gal. 3:17). Paul hears Gen. 12 as preaching the gospel ahead of time through God's blessing on Abraham: "I will bless those who bless you, and the one who curses you I will curse; and in you all the families of the earth shall be blessed" (Gen. 12:3; cf. Gen. 18:18; Ps. 72:17). These "families of the earth" include the Galatians, who are also blessed in the substance of Abraham's faith, the messianic promise.[27]

The English of the NRSV gives four words to express the single Greek verb *proeuēngelisato* ("to preach in advance," AT). Paul wants to make clear that he is not reshaping, adding to, or reinterpreting scripture; the gospel is *precisely* the same story in which the promise to Abraham is Christ the seed.[28] The Galatian churches succumb to circumcision precisely because they do not discern this continuity, and their lack of discernment sparks the pastoral occasion of the letter. Scripture itself declares the gospel beforehand, and Paul understands himself to be simply passing on what he has learned.

3:9 those who believe are blessed with Abraham who believed—Paul brings to a soft pause the topic of Abraham as an example of justification by

---

26. The NRSV translates the Greek word *huioi* (lit., "sons") as "descendants." While this successfully removes gender, it misses Paul's argument throughout Galatians about the two sons of Abraham: Isaac and Ishmael. The fact that the identity of these two specific sons, not descendants or children in general, is at the heart of the problem in Galatia complicates inclusive translation.

27. But because of this typological reading of the Abraham stories, the point here is not reducible to family lineage. *Pace* Wright, who says, "The subject of this chapter is not 'how people get saved' but 'how Abraham gets his promised family' and 'how this family is to obtain the inheritance.'" Wright, *Galatians*, 190.

28. Barclay offers a different opinion: "The narratives of Israel are refashioned around Christ. If the *characters* are shared with some of the varied narratives current in Second Temple Judaism, the *plot* is new; it is doubtful if it makes sense to speak of Paul's inhabiting the 'same' story." *Paul and the Gift*, 415.

faith: Gentile election apart from circumcision. This verse closes the inclusio material begun in 3:6 and opens a subsequent inclusio that will end at 3:14, where Abraham's name returns. In the material between 3:9 and 3:14, we hear Paul's discussion of the curse of the law (3:10–13).

3:10 For all who rely on the works of the law are under a curse; for it is written, "Cursed is everyone who does not observe and obey all the things written in the book of the law"—To show the inverse relationship between law observance and righteousness, Paul builds a quotation from excerpts of Deuteronomy. From Deut. 27:26 he emphasizes the first word, "cursed." From Deut. 28:58 he adds the qualifier "all."[29] The second part of the construct adds an allusion to the exodus narrative.[30] The constructed quotation thus emphasizes not the danger of the law per se but the danger of not observing *all* of it. A curse falls on the people of Israel when they do not observe the entire law. This does not pertain to Gentiles, unless they, too, take on law observance.

Christ as the righteous promise becomes curse on the cross as he takes on the cursed condition of Adam and Eve (Gen. 3:15–19) and dies the cursed death that we in them bear (Gen. 2:17). As the law himself (Gal. 6:2), Jesus releases humanity from the curse of the law.[31] His cursed body on the cross brings the blessing of Abraham to the Gentiles through the power of the Spirit.

But this makes sense only if we remember what "curse" means in the context of the Hebrew Bible. The scriptural career of the word "curse" in Gal. 3:10–13 (*katara, epikataratos*) sets the stage for what disobedience to God's command means in both the universal and the particular covenants. Introduced in Gen. 3:14–19, the word "curse" indicates the punishment on our first parents for their original disobedience. The curse in the garden consigns the serpent to the status of the vilest of all creatures: it will eat dust and slither on its belly (Gen. 3:14). The woman is cursed in the increase (*rabah*, "multiply") of her birth pains (Gen. 3:16), the inverse of her earlier blessing: "be fruitful and multiply" (*rabbah*, "multiply," Gen. 1:28). The man's curse falls not directly on him (*adam*) but on the ground (*adamah*) from which he was formed; the

---

29. *et-kol-dibre hatorah*, MT; *panta ta rhēmata tou nomou*, LXX; "all the words of the law" (AT).

30. See Deut. 28:58–68; Exod. 7:14–12:32.

31. Even though Paul and James are often read as polar opposites on justification, regarding the cursing potential of the law's incomplete observance they are in agreement: "For whoever keeps the whole law but fails in one point has become accountable for all of it" (Jas. 2:10). And even though James holds the law to be "royal" (2:8) and freeing (2:12), it nevertheless convicts those who transgress (2:9).

ground that had previously been their source of nourishment is now rendered foul (Gen. 3:17). Yet, even God's punishment of the man and the woman embraces an element of mercy. While the pair is cast out of the garden and away from the tree of life, the flaming cherubim protect them from reentering paradise lest they live eternally in an accursed state of eternal death in the presence of the tree of life (Gen. 3:24).[32]

The curse returns in the story of the next generation's fratricide (Gen. 4:10–16). The Lord favors the younger brother Abel's sacrifice (meat) over the older brother Cain's (grain); Cain's jealousy gives rise to murderous violence. Abel's blood cries out for justice from the very same ground that Cain had tilled for his grain sacrifice. The Lord curses Cain, sending him away from the land, giving him a life sentence. But again, even here, the curse of exile is ultimately attenuated by God's mercy: the Lord gives Cain a "mark" (*ot*), identifying him lest those who encounter him exact punishment on him, perpetuating his crime and taking his guilt upon themselves. Cain's mark performs a similar function for him as do the cherubim for his parents.

Elsewhere in the Hebrew Bible, this word "mark" or "sign" (*signum*, VG; *ot*, MT; *sēmeion*, LXX) can also refer to God's blessings. The bow in the sky after the flood is a sign (*ot*) of the covenant with all flesh through Noah (Gen. 9:12–17, the universal covenant). Circumcision itself will be the sign (*ot*) of the covenant with Abraham (Gen. 17:11, the particular covenant). The blood of the Passover lamb on the doorposts is a sign (*ot*) of God's salvation.[33] Curse and blessing are in a profound sense linked in Israel's life before God. The God of Israel is the one who brings life out of death, blessing out of curse (Deut. 11:26–28).

3:11 no one is justified before God by the law; for "The one who is righteous will live by faith"—Galatians 3:11 offers a prooftext to expand on the implicit claim that Abraham's justification is by faith specifically in Jesus Christ. Paul moves quickly from a negative statement in the first half of 3:11 ("No one is justified before God by the law") to a positive statement supplied by a quotation of the second half of Hab. 2:4 ("The one who is righteous will live

---

32. In the Vulgate, the garden is *Paradisum* (Gen. 2:8). See also 2:15; 3:23–24. When Cain is finally expelled in Gen. 4:16, the Vulgate refers to the location as *Eden*.

33. "The blood shall be a sign for you on the houses where you live: when I see the blood, I will pass over you, and no plague shall destroy you when I strike the land of Egypt" (Exod. 12:13, the particular covenant).

by faith").[34] While the focus of Hab. 2:4–5 is human pride that leads to death, the piece quoted is set within the context of eschatological hope.[35] With the future tense from Hab. 2:4, Paul folds into Gal. 3:11 this hope of resurrection life in Christ: "The one who is righteous *will live* by faith." Both the larger context of the Habakkuk quotation and the future tense of its verb "to live" form a prooftext not only for justification by faith but also for the resurrection of the dead: the righteous *will live*.

Paul has already shown that resurrection life is not only a future event but a present reality even now as he dwells in Christ and Christ in him (Gal. 2:19–20). The life that the righteous *will live* is the antithesis of the earlier multiple references to curse and blessing in Gal. 3:10–14. Jesus's death on the cross is the curse slain by his resurrection, in which the righteous shall live by faith in him. This emphasizes Paul's understanding of the eschatological quality of Abraham's trust in Christ and the prophetic nature of the Abraham story.

The future verb tense in Hab. 2:4 is found in the Greek Septuagint, Paul's Bible. But in the Hebrew at Hab. 2:4, the verb "lives" is a *qal* and indicates no future aspect. The Septuagint and Masoretic Text also witness to different traditions regarding the pronoun that accompanies the noun "faith." While the Masoretic Text gives us "by *his* faith," the Septuagint gives "by *my* faith" (*ek pisteōs mou zēsetai*).[36] But Paul omits the pronoun entirely, giving us simply "the one who is righteous will live by faith" (*ek pisteōs*; see Gal. 2:16; 3:7–9).[37] By leaving out the pronoun "my" at "faith," Paul allows us to hear the implicit claim that the faith of Abraham is indeed Abraham's, but not his alone. It is the faith also of those who believe in the promise of Christ. Those who share Abraham's belief in Christ also share his blessing of being reckoned as righteous

34. Paul quotes Hab. 2:4 also in Rom. 1:17 as a prooftext for the power of the gospel to justify both Jew and Gentile in Christ.
35. "I will stand at my watchpost, and station myself on the rampart; I will keep watch to see what he will say to me, and what he will answer concerning my complaint. Then the LORD answered me and said: 'Write the vision; make it plain on tablets, so that a runner may read it. For there is still a vision for the appointed time; it speaks of the end, and does not lie. If it seems to tarry, wait for it; it will surely come, it will not delay'" (Hab. 2:1–3). See Hays, *Echoes of Scripture*, for how the larger context of a quotation or allusion can be indicative of the sense of a sentence.
36. As in 2:16, we are presented here with a choice between an objective and subjective genitive: "will live by faith in me" (objective genitive) or "will live by my faith" (subjective genitive).
37. The NRSV of Hab. 2:4 renders the Hebrew pronoun as "their," though it is properly translated as "his." This confuses the reader. Paul does not use a pronoun here at all. His words correspond neither to the LXX nor to the MT. For introductions to the development of the Christian use of both the LXX and the MT, see McDonald, *Formation of the Bible*; and von Campenhausen, *Formation of the Christian Bible*.

before God by the cross of Jesus on which the Lord became our own curse, destroying it in his resurrection life. This is the gospel preached beforehand to Abraham. This is the blessing for all who share in Abraham's faith in Christ.

3:12 But the law does not rest on faith; on the contrary, "Whoever does the works of the law will live by them"—Paul showed in Gal. 3:10 that the law declares itself to be a curse to those who fulfill it only partially (Deut. 27:26; 28:58). In 3:11 he reads the prophet Habakkuk as declaring that the righteous will live by faith. The law does not depend on faith, nor does it give life.

3:13 Christ redeemed us from the curse of the law by becoming a curse for us—for it is written, "Cursed is everyone who hangs on a tree"—Paul brings forward the word "curse" from Gal. 3:10, linking it to the imagery of the tree: for Paul, the cross. He quotes the statute from Deuteronomy requiring that the body of the criminal executed by hanging be removed from the tree and buried before sundown that same day lest the body "defile the land" (Deut. 21:23). The word "tree" in the context of Deut. 21:23 refers to the gibbet, the site of the capital punishment. The immediate theological context of that verse is *halakic* purity, specifically regarding the land. For Paul, the tree on which the body is left to hang that defiles the land typologically recalls the tree of the knowledge of good and evil in Gen. 3. Paul sees the tree of Deut. 21:23 as a type of the cross, and its defiling of the land as a type of Jesus's crucifixion. Christ became curse on our behalf, taking on himself the curse of Adam and turning it into blessing on the cross. In this way, the blessing of Abraham comes to the Gentiles, even those of Galatia (Gen. 3:14–19; Gal. 3:14).

tree—Galatians 3:13 may be our earliest written reference to the cross as antitype of the tree of life in the garden of Eden.[38] In the garden, there are many trees "pleasant to the sight and good for food" (Gen. 2:9). But only two are given a specific name: the tree of life in the middle of the garden and the tree of the knowledge of good and evil.[39] After Gen. 2:9, mention of the

---

38. Peter's sermon in Acts 10:36–42 also uses the image of the cross as tree. The image runs throughout the history of Christian interpretation and art. Just two examples are the hymn "Jesus Christ the Apple Tree" and James Cone's *The Cross and the Lynching Tree*. The first is cross-testamental, typologically linking the grace of the tree of life to the cross of Calvary; the second is extratestamental, typologically linking Jesus's murder on the cross to the lynching tree of white supremacist execution of Black people in America.

39. Tree of life: Gen. 2:9; 3:22, 24; tree of knowledge: Gen. 2:9, 17; 3:3 (implied).

tree of life recedes from the narrative, returning in Gen. 3:22 (and again in Rev. 22:2). God prohibits the first parents from eating the fruit of the tree of the knowledge of good and evil, but after their disobedience, along with the ensuing curses, the narrator turns the reader's attention back to the tree of life (Gen. 3:1–19). The tree of the knowledge of good and evil then recedes entirely from the Genesis story, subsumed by the tree of life. For Paul, the cross is the tree of life; life has the last word. Genesis 3 bears the curse as well as the promise of resurrection.

Jesus takes on the curse of the law specifically as an outlaw. He was not born cursed; he becomes cursed. If Jesus had been born cursed, he would have no power to save.[40] Paul's imagery in Gal. 3 of Jesus's cross as the tree of execution links the statute in the last book of the Torah with the tree of life in the first book of the Torah.[41] The tree of life bears its fruit in due season (Ps. 1:3); the crucified Jesus gives the blessing of life and the fruit of his Spirit (5:22–23).[42]

Paul's linking the cross to the cursing tree of Deuteronomy prepared the way for (at least) two streams of patristic interpretation. One links the tree of Ps. 1 as a type of both the tree of life in the garden and the tree of the knowledge of good and evil with the antitype of the cross of Christ; the other stream developed into the protoevangelium tradition, itself a version of typology. An example of the first is the sixth-century hymn attributed to Fortunatus woven into a contemporary hymn: "Faithful cross above all other, one and only noble tree! None in foliage, none in blossom, none in fruit thy peer may be: sweetest wood and sweetest iron! Sweetest weight is hung on thee."[43] The second, the protoevangelium, can be seen as a development from the thematic movement in Gal. 3:13. That the first tree (death) is overtaken by the second tree (life) is formally parallel to the scene of God's cursing in Gen. 3 with its announcement of the victory of Eve's seed even before the curse itself is leveled: "He [Eve's seed] will strike your [the serpent's] head, and you [the serpent] will strike his [Eve's seed's] heel" (Gen. 3:15).[44] Christ is the seed who will

40. This distinction in Gal. 3:13 is especially important to Jerome; see *Commentary on Galatians*, 144.

41. Deut. 21:23; Gen. 2:9. This is an example of typology functioning intratestamentally within the Old Testament.

42. Augustine, *Augustine's Commentary on Galatians*, 161.

43. Episcopal Church, *Hymnal 1982*, #165, verse 4.

44. This theme is also parallel to the motif of *felix culpa* ("Oh happy fall!"). Augustine, *Enchiridion on Faith, Hope, and Love* 8; Aquinas, *Summa Theologiae* III.1.3, ad. 3. There are some liturgies that continue to use this typology—e.g., the *Exsultet* in the Easter Vigil. See *Book of Common Prayer*, 286–87.

crush the deadly serpent under his feet. This tradition finds its roots (at least) in Gal. 3:10–13. Paul's typological reading of the cross as the tree of life may even chronologically precede his Adam-Christ typology.[45]

While Deut. 21:23 links the leaving of an executed criminal on the tree to the defilement of the land, Paul does not mine the second half of the verse here in Gal. 3:1.[46] The defilement of the land in the second half of the Deuteronomy verse is less important to his typology. His main interest lies in the christological elements in the earlier part of the verse: curse, hanging, and tree. In the Gospels, the disciples implicitly observe the statute proscribing the defilement of the land: they remove Jesus's halakically unclean corpse from the cross. Preventing the defilement of the land of promised rest, they move to their hasty and temporary pre-Sabbath burial.[47] At dawn on the third day, intending to finish the burial properly, they go to the tomb; to their great surprise they find no corpse. For Paul, the first half of Deut. 21:23 speaks of Jesus's cursed death; for the Gospels the second half of the verse implicitly tells of the disciples' obedience to the statute.

In John, Jesus is presented as a condemned criminal on trumped-up charges punishable by death: "The Jews answered him, 'We have a law, and according to that law he ought to die because he has claimed to be the Son of God'" (John 19:7). He is innocent if either the *charge* is untrue (i.e., he did not claim to be the Son of God) or the *claim* is untrue (i.e., he is not the Son of God). While the Gospels are inconsistent as to the exact charge, whether religious or political offense, all implicitly assume the truth of the claim itself: Jesus is the Son of God. Moving now from the Jewish council to the Roman authorities, Jesus is condemned unjustly as a criminal. In Luke's passion narrative Jesus is declared innocent five times by three individuals. Pilate says that Jesus has done nothing wrong and announces to the crowd that Herod also has found no fault

45. "Yet death exercised dominion from Adam to Moses, even over those whose sins were not like the transgression of Adam, who is a type of the one to come" (Rom. 5:14) and "For as all die in Adam, so all will be made alive in Christ" (1 Cor. 15:22).

46. The full verse reads: "His corpse must not remain all night upon the tree; you shall bury him that same day, for anyone hung on a tree is under God's curse. You must not defile the land that the LORD your God is giving you for possession" (Deut. 21:23).

47. "When it was evening, there came a rich man from Arimathea, named Joseph, who was also a disciple of Jesus. He went to Pilate and asked for the body of Jesus; then Pilate ordered it to be given to him. So Joseph took the body and wrapped it in a clean linen cloth and laid it in his own new tomb, which he had hewn in the rock. He then rolled a great stone to the door of the tomb and went away" (Matt. 27:57–60). Details of a hasty burial find their way into all the Gospels: Mark 15:42–46; Luke 23:50–54; and John 19:38–42.

in him (Luke 23:4, 14–15, 22). One of the criminals crucified nearby cries out
from his own cross that Jesus is innocent (Luke 23:41). The centurion present
at the cross declares that Jesus died an innocent man (Luke 23:47). Karl Barth
links this innocent-yet-guilty pattern to Gal. 3:13 in his larger discussion of
Chalcedonian Christology: "[Christ] bears away the sin of the world, but He
does not bear it (John 1:29). It can all be summarised in the terrible saying
of Gal. 3:13, *genomenos hyper hēmōn katara* [becoming curse on our behalf],
that He was innocent without sin of His own, that the whole accusation does
not touch Him but us."[48]

The blood of the innocent Jesus cries out from the ground like the blood of
Abel, the younger brother slain by the elder who should have protected him.
But, according to Hebrews, Jesus himself is the mediator and content of the
covenant of Abraham, and his own sacrifice on the cross sheds "blood that
speaks a better word than the blood of Abel" (Heb. 12:24). The risen Jesus
declares that scripture announced in advance that the Messiah must suffer in
order to pardon the sins of the world.[49] "It is not wonderful, therefore, if he
who overcame death by death and sin by sin and the serpent by the serpent,
overcame the curse by the curse. Not only that, but death is cursed, sin is
cursed, the serpent is cursed, and all these things are triumphed over in the
cross."[50] "Cursed is everyone who hangs on a tree" (Gal. 3:13).

**3:14 in order that in Christ Jesus the blessing of Abraham might come
to the Gentiles**—While there are episodes in Acts in which Paul preaches in
synagogues and Peter evangelizes Gentiles, Paul identifies himself specifically
as apostle to the Gentiles (Gal. 1:16; 2:2, 8–9; Rom. 11:13). He defends the
Gentile Christians in the controversy with Peter in Antioch (2:12, 14). The
Genesis stories that Paul interprets in Galatians point to God's promise to
Abraham that the Gentiles will be blessed in his seed (Gen. 12:3; 18:18; Gal.
3:8–9, 14). The inclusion of the Gentiles in the people of God is inextricably
bound to Abraham's blessing, his faith in Christ the seed, and the promise of
the Spirit (Gal. 3:2–5; 5:22–24).

48. Barth, *CD* I/2, 152.
49. "Thus it is written, that the Messiah is to suffer and to rise from the dead on the third day,
and that repentance and forgiveness of sins is to be proclaimed in his name to all nations, beginning
from Jerusalem" (Luke 24:46–47).
50. Augustine, *Augustine's Commentary on Galatians*, 163.

3:15 a person's will—The word "will" (*diathēkē*) can refer to a covenant in the religious sense, such as God's covenant with Abraham. The words "promise" and "blessing" also nest within this religious context.[51] The covenant with Abraham is a promised blessing. A promise broken is no longer a promise but rather a betrayal; by nature, God is faithful and remembers his covenant.[52] But the word "covenant" (*diathēkē*) can also have a secular sense, referring to a legal document, a last will and testament. Paul uses the secular sense of the word to illustrate the religious sense. Once a will is ratified, says Paul, it cannot be changed or canceled. This is what the Galatians must understand: their inheritance through Abraham does not mean that God has changed tack. There is a significant overlap between Paul's two uses of the word "covenant" in chapter 3: in both contexts nothing is in effect until a death occurs, until blood is spilled.[53] For Paul, Jesus's death on the tree is the blood of the new covenant spilled.[54]

3:16 Now the promises were made to Abraham and to his offspring; it does not say, "And to offsprings," as of many; but it says, "And to your offspring," that is, to one person, who is Christ—The NRSV translation is a helpful foil again here precisely because it highlights for us Paul's key points. In translating Paul's word *sperma* as "offspring" in 3:16, 19, 29, the NRSV inadvertently masks Paul's main observation: the promise in which Abraham believes is the Christ, not Abraham and his family.[55] Paul is speaking at this point not about Abraham's justification by faith, nor the general concept of the workings of justification as in 3:6–7, but about the specific content of Abraham's faith: the Messiah. Even before the covenant, when

51. *Epangelia*, 3:14, 17–19, 29; 4:23, 28; *eulogia*, 3:8–9, 14.
52. "Then will I remember my covenant with Jacob; I will remember also my covenant with Isaac and also my covenant with Abraham, and I will remember the land" (Lev. 26:42).
53. Heb. 9 reads like an interpretation of Gal. 3: "For this reason he is the mediator of a new covenant, so that those who are called may receive the promised eternal inheritance, because a death has occurred that redeems them from the transgressions under the first covenant. Where a will is involved, the death of the one who made it must be established. For a will takes effect only at death, since it is not in force as long as the one who made it is alive. Hence not even the first covenant was inaugurated without blood" (Heb. 9:15–18).
54. See Luke 22:20; 1 Cor. 11:25; 2 Cor. 3:6; quoting Jer. 31:31; Heb. 8:8, 13; 12:24. The early church gathered its own writings as New Testament (new covenant), *kainē diathēkē*.
55. The NRSV is not alone in rendering this word as "offspring." The RSV, ESV, and NET do so as well, while the KJV, CJB, ASV, BBE, NIV, and WEB use "seed."

Abraham was still a Gentile, he believed in the messianic promise.[56] Translating *sperma* as "offspring" muffles this messianic claim, making it difficult to hear the interplay of "seed" and "promise" that is central to Paul's use of the stories of Abraham.

In the Septuagint the word translated here as "offspring" (*sperma*) is a singular noun. The word used in the Hebrew Masoretic Text is also a singular noun (*zera*). While the singular Greek word Paul himself uses can be translated into English as "offspring," as does the NRSV, and read as a collective noun of many members, this does not seem to be Paul's intention.[57] In English there is no plural for the noun "offspring," as is clear from the NRSV's tangled translation of Paul's own convoluted construction at 3:16.[58] Paul distinguishes the singular from the plural in Greek to underscore his messianic claim: "to one person, who is the Christ."

This is not a minor point. Paul uses the word "seed" primarily because of the biblical context of promise: agricultural germination and growth. In Galatians, the themes of barrenness and fecundity, conception and gestation, and long-awaited birth are undergirded by the biblical narrative's focus on biological promise. A glance at the scriptural career of the word "seed" will help us hear how Paul uses this word as a specifically messianic term linked with the concept of promise, especially in his distinction of the third and fourth episodes of the promise in Gen. 15 and 17.

The first appearance of the word "seed" in the plot of scripture is, not surprisingly, in the creation story: God brings forth vegetation with its seed in it for increase of life (Gen. 1:11, 29).[59] The narrator's remark in Gen. 1:11 that the plants are created "yielding seed" shows that the promise of life is not an afterthought but is God's determination from the very outset of creation. The plants yielding seed promise both the continued generation of the plants themselves and the provision of nourishment for the living creatures.

56. Paul is not the only voice in the New Testament to declare that the content of Abraham's faith is messianic: "Your ancestor Abraham rejoiced that he would see my day; he saw it and was glad" (John 8:56); "Before Abraham was, I am" (John 8:58).

57. In Aramaic and Hebrew, the singular noun "seed" can refer collectively to family. Wright, *Climax of the Covenant*, 162–68; Boyarin, *Radical Jew*, 145, 302n19. While this is lexically valid, translating "seed" as "family" obscures Paul's insistence in 3:16 that Abraham's faith was precisely in his singular seed, the Christ.

58. Not only in English but more importantly in the Hebrew, Greek, and Latin texts (*zera*, MT; *sperma*, LXX and NA[28]; *semen*, VG).

59. "Seed" here is singular.

The word "seed" next appears at the episode of the fall in the garden of Eden (Gen. 3:15).[60] The context is less directly one of fecundity but is nevertheless agricultural: the garden was earlier described with fruit trees and rivers (Gen. 2:8). But even before God creates vegetation, human life is promised in the simple comment that there was no one yet to tend the garden; the implication is that someone yet to come will fulfill this task (Gen. 2:5). This detail itself points to promise: the human creature *adam* will be placed in the garden specifically to fill this role ("to till and keep it," Gen. 2:15). But although the garden has been described as a fertile locale—the leaves are even large enough to hide the pair's shame (Gen. 3:7)—after their disobedience the word "seed" no longer indicates the site of agriculture, nutrition, or reproduction (3:15). At this point the context becomes degradation and pain, beginning with God's curse. For the disobedience of Eve and Adam, God first curses the serpent: "I will put enmity between you and the woman, and between your seed and hers; he will strike your head, and you will strike his heel" (Gen. 3:15 AT).[61] Then Eve hears her punishment; she will deliver the next generation in agony (Gen. 3:16). Adam's burden is in the multiplication of his toil in farming the once-fertile soil; before it produced nourishment, but now it will bring up thorns and thistles (Gen. 3:18). After their disobedience, both Adam and Eve are left with heavy labor, each in their own way. Even so, the (singular) seed of Eve will ultimately conquer the (singular) seed of the serpent. While the serpent's wounding Eve's seed is not light (3:15), the promise has been declared in the victory of her own seed over the serpent's seed. Her (single) seed is the Christ, who will vanquish the serpent's seed, death itself. The gospel is promised even before the punishment is laid on Eve and Adam: grace is prevenient. In the allegory of chapter 4, Paul will show how Eve's seed is a type of Isaac, who in turn is a type of Christ, the antitype and ultimate victor.

The word "seed" then points explicitly to the stories of the election of and promise to Abraham. The motif ties the creation stories, where we first found the seed (universal covenant), to the story of Israel (particular covenant). The link between these two covenants is integral to Paul's preaching to the Galatians: the election of Israel is specifically in the promised seed of Abraham, the Christ.

60. Here we find the first instance where the NRSV chooses to translate *sperma* as "offspring." The RSV uses "seed" to translate *sperma* at Gen. 3:15 but "offspring" in Paul's quotations in Gal. 3:16, 19, 29.

61. The word "seed" is again in the singular (*sperma*, LXX; *zera*, MT). While at this point in the narrative the figures do not have names, I will refer to them by the names they acquire after the curse.

In what I am calling the first episode the promise is threefold: land, progeny, and blessing to the nations. The Lord calls to Abram: "Go from your country and your kindred and your father's house to the *land* that I will show you"; "I will make of you a *great nation*" (*goy*, MT; *ethnos*, LXX); "in you all the families of the earth shall be *blessed*" (Gen. 12:1–3).[62] We do not yet hear the word "seed," only "nation" (*ethnos*).

This detail presents a lexical and theological puzzle that complicates translation. The Hebrew word often translated in English as "nation," *goy*, is *ethnos* in the Septuagint. Paul will use this word, usually translated "Gentile" in English, as a counterpart to "Jew." But at Gen. 12:2 it is clear that the word *ethnos* includes the nation of Israel. As the biblical narrative moves forward, the word *ethnos* no longer refers to Israel but to the not-Israel; this is not the case here. The complication deepens: in the Hebrew Bible, some of these *ethnē* descend from Abram through Hagar's son Ishmael (Gen. 17:16; →1:17). The promise for the great nation from Abram's loins points typologically to the promise of the "seed" in Gen. 15, the key episode for Paul's preaching to the Galatians.

The second episode of the promises (Gen. 13:14–17) leaves out the blessing on the nations and reorders the other promises. Paul is less explicitly interested in this episode, even though it implicitly underlies his preaching to the Galatians. The promises of land and seed are richly interwoven: the promise of the seed (*sperma*; 13:15–16) is sandwiched between two promises of the land (13:14–15, 17). Here the promised people are not referred to as a *goy* ("nation," 12:2) but *zera*, "seed." This seed (singular) will be as innumerable as the dust of the earth: "The LORD said to Abram . . . , 'Raise your eyes now, and look from the place where you are, northward and southward and eastward and westward; for all the land [*gē/ha'arets*] that you see I will give to you and to your seed [*sperma/zera*, singular; NRSV "offspring"] forever. I will make your seed [*sperma/zera*] like the dust of the earth [*gē/ha'arets*] so that if one can count the dust of the earth [*gē/ha'arets*], your seed [*sperma/zera*] also can be counted. Rise up, walk through the length and the breadth of the land [*gē/ha'arets*], for I will give it to you'" (Gen. 13:14–17 AT).

The third episode of promises in Gen. 15:2–23 is also twofold but is significantly expanded. At Gen. 15:4 the word "heir" appears (*klēronomēsei*, LXX; *yirash*, MT), but in the following verse this heir is identified as "seed" (*sperma*,

---

62. The promise of land is recounted five times in the Abram/Abraham stories: Gen. 12:7; 13:14–18; 15:7, 18–21; 17:1–8.

LXX; *zera*, MT; NRSV, "offspring"). This seed will be as numerous as the stars (Gen. 15:5; see also 22:17). The Lord will give Abram a land. Added here is the detail of its boundaries: it will stretch from the Nile to the Euphrates (Gen. 15:7, 18–21). The tribes originally occupying the land are now mentioned, foreshadowing the future threats to the promise. In this dialogue with the Lord, Abraham registers his complaints, doubts, and objections. In this episode bracketed between the two promises of progeny and land lie the key terms for Paul's interpretation in Galatians: righteousness and faith. "And [Abram] believed the LORD; and the LORD reckoned it to him as righteousness" (Gen. 15:6; Gal. 3:6).

In Gen. 15:2 we hear Abram's complaint to the Lord God: despite the earlier promises, Abram continues without an heir.[63] "You have given me no seed [*sperma/zera*], and so a slave born in my house is to be my heir" (Gen. 15:3 AT). The Lord responds that Abram will indeed have an heir of his own body (Gen. 15:4). The slave born in his house, Eliezer of Damascus, is the non-seed; he is not Abram's biological son or his heir. Eliezer foreshadows Ishmael, who is the biological non-heir. The Lord brings Abram outside and tells him to try to count the stars: Abram's descendants (*sperma/zera*) will be as numerous as this starry band. There is an ambiguity built into the use of the word "seed" at this point: the single seed refers to something uncountable.[64]

In the fourth and theologically central episode in Gen. 17, even before God covenants, he promises.[65] This is the story that opens the particular covenant with the election of Abram. Unlike Gen. 15, with its detailed promise of the land, Gen. 17 shrinks the promise of the land to fill just one verse (17:8),

---

63. Gen. 15:2 is one of the relatively rare instances in the Hebrew Bible where the tetragrammaton, *YHWH* (transcribed in English as "LORD"), appears second in the construct of the divine name. Whereas it usually precedes its counterpart, *Elohim* ("God"), here *YHWH* comes second preceded by *Adonai* ("my Lord"). The usual construct is transcribed "LORD God," but at Gen. 15:2 the name is transcribed "Lord GOD." That this anomalous usage (appearing in the Hebrew Bible only some sixty times) should be embedded in Gen. 15, a text so theologically rich in the promise of the covenant, impacts our reading of Paul's theological use of the narrative suppression of the divine name in Gen. 17. There it underscores the christological nature of the messianic gift of the seed to all, Jews and Gentiles alike, as in the dual missions of Peter and Paul. Thanks to Michelle Knight for her clarification of the number of occurrences in the Hebrew Bible of the less common construction of the divine name.

64. See also Gen. 15:13, where we find the ambiguous nature of the word "seed," which is singular yet clearly also collective. The seed is likened to the dust of the earth (Gen. 13:16), the stars of the sky (15:5), and the sand of the seashore (22:17).

65. One interesting detail in Gen. 17, where the particular covenant is given, is that the divine name drops out of the narrative after 17:1. The narrator identifies the divine voice as the Lord in 17:1, but then introduces himself: "I am God Almighty" (*El Shaddai*). The divine name does not return to the narrative until Gen. 18:1.

while the promise of descendants and the command to circumcise will fill five verses (17:10–14).

At Gen. 17:5, God (*El Shaddai*) changes Abram's name to Abraham, promising that he will be the father of many: "No longer shall your name be Abram [*'avram*], but your name shall be Abraham [*'avraham*] for I have made you the father [*av*] of a multitude of nations [*ethnōn/goyim*]" (AT).[66] The name of the patriarch up to this point had been Abram in the episodes in Genesis; however, Paul uses the patriarch's covenant name to refer to him throughout: Abraham.[67] Paul's narratival dislocation of the name is no doubt intentional, for it highlights the content and goal of his preaching to the Gentiles.

Paul's use of the patriarch's covenant name Abraham in Galatians is significant for at least two reasons. First, the chronological relationship between election and circumcision is key to Paul's overall argument. The rite of circumcision is given to the patriarch only after God renames him at the gift of the covenant, where Abram becomes Abraham.[68] That the Gentiles in Galatia do not grasp the theological import of this chronology has resulted in their being confused by the teaching of the Third Party, who impose circumcision. Paul needs to remind the Galatians from scripture that the promise of the seed (Gen. 15:5; Gal. 3:16) precedes the giving of the statute of circumcision (Gen. 17:11). Second, Abram's new identity as Abraham, "father of many," indicates the promissory nature of God's covenant with the nations through Christ, including the Gentiles in Galatia. They are among the nations who, apart from the promise of Christ, are strangers to the covenant of election (Gen. 17:4; *ethnē*, LXX; *goyim*, MT; Eph. 2:12). Through Christ they are members of the particular covenant of election.

God renames Sarai at 17:15. Now she will be Sarah. Whereas the change in Abraham's name is marked with a change in identity (he becomes the "father of many"), the significance of Sarah's name change is left in the shadows. And even though she is renamed, Paul himself does not use her name at all throughout Galatians; he refers to her simply as "free," "our mother," the "free woman," and the "Jerusalem above" (Gal. 4:23, 30–31; 4:26). In both Genesis and Galatians, the seed cannot be delivered except through Sarah's own body.

---

66. The pun on Abraham's name makes use of the same root we found in Gen. 2 and 3: *rabah*, "to multiply."

67. As I read the earlier stories of election, I will refer to the characters by their names in the narrative setting: Abram and Sarai. Where I read Paul, I will follow his use of the names: Abraham and Sarah.

68. Paul takes this chronology to be theologically significant also in Rom. 4:10–12.

While Hagar's very presence in the narrative is both a threat to the promise and the engine of the story of Abraham's family, Hagar's own name remains unchanged throughout. This foreshadows the complexity of her specific role in the particular covenant. Hagar's role points to Sarah's own crucial role in the story of election: the promised son comes *not through Hagar* but specifically through Sarah. The promise is fulfilled neither in Eliezer of Damascus nor in Abraham's first son Ishmael. Even though the former is not Abraham's biological son and the latter is, neither of them is the son of the promise; neither is born of Sarah. The seed will come specifically through Sarah's womb, not Hagar's (Gen. 17:16, 19, 21). Abraham himself is in effect a third wheel at this point in the story. The details regarding Sarah's infertility and Hagar's birthing of Abraham's firstborn will become key indicators of the complexity of God's promises and providence as Paul moves into the allegory of Gal. 4.

At the apex of the fourth episode of the promise, Abraham steps from the universal into the particular covenant in which he is given the command to circumcise. But God's covenant with Abraham is not limited to him or even to his biological descendants; it includes also the slaves born in his house and any slaves he will acquire. All of them must be circumcised (Gen. 17:12–13). The fact that the seed itself is promised before the rite is commanded expresses the overflowing abundance of God's grace, which Paul understands in specifically messianic terms.[69]

Abraham fits the typology that Paul employs with the Galatians for (at least) four reasons: (1) Abraham is a Gentile when God calls him out from Ur; (2) Abraham's faith in the promised Messiah makes him righteous in God's sight; (3) his righteousness is declared before the covenant rite is given; and (4) this all occurs long before the law of Sinai is revealed. In Abraham's faith, righteousness is bound to Christology and hence points to ecclesiology. Abraham is the ecclesiological figure par excellence in whom the Galatians are to find not only their messianic faith but also their own election as Gentiles in Christ apart from circumcision.[70]

---

69. "And I will make my covenant between me and you, and will make you exceedingly numerous" (Gen. 17:2). The construct "exceedingly numerous" (*sphodra sphodra*; *bimeod meod*) occurs twice more in chapter 17 at verses 6 and 20.

70. Hebrews 11 also presents an ecclesial use of the figure of Abraham: "By faith Abraham obeyed when he was called to set out for a place that he was to receive as an inheritance; and he set out, not knowing where he was going. . . . For he looked forward to the city that has foundations, whose architect and builder is God. By faith he received power of procreation, even though he was too old—and Sarah herself was barren—because he considered him faithful who had promised. Therefore from

We encounter a fifth episode in Gen. 18:1–15 that also points to the episode of the long-awaited birth of Isaac narrated in Gen. 21. In Gen. 18, the promises of land and progeny recede and the plot now centers on the promised son. Sarah's incredulity over the promise's seeming impossibility (Gen. 18:12–15) anticipates her laughter after his birth (21:6–7). While Gen. 18 plays a minimal role in Gal. 3, a small detail in Gen. 21:9–10 about Sarah's reaction to the boys will play a key role in Paul's allegory in Gal. 4.

A sixth episode of the promise narrated in Gen. 22 is strikingly different from the preceding episodes; the promised son is at the center of impending doom. God commands that Abraham sacrifice his own son. The most dire threat to the covenant in the entire Hebrew Bible, the Sacrifice (Binding, *Akedah*) of Isaac makes the threat of Sarah's infertility pale in comparison. God commands; Abraham obeys; God spares; Abraham's hand is stayed; the declaration of the promise is reiterated.[71] Disaster averted. But the fact that Paul does not allude to this final episode in Galatians is theologically provocative, especially given the embryonic christological typology of Gen. 22 (Heb. 11:17; James 2:21) that will blossom in the later tradition. But we can safely assume that the passage does not serve the pastoral needs of the Galatians' situation. The fact that Paul omits the story in recounting the promise is an additional sign that he is not writing a theological tract but a pastoral response to a specifically fraught intracommunal situation.

3:17–18 the law, which came four hundred thirty years later, does not annul a covenant previously ratified by God, so as to nullify the promise— Here Paul circles back to the idea of the covenant in its religious sense and to the significance of the chronological ordering of the episodes of the promise. Because the law was given centuries after the rite of circumcision, it cannot cancel God's promise to Abraham, which came before circumcision. The Galatians have been declared righteous in God's sight apart from law observance because they believe in the same promise that Abraham believed prior to the covenant rite of circumcision.

---

one person, and this one as good as dead, descendants were born, 'as many as the stars of heaven and as the innumerable grains of sand by the seashore'" (Heb. 11:8–12).

71. "I will indeed bless you, and I will make your offspring as numerous as the stars of heaven and as the sand that is on the seashore. And your offspring shall possess the gate of their enemies, and by your offspring shall all the nations of the earth gain blessing for themselves, because you have obeyed my voice" (Gen. 22:17–18).

The idea that the law came 430 years after the promise to Abraham is not unique to Paul. The Torah tells that the people of Israel lived in slavery under Egypt for 430 years before being freed.[72] Their freedom and the gift of the law are theologically linked, not opposed to each other. Paul draws to a close his earlier illustration: the law does not abrogate the promises of God's covenant.

While Gal. 3:17 speaks of the theological relation of law and promise from the standpoint of the law, Gal. 3:18 approaches the relationship from the standpoint of the promise. The "if" is contrary to fact: if inheritance came through the law (which, of course, it did not; the law came 430 years later), then it would not come through the promise (which, in fact, it did). How could the inheritance then be through the law? (It was not.) It was through the promise that infraseded (defined in the epilogue) the Christ.

3:19–22 Why then the law? It was added . . . —This rhetorical question points to the law's place in the chronological/providential ordering of sin, promise, and covenant election: the law is an intermediary. Paul will soon tell us that the law is a temporary guide (3:24–25). If Paul judged the law to be temporary, why did he approve of Peter's mission to the Jews? One possible answer is that he sees the law as temporary in the economy of God, but Jews can observe it with no violation of the gospel as long as they know they are not declared righteous before God except through Jesus Christ.[73]

Paul's statement that the law came "through angels by a mediator" (3:19) corresponds to Stephen's words in Acts 7. In the speech that results in his martyrdom, Stephen refers to the law as the "living oracles" of Sinai that were given through the mediation of an angel in the flames of the burning bush.[74] Stephen begins his recitation of salvation history with Abraham, moving through the Law and Prophets, and from David to Solomon. For Paul, the messianic tie

---

72. "The time that the Israelites had lived in Egypt was four hundred thirty years. At the end of four hundred thirty years, on that very day, all the companies of the LORD went out from the land of Egypt. That was for the LORD a night of vigil, to bring them out of the land of Egypt. That same night is a vigil to be kept for the LORD by all the Israelites throughout their generations" (Exod. 12:40–42).

73. This was the suggestion of Augustine, over against Jerome (→3:25). According to Sanders's characteristics of covenantal nomism, Augustine's idea would have corresponded to Second Temple Judaism. See Sanders, *Paul and Palestinian Judaism*, 422. In Romans, the law reveals sin but is not itself sin (Rom. 3:20; 4:15; 5:13; 7:7). The law increases transgressions (Rom. 5:20; 7:8) and brings death (Rom. 7:9–11). In Romans, as in Galatians, the law is temporary (Rom. 7:1).

74. Acts 7:38; cf. 7:30, 35. In the Exodus scene, the angel plays only a small role (Exod. 3:2).

of the law is not to the person of David, but far before that, to King David's greater son, Christ (see Luke 1:32–33).

3:20 a mediator involves more than one party; but God is one—The declaration "God is one" forms the backbone of Israel's confession: "Hear, O Israel: The LORD our God is one LORD" (Deut. 6:4 RSV). The Shema (the first word of the verse is *shema*: "hear," "observe") is one of the key prayers, linking the confession of the unitary identity of the Lord with Israel's call to love the Lord (Deut. 6:5).[75] But at the episode of the giving of the law on Sinai we find three main characters: the Lord, the angel, and Moses (Exod. 3:1–6). Moses serves as a mediator as he passes on the law to the people: "When Moses had finished speaking with them, he put a veil on his face; but whenever Moses went in before the LORD to speak with him, he would take the veil off, until he came out; and when he came out, and told the Israelites what he had been commanded, the Israelites would see the face of Moses, that the skin of his face was shining; and Moses would put the veil on his face again, until he went in to speak with him."[76] But does the Lord need a mediator in the giving of the law, the Lord's own divine word? What is the role of the angel in the scene? Paul implies that the law bears an internal contradiction: God depends on a mediator to give his divine word to the people, and yet God is one and needs nothing.

Augustine, reading Gal. 3:19–20 in light of 3:16, takes the mediator to be Christ. He reads 1 Timothy as a prooftext: "For there is one God; there is also one mediator between God and humankind, Christ Jesus, himself human, who gave himself a ransom for all" (1 Tim. 2:5). Augustine also reads John 1:1 as key to Gal. 3:19–20: "And so God's only Son became the mediator between God and mortals when the Word of God, God with God [John 1:1] both laid down his majesty to the level of the human and exalted human lowliness to the level of the divine, in order that he—a human being who through God was beyond human beings—might be the mediator between God and human being."[77] This does not seem to be Paul's reasoning. Whoever the mediator is, Paul makes clear that it is not Christ, the "seed." Christ is the *terminus ad quem*, the goal, summary, and content of the law (Gal. 5:14; 6:2; see also Rom.

75. The Shema is, for devout Jews, the prayer said first upon rising and last before sleeping.
76. Exod. 34:33–35; see also Lev. 26:46; Deut. 5:4–5; Num. 36:13; 2 Cor. 3:13–16; Philo, *Life of Moses.*
77. *Augustine's Commentary on Galatians*, 164n101, 165n102.

10:4). Christ is not a go-between, a separate party, but is himself that very promise guarded by the law.

3:21 Is the law then opposed to the promises of God?—If God is one, God's will is one and cannot be self-contradictory. God's gifts cannot be mutually canceling; neither is his work in creation zero-sum. The law does not displace the promises because it was given after the promise, and God's promise abides. While the law is not opposed to the promise, it neither gives life nor bestows righteousness. The law restrains from sin, but Christ brings life (Gal. 3:19, 22; 2:19–20; 6:14–15).

3:22 But the scripture has imprisoned all things under the power of sin, so that what was promised through faith in Jesus Christ might be given to those who believe—The word "scripture" is the grammatical subject of the sentence; it serves to "imprison all things under sin." The same word "imprison" appears at the confluence of human disobedience and divine mercy rather than sin in Rom. 11:32: "For God has imprisoned all in disobedience so that he may be merciful to all." Both verses point to God's grace. The noun "power" is supplied by the NRSV but is missing from the Greek. The English gives the impression that sin is an agent with its own force, but here the law is said specifically *not* to have power to give life. For Paul, the word "scripture" (*hē graphē*) refers to the Law and the Prophets, the canon in Paul's day.[78] The image of scripture imprisoning under the power of sin seems to indicate its opposition to the promise. But is this what Paul has been saying? Jerome exposes the theological problem here and relies on the rule of faith to guide a fruitful interpretation (→2:2, 5; 5:6; 6:16).

We should not surmise that Scripture is the author of sin because it states that the whole world is a prisoner of sin. It conveys the commandments prescribed by the Law and condemns sin but it is not the cause of sin any more than a

78. "Scripture" in Second Temple Judaism is designated by the terms "the law and the prophets" (e.g., Sir. 0:1, 8–9; 2 Macc. 15:9; 4 Macc. 18:10). Paul uses the phrase in Romans: "But now, apart from law, the righteousness of God has been disclosed, and is attested by the law and the prophets" (Rom. 3:21). It appears on the lips of Jesus: "On these two commandments hang all the law and the prophets" (Matt. 22:40); "Do not think that I have come to abolish the law or the prophets; I have come not to abolish but to fulfill" (Matt. 5:17). This evidences the canon's development at the time of the earliest Christian writings. See also Matt. 7:12; 11:13; Luke 16:16; 24:44; John 1:45; Acts 13:15; 28:23.

judge is the author of a crime for subduing malefactors. The judge imprisons them and by his legal authority pronounces them to be dangerous, but he leaves open the option of showing mercy and absolving the guilty from their initial punishment, if he so desires.[79]

3:23–24 Before faith came . . . the law was our disciplinarian until Christ came—The content of Abraham's faith comes precisely in Christ. The translation of the word *paidagōgos* (NRSV: "disciplinarian") introduces a problem. For the English reader, the word "disciplinarian" often carries a negative connotation that is not present in the Greek. A *paidagōgos* is a slave who serves as a guardian of a minor but does not primarily have the function of exacting discipline. Neither is the person properly a teacher.[80] The *paidagōgos* is something in between, yet more.

Translating the word as "disciplinarian" misses the chronological limitation of the role of the *paidagōgos*, who is relevant only for a discrete period of time in the youth's life.[81] The *paidagōgos* is not necessary while the child is an infant, but serves only during the years between youth and adulthood. When the minor comes of age, the *paidagōgos* steps aside, no longer needed. The clauses sandwiched between 3:19 and 3:25 make statements specifically about release from the law. Thus the *paidagōgos* embodies the temporal, constrictive, and character-shaping qualities of the law that Paul tries to express.

3:25 But now that faith has come, we are no longer subject to a disciplinarian—Because Paul is speaking to Gentile Christians in Galatia, he seems to leave unaddressed the role of law observance in the religious life of Jewish Christians. Given the mutual accord between Peter and Paul of their two distinct missions, Peter to the Jews and Paul to the Gentiles, it is imaginable that Paul might have spoken about the law differently to the Jews than he does to the Gentiles in Galatia. However, we have no direct evidence of what Paul might have thought the role of the law should be for Jewish Christians, because there were none in Galatia.

This question occupied some of the disagreements between Augustine and Jerome. Augustine argues for the validity of Jewish Christian observance of the law, as long as those who observe it know that they are not made righteous in

79. Jerome, *Commentary on Galatians*, 149–50.
80. In the ancient world, only boys needed this kind of slave, since girls would not have been sent to school. The category of the *paidagōgos* itself is gendered.
81. Because its English cognate "pedagogue" is not much more helpful for the English reader, I leave the word untranslated.

observing it.[82] However, Jerome characteristically disagrees: "I, on the contrary, shall maintain, and, though the world were to protest against my view, I may boldly declare that the Jewish ceremonies are to Christians both hurtful and fatal; and that whoever observes them, whether he be Jew or Gentile originally, is cast into the pit of perdition. 'For Christ is the end of the law for righteousness to every one that believes' [Rom. 10:4]."[83] But neither Augustine nor Jerome speak of Gentile observance of the law, which is Paul's main concern here. What he means by the release from the temporary role of the *paidagōgos* will become clearer in the next several verses.

3:26 for in Christ Jesus you are all children of God through faith—At 3:23 Paul switched from the third-person singular to the first-person plural. Here at 3:26 he switches again, now to the second-person plural, addressing the Galatians directly. He picks up the thread of the ecclesial identity of the Galatians in Christ: they are children of God through faith even though they have no biological claim to this inheritance (→2:15). The theme of adoption will return at Gal. 4:5 in the liturgical context of prayer (4:6: "Abba! Father!"; see also Rom. 8:15). Christ is the seed promised to Abraham, and all who share the patriarch's faith in Christ are children of God through him, including the Gentile churches of Galatia. They are adopted into the family of Abraham as children of God through Christ without the requirement of circumcision.

3:27 As many of you as were baptized into Christ have clothed yourselves with Christ—In 3:26 those who are "in Christ" are children of God through faith; this form of adoption is precisely through the church. While in 3:27 this inclusion comes through baptism, we find no liturgical setting specified apart from what may be indicated by the term "baptism." Paul does not refer to the administration of the rite of baptism, nor does he use a baptismal formula— for example, the triune name of God (→3:28). In the following verse he will employ a triadic statement formed by three couplets, but it serves no liturgical purpose in these verses.

Nevertheless, it is clear from this verse that baptism is a rite familiar enough to the Galatians that Paul does not have to explain its meaning or describe it. He says simply that they are "baptized into Christ" (*eis Christon ebaptisthēte*).

---

82. Augustine, *Letters* 28, 40, 71.
83. Jerome, *Letter 75*, 4.14 (*NPNF*[1] 1:338). I myself do not agree with Jerome's interpretation of Rom. 10:4.

Paul refers to Christian baptism with the imagery of putting on clothing or
getting dressed to symbolize the Christian's dying and rising with Christ.[84]
Again, this is likely to have been familiar to the Galatians, since Paul does not
explain it. He merely drops reference to it.

The early church adopted clothing imagery in its baptismal practice: wrap-
ping the baptizand in white cloths or towels signified death and resurrection
to new life.[85] The garments function typologically on several levels. They are
Jesus's clothes stripped from him at the cross; they are his grave shroud and the
cloths that bind his head at his burial (John 20:5–7). The baptismal clothes
are the white robes of the twenty-four elders around the throne of the Lamb
(Rev. 4:4; 7:13–14; 22:14). Like the martyrs, the baptized are clothed in the
resurrection life of Christ. Paul's typological presentation of baptism as being
clothed in Christ is a form of theological interpretation that prepares not only
for his figural reading of the Abraham stories in chapter 4 but also for the
tradition that follows him.[86]

Early Christian art evidences a rich typological understanding of baptism as
a sacramental participation in the death and resurrection of Christ. Here again
we encounter Noah; he appears in the early Christian frescoes where scenes
of the floodwaters and the ark's safe landing on dry ground are presented as
types of baptism in which the Christian is plucked from the waters of death to
new life, like this first righteous Gentile Noah.[87] The baptized are held safe in
the ark, a type of the church (1 Pet. 3:18–21). The Galatians have not simply
changed their clothes; in baptism, they participate in the new creation (Gal.
6:15).[88] They are a new people, and as children of Abraham they bear the
resurrected identity of the "Israel of God" (3:28; 6:16).

**3:28 There is no longer Jew or Greek, there is no longer slave or free,
there is no longer male and female; for all of you are one in Christ Jesus—**
The subject matter of the entire letter to the Galatians is announced in this
benediction-like verse pointing to the believer's identity in Christ.[89] There is

84. "Do you not know that all of us who have been baptized into Christ Jesus were baptized into
his death?" (Rom. 6:1–4; see also Gal. 2:19–20; Eph. 4:24; Rom. 13:14).
85. Senn, *Christian Liturgy*, 150–51.
86. See also Gal. 3:13; 2:20.
87. This may also be an expansion on Rom. 6:3–4, where baptism is portrayed as burial with
Christ and resurrection to new life in his resurrection.
88. See also Rom. 6:4 and 2 Cor. 5:17.
89. For another view, see Harker, *Colonizers' Idols*, 41.

new creation (Gal. 6:15), not universalism nor "coercive sameness."[90] In fact, such coercion is the prime offense imposed by the Third Party as they require the rite of circumcision for Christian conversion of Gentiles (6:13). This coercive sameness is precisely what Paul wants the Galatians to reject.

Paul's triadic declaration is composed of three couplets. The first two couplets perform a different function from the third. To specify, I will refer to the first two couplets as binaries: they indicate an opposition, a this *or* a that. The final couplet, however, is not a binary: it indicates a pairing, a this *and* a that.[91] Unlike the first two couplets, the final is gendered, two nouns joined with the simple conjunction "and" (*kai*). The first couplet, the binary Jew/Greek, bears on election, the presenting pastoral issue in Galatia. The second couplet, the binary slave/free, speaks to the sociological situation of the Galatians. The nonbinary third couplet is the pairing of male *and* female. It speaks primarily of created identity and eschatological blessing, not gender identity per se.

In order to understand Paul's triadic declaration, we can compare it to two ancient prayers: a pagan prayer attributed to Socrates and a rabbinic blessing in the Talmud. Socrates incorporates three binaries in giving thanks to Fortune for (male) identity, in this order: "First, that I was born a human being and not one of the brutes; next, that I was born a man and not a woman; thirdly, a Greek and not a barbarian."[92] But the second prayer is more relevant to our reading of Paul.[93] The Talmudic blessing gives thanks for how God has *not* created the one who prays, in this order: *not* a Gentile, *not* a woman, *not* a slave ("brutish man").[94] While in the Talmudic prayer the binaries are not specifically articulated, they are clearly implied: Blessed is God that I *am* a Jew and *not* a Gentile; that I *am* a man and *not* a woman; that I *am* free and *not* a brute. A version of this prayer remains among the traditional daily prayers of devout male Jews to this day. The English translation is as follows:

90. This phrase comes from Boyarin, *Radical Jew*, 236.

91. The Greek, Hebrew, and Latin texts of Gen. 1:27 all agree with Paul in this pairing: *arsen kai thēlu*, LXX; *zakhar unqevah*, MT; *masculum et feminam*, VG.

92. Credited to Socrates (fifth century BCE) by historian Diogenes Laertius (third century AD). Diogenes Laertius, *Lives of Eminent Philosophers* 1.33 (Hicks, 35).

93. It is fair to assume that, like other traditions recorded in the Talmud, a version of this prayer would have circulated prior to its being recorded in written form. Paul may even have been familiar with such a proto-rabbinic tradition.

94. "[Blessed art thou] who hast not made me a heathen, . . . who hast not made me a woman, and . . . who hast not made me a brutish man." *The Babylonian Talmud: Seder Kodashim* 43b–44a (trans. Epstein, 264).

Praised be you, *Adonai* our God, King of the universe, because you have not made me a Gentile. Praised be you, *Adonai* our God, King of the universe, because you have not made me a woman. Praised be you, *Adonai* our God, King of the universe, because you have not made me a slave.[95]

These two prayers each bear similarities to and differences from Paul's declaration in Gal. 3:28. First, while all three are triadic in form, Paul is not offering a prayer of thanksgiving, as do the triads of Socrates and the Talmud. Indeed, Paul is not offering a prayer at all: he is addressing neither Fortune nor the Lord (*Adonai*), but simply the Galatians. Second, while Socrates's prayer has three binaries, and three binaries are implied in the Talmudic blessing, Paul's triad has only two binaries. Third, unlike the Talmudic blessing with its three implied binaries, the two binaries that Paul incorporates are explicitly articulated: *this and not that.* Fourth, whereas both the Talmudic blessing and the Socrates prayer are voiced by males with reference to male identity, the addressees of Paul's declaration are not gender-specific. Fifth, whereas Socrates's thanksgiving and the Talmudic blessing place the gendered binary in the center of the three, Paul's gendered couplet comes last, closing the triad.[96] Sitting in the final position, Paul's gendered couplet gains rhetorical force over the two preceding binary couplets, thus emphasizing that it is not a binary. Sixth, this force is created by the coordinating conjunction "and." Therefore, it is precisely the gendered pairing in the final position of Paul's triadic declaration that governs the force of the entire verse.

The final observation leads us to the original narrative location of the phrase "male *and* female": the creation of humanity in Gen. 1:27 with its own pairing of male *and* female. In addition, the gendered pairing in Paul's triadic declaration echoes the narrator's comment in Genesis that humanity is created in the *image and likeness of God*, the image located definitively in the intimate union of male *and* female. This image is understood in the Christian tradition to be specifically in and through Christ, linking the first creation to the new creation, ecclesiology to eschatology (Gal. 6:15).

At Gen. 1:27, the narrator tells us that God creates the single, unitary,

---

95. Hertz, *Authorised Daily Prayer Book*, 18–21, in Stern, *Jewish New Testament Commentary*, 555. Various communities revise the gendered prayer.

96. Interestingly, there is an ancient Jewish authority that, like Paul, places the gendered blessing in the final position. See t. *Berakhot* 6.18: "Praised [be Thou, O Lord . . .] who did not make me a gentile"; "Praised [be Thou, O Lord . . .] who did not make me a boor"; "Praised [be Thou, O Lord . . .] who did not make me a woman." Neusner and Sarason, *Tosefta*, 40. See also Levine and Brettler, *Jewish Annotated New Testament*, 339.

nameless, and non-gender-specific *adam* in God's own image, and only later does this non-gender-specific *adam* become distinctly gendered as a pairing: male and female (*zakhar uneqevah*). Being created in the image of God is fundamentally tied to this pairing-in-differentiation (see also Gen. 5:2). Paul sends the Galatians back to this story of the created order, where the first human relationship springs from the gendered pairing created specifically *in the image of God*, a typology of Christ and the church (Col. 1:15; Eph. 5:29–32).

Another observation important to Gal. 3:28 that Paul suggests from the opening chapters of Genesis (the universal covenant) is that the gendered pairing is the sole distinction among humans as God declares all creation good (Gen. 1:31). At this point in the narrative, there are no racial distinctions, no socioeconomic divisions, no tribal identities. Only after the curse and the pair's exile from their garden home do we find the entrance of taxonomies of race, clan, class, and occupation. Only after the exile from the garden does the text tell us that Abel is a shepherd and Cain a farmer (Gen. 4:2). Enoch built cities (4:17). Jabal was a nomad (4:20). Jubal was a musician (4:21). Tubal-Cain was a smith (4:22). The force of these fallen human divisions gathers momentum as the narrative moves forward. This is important: that these post-curse distinctions of Jew/Greek and slave/free are not original to humanity's creation in the image of God is the engine of Paul's two binaries in Gal. 3:28. Human divisions that enter the biblical narrative after the fall story are not integral to human blessedness; the original pairing of the male *and* female in the image of God (for Paul, in Christ) does participate in this original blessing.

Contemporary interpreters of Gal. 3:28 sometimes read it as a resource for empowering a vision of justice, inclusivity, and diversity.[97] In these readings of Gal. 3:28, baptism promotes equality in various arenas: gender, race, nationality, and sexuality. This interpretation appeals to the gospel's concern for the health and well-being of the "least of these my brothers and sisters," an integral part of Christian mission (Matt. 25:31–46). I am drawn to this interpretation because of its passion for social justice. However, it mistakenly rests on an implicit reading of all three couplets as binaries, focusing on the declaration of "no longer." In this kind of social justice interpretation, the three couplets do risk promoting what the triad seeks to correct: christological "coercive sameness."[98]

97. See, e.g., Bedford, *Galatians*, 97–107 and the literature indicated there.
98. For those who argue from a close reading (all are men!) that the third couplet does speak of an equality between the sexes, see Meeks, "Image of the Androgyne"; Scroggs, "Paul and the Eschatological Woman"; Betz, *Galatians*.

However, a close reading of the text complicates this conclusion: the final pairing is not equalized as we might think, but is transformed in Christ.[99] The relationship between male and female is returned to its original blessedness, granted in Christ an eschatological identity (see 6:15). Through baptism, even this eschatological identity does not fundamentally displace the human creature from its created identity, an original blessing that points to the relationship between Christ and the church. In baptism, Christ claims us as bone of his bones and flesh of his flesh (Gen. 2:23). Precisely as that bone and as that flesh the church is transformed from glory into glory.

While successful at offering a gender-neutral translation, the NRSV muffles the echo in Gal. 3:28 to Gen. 1:27. Here is the NRSV English of Gen. 1:27:

> So God created humankind in his image,
>   in the image of God he created them;
>   male and female he created them.

Unfortunately, obscuring gender here impedes our ability to pass along the verbal sense of the passage. A translation closer to the words (that unfortunately does not exclude gendered language) gives a different sense entirely. Here is my own translation with interpolated Hebrew transliteration:

> So God created the human one [*ha-adam*] in his image;
>   in the image of God he created him [*oto*; the Hebrew pronoun is the
>   singular male];
>   male and female he created them [*otam*].

The Hebrew, Greek, and Latin all agree: before the human creature is declared to be two, the text includes the detail that the human is made in the image of God. Indeed, there is no "them" until they are announced precisely as male *and* female in the divine image.[100] This is lost in the NRSV.

Another difficulty in many of the English translations is the introduction of the temporal rendering of the negations ("no longer") when they can be

---

99. See also Rom. 12:6–8; 1 Cor. 12:12–31; Eph. 4:11–13. Even there we find no coercive sameness but a diversity that serves specifically the unity of ministry in Christ's name.

100. The text does not suggest that Christian communities should exclude people of differing sexual identities. This issue is as far from the text's orbit as one could imagine. Reading a text is different from using a text; we must read it carefully first.

more logically translated with nontemporal negations ("neither/nor").[101] The temporal rendering is not lexically required, and because it obscures the force of Paul's gendered pairing at the end of the triad, I find it is not helpful for rendering the sense of the phrase. While at 3:28 Paul uses the nontemporal negative *ouk* ("not"), elsewhere he gives the temporal negative *ouketi* ("no longer"; 2:20; 3:18). The difference in context between 3:28 and at 2:20 and 3:18 allows for a justifiable translation of the negatives in the triad at 3:28 as nontemporal. This would give us "not" (*ouk*) without the temporal sense of "no longer" (*ouketi*).[102] The nontemporal negative reading of the couplets makes more sense of Paul's triadic declaration with its gendered couplet in the final position, linked narratively with its echo of the created order in Gen. 1:27.

This is not merely a lexical quibble. The allegory in chapter 4 would make absolutely no sense if the pairing of "male and female" were "no longer." While the Corinthians are clearly troubled by sexual misbehaviors, this does not seem to be the Galatians' problem.[103] In Galatia the misunderstanding of Christian freedom centers not on sexual ethics but more significantly on ethnic/religious identity. Paul's interpretation of the Genesis stories in Gal. 4 is so entirely saturated by concern with fertility, infertility, semen, wombs, conception, and birth that it is hard to imagine Paul wants to tell the Galatians that distinctions between male and female are actually *undone* in baptism. The focus on the gendered pairing in the final couplet at 3:28 recalls the previous verse: baptism into Christ (3:27). It also highlights Paul's declaration of the church's oneness in Christ. They are Abraham's seed, heirs according to the promise (3:29 AT). The pairing participates in the new creation, but not because the first creation is undone. Baptism brings humanity as male *and* female created in the image of God into the heavenly dwelling, the Jerusalem above, the church (2 Cor. 5:1–5; Gal. 4:26).

Paul rejects Gentile circumcision not because it is a "gendered" rite. Paul is not concerned over the question that the rite problematizes equality, insofar as it is given to only one of the sexes. But this does not mean we should not

101. See BDAG 266, 592.

102. The BBE, KJV, Douay-Rheims, Geneva, Bishops, Tyndale, RSV, CJB, NET, and WEB include a nontemporal "neither/nor" and give "male *nor* female." The ASV, ESV, and NIV give nontemporal negatives and offer the pairing "male *and* female." The NRSV uses a temporal negative: "no longer/or," and gives the pairing "male *and* female."

103. For the Galatians, even their sexual profligacy, addressed in chapter 5, seems to focus on male/female relations; gendered life in Christ remains.

ask the question: Why, indeed, is the rite of the covenant given to only half of the population? While female circumcision was not unknown in the ancient world and is still (rarely) encountered in the modern world, it was not practiced in Paul's day, nor is it practiced now among the covenant people of Israel.[104] The fact that female descendants of Abraham are not circumcised but are not thereby disqualified from religious status and life within the covenant people might itself be seen as a type of baptismal identity that unites male and female without annihilating gender.

The creation of "male *and* female" in the image of God is a type of baptism into Christ. The unity-in-differentiation of male *and* female is blessed specifically in their common task of continuing God's creative work, and their blessing as male and female is precisely in their generative capacity: "God said to them, 'Be fruitful and multiply'" (Gen. 1:28).[105] In Genesis the pair shares this blessing and vocation with all other creatures; in this, they are more like than unlike the plants and other living creatures.[106] However, unlike the other creatures, the "male *and* female" come into relationality with each other precisely where they are said to be created in the image of God. Because Christ himself is the image of God (Col. 1:5), the pairing in his image is drawn into the eschatological reality of Jesus's risen life. Baptism is the sacrament of this eschatological reality.

3:29 And if you belong to Christ, then you are Abraham's offspring, heirs according to the promise—That Jesus Christ is the son and seed of Abraham is a statement so basic to the gospel that the New Testament opens with it.[107] While the word "seed" in 3:29 is in its usual singular, because it stands in apposition to the plural pronoun "you," it takes a plural verb form and pronoun. This is the only time in the entire letter where the noun "heir"

---

104. For an extensive study of this idea, see Cohen, *Why Aren't Jewish Women Circumcised?*

105. I am *not* suggesting that the text says that individuals who do not conceive, birth, and/or nurture the next generation from their own bodies are not made in the image of God. I am simply pointing out that in the text the blessing that the human pair shares with all other living creatures is expressed as a participation in God's creative task of furthering life. This, of course, can be true of any human, individual or yoked. The Christian tradition, particularly the monastic tradition, has affirmed the blessings of the non-yoked (celibate) life as well as that of the sacrament of marriage. With contemporary technologies, human biological creative capacity extends to any gender.

106. For example, with the plants and trees with their seed and fruit (Gen. 1:11–12) and with fish and fowl (Gen. 1:21–22).

107. "An account of the genealogy of Jesus the Messiah, the son of David, the son of Abraham" (Matt. 1:1).

occurs in the plural: "And if you belong to Christ, then you are Abraham's seed [*sperma*, singular], heirs [*klēronomoi*, plural] according to the promise" (AT).[108] Here the ecclesial referent joins the messianic: the church is created from the side of Christ as "bone of my bones and flesh of my flesh" (Gen. 2:23).[109]

108. In Gal. 4:1 and 4:7, however, the word "heir" in Greek appears in its singular form, where it has a christological function. The word also occurs in a nominal verbal form at 3:18 and appears in the future tense at 4:30 and 5:21.

109. It is in part for this reason that the church is referred to with female gendered language.

GALATIANS 4

Chapter 4 includes some of the richest Christology in all of Paul's writings, most explicitly in 4:1–7. We learn more about the Galatians' religious life and Paul's assessment of it in 4:8–11. After pastoral exhortation (4:12–20), Paul turns to the Abraham stories in Gen. 16 and 21, giving an allegorical interpretation (4:21–31). Paul is telling the Galatians that, even though they are Hagar's children "in the ordinary way,"[1] in Christ they are children of Sarah; like Isaac, they are elect in the promise to Abraham. This coheres with all that has preceded it in the letter, and the allegory brings the first four chapters of the letter to its climax.

4:1 My point is this: heirs, as long as they are minors, are no better than slaves, though they are the owners of all the property—This verse bridges chapters 3 and 4. The language of inheritance again combines religious and secular contexts. In chapter 3, Paul made analogies between the law and a will (3:15–18) and between the law and a disciplinarian (3:23–25). In chapter 4, Paul now turns to another legal context to speak of the coming of Christ: that of guardians and trustees (4:1–3). Again, the NRSV translation is helpful here as a foil. In the attempt to offer a gender-neutral translation it again distorts the plain sense, obscuring Paul's larger argument. Noticing a simple

---

Parts of this chapter appeared in Kathryn Greene-McCreight, "Figured In: Nonliteral Reading, the Rule of Faith, and Galatians 4," in *The Identity of Israel's God in Christian Scripture*, ed. Don Collett, Mark Elliott, Mark Gignilliat, and Ephraim Radner, Resources for Biblical Study 96 (Atlanta: SBL Press, 2020): 339–53; and Greene-McCreight, "Born of Woman, Born under the Law: A Theological Exegesis of Galatians 4:4," *Pro Ecclesia* 31, no. 1 (2022): 33–40, https://journals.sagepub.com/doi/full/10.1177/10638512221076356.
   1. Translation from Sacks, *Not in God's Name*, 95. I rely on this translation in my comments on the allegory, particularly in my discussion at 4:23.

distinction between Greek and English grammar will help us see the problem in translating here: Greek nouns and pronouns are gendered regardless of any correspondence or lack thereof to physical gender; though English nouns are not gendered, singular pronouns are. For example, some of the crucial terms in 4:1 are as follows: *klēronomos* (heir), *doulos* (slave), *nēpios* (minor), and *kyrios* (owner). In Greek, all of these words are masculine singular nouns and take corresponding masculine articles and pronouns. In English, the third-person singular pronoun is gendered (she/he), but its corresponding third-person plural is nongendered (they). So, to avoid gendered translations, the NRSV gives us plural nouns in place of the Greek singular nouns. Unfortunately, as we saw at 3:28, this effaces christological and ecclesial referents that belong properly to the text (→3:28–29).

4:2 guardians and trustees—This is no succession narrative; the Father does not pass the baton to the Son, as though resigning from his role. The Son does not enter the scene at the fullness of time as one previously unknown; the incarnation does not introduce a new character. The arrival of the incarnate Son, the heir and lord (*kyrios*; NRSV "owners") and slave, is not discontinuous with the work of the Father. Paul does not portray the Father as bestowing anything on the Son, either earthly or spiritual.[2] The Father simply fixes the time when the minor will be given the inheritance by the trustees. The time set by the Father (4:2) points to the "fullness of time" when God chooses to send the Son (4:4) and to the eschatological promise of the heavenly Jerusalem (*anō Ierusalēm*; 4:26).

The word "until" (*achri*) breaks the flow of the sentence and the time of which it speaks into two periods: a before and an after. A future time is opened that will be both different from and yet continuous with the past. The covenants are distinct in chronology but are one in substance (3:6–9; 4:1, 24).[3] Paul states that the old is temporary (3:17–25; 4:2), but the new lives into freedom of the Spirit (5:1, 13, 22–24). The little word "until" points to the time of the sending of the preexistent Christ "born of woman."[4] As the mother of the one born under the law (4:4), this woman herself unites law and grace, grace and law.

2. Unlike in Phil. 2:9.
3. Calvin, *Institutes* 2.10.2.
4. The Greek here has no article and could be translated literally as "born of woman" (*genomenon ek gynaikos*; →4:4).

4:3 while we were minors, we were enslaved to the elemental spirits of the world—Here again we come upon a plural pronoun: "we" (*hēmeis*). Paul includes himself among the Galatians.

The term "elemental spirits" will reappear at 4:9 to refer to the reality that binds the Galatians to their former pagan identity.[5] These elemental spirits fall into the same category for the Galatians as does the circumcision that the Third Party wants to impose on them—a formal equivalent of their relapse into paganism. While these elements are "weak" (4:9), they have the power to enslave (4:3).[6] They are lower cosmic powers; they are "godlings."[7] Being less than God, they cannot ultimately oppose God.[8] They do, however, oppose the freedom of the Galatians.

4:4 But when the fullness of time had come, God sent his Son, born of a woman—The fullness of time is both the ordering of events in time and the gathering of all things in heaven and on earth into the eternal plan of God (1:4; 4:22–5:1).[9] The fullness of time sets forth Christ's double birth: the eternal and the temporal. Referred to in the tradition as the *duplex nativitas*, this claim to Christ's double birth points not to the two natures of Chalcedon but to the one Christ who is born of the Father in eternity and of the womb of Mary in the fullness of time.[10] Because the temporal birth is the eternal will of the Father, Mary's delivery adds nothing to the Son. Arius notwithstanding, there was no time that he was not. And yet Jesus is truly born of a woman, truly in the fullness of time. All human history bends toward this fullness of

5. These may refer to the four elements of the ancient world—earth, water, air, fire—the imbalance of which brings disease (de Boer, "Meaning of the Phrase," 207; Barclay, *Paul and the Gift*, 409n45). They could also refer to the luminaries: sun, moon, and stars (Wright, *Galatians*, 251).

6. In Colossians, elemental spirits are linked to human tradition and deceit, and as such, they enslave. "See to it that no one takes you captive through philosophy and empty deceit, according to human tradition, according to the elemental spirits of the universe, and not according to Christ" (Col. 2:8); "If with Christ you died to the elemental spirits of the universe, why do you live as if you still belonged to the world?" (Col. 2:20).

7. I am borrowing this term from Fredriksen, "Gods and the One God."

8. "I am the LORD, and there is no other; besides me there is no god. I arm you, though you do not know me, so that they may know, from the rising of the sun and from the west, that there is no one besides me; I am the LORD, and there is no other. I form light and create darkness, I make weal and create woe; I the LORD do all these things" (Isa. 45:5–7).

9. See also Eph. 1:10.

10. Augustine, *Sermons* 186.3; 189.4; 190.4; 196.1; John of Damascus, *Exact Exposition of the Orthodox Faith* 3.7.12; Aquinas, *Summa Theologiae* III.35.2–3; I.43.2, ad. 3; Martin Luther, *Enarratio 53 cap. Essaie prophetae*; Barth, *CD* I/2, 138–39. Thanks to Phil Cary for pointing me to the Augustine sermons.

time, and all history since then finds its reference point in the ineffable-yet-everyday human birth. This event interprets all other world-historical events: "That Jesus had been born in the fullness of time meant that all things which had gone before seemed to conspire toward the realization of the event. Not only the religion of the Hebrews but the philosophy of the Greeks also was now intelligible as prophecy of the coming of a great salvation."[11] The fullness of time both creates the condition for the sending and is the sending itself (Gal. 4:5; Eph. 1:7–11). The incarnation is no afterthought, no alteration of God's will, no change of the divine mind. It is precisely God's fulfillment of his own first accords and promises: "God said, 'Let there be light'; and there was light" (Gen. 1:3). The fullness of time is from eternity and yet lies in the manger of King David's city.

These four simple words "God sent his Son" express the one single divine will and act of both sending and coming that composes the divine self-giving.[12] The Father sends; humanity receives but does not invite. The Son is sent uncoerced.[13] The past and present tenses of the verbs in 4:4 point to a shift in time that is at its fulcrum: the birth of the Son (Gal. 3:8, 23). This arrival is before all time in its fullness but takes place in time: "*when* the fullness of time had come."

Galatians 4:4 is one of many texts in the Bible with trinitarian instincts.[14] This is not simply because the names Father, Son, and Spirit appear here.[15] These trinitarian instincts emerge specifically in the actions and relations of the divine persons.[16] The Father (4:2, 4, 6), the Son (4:4), and the Spirit (4:6; cf. 3:3, 14; 4:29; 5:5, 16–25) are one in both the will and act of God's sending. The Son comes in the fullness of time, of a woman's womb, under the law's statutes. And yet the incarnation alters nothing in the Son, nor in the Father or the Spirit. Within history, yet beyond it, the eternal plan of God draws the Gentiles into the elect people of Abraham through God's promise of the Christ.

The sending is fixed not only to a date in history but also to a people and a place. Ethnicity, land, and gender participate in the fixedness of the sending

---

11. Niebuhr, *Meaning of Revelation*, 112.
12. In Greek the clause is composed of six words: *exapesteilen ho theos ton huion autou.*
13. Christ's will is one with the Father's: he "gave himself" (Gal. 1:4; see also 2:20).
14. Rowe, "Biblical Pressure."
15. Yeago, "New Testament and Nicene Dogma."
16. Swain, "Heirs through God"; Hill, *Paul and the Trinity*; Schweizer, "God Sent His Son."

of the Son: Jesus arrives in a specific family—namely, Mary's. Just as Isaac, the son of the promise, cannot be born of any mother but Sarah, so also the Son of God cannot be born but of a specific woman, more precisely a woman under the law. This is the same woman who heard the promise announced and accepted the commission uncoerced.[17]

Following Paul's earlier illustration of the *paidagōgos* in 3:24–25 and the image of guardians and trustees (3:23; 4:2), he might logically have added here something like "when we came of age" or "when we reached majority." But the subject of the verb here is God, and the larger context of the verse is the Father's will. Mary's role is a free self-surrender to the commission of God, just as the will of the Son is one with the will of the Father. In the sending, the Father forces neither the woman nor the son she bears.

Any kind of sending necessarily involves a transfer from one "place" to another, and in this specific sending of the Son there is movement: from eternity, into our own time, our own place. The sending of the Son into time and space means that neither God the Father nor God the Son is identical to that time and space. God the Father is transcendent over time and space, specifically in and through this very act of sending the Son.

The sending into time therefore also points to the Son's preexistence: Christ is sent in the fullness of time into history from eternity.[18] The claim to Christ's preexistence is a logical outworking of 4:4. "If we understand eternity as pre-time—and we must understand it in this way—we have to recognize that eternity itself bears the name of Jesus Christ."[19] The fullness of time is therefore the eternal plan and purpose of God to which the whole covenant arcs (Gal. 5:14; Rom. 13:9; Eph. 1:10). As the eternal divine will, the sending is both an eschatological sign and a gynecological miracle. This sending itself is a delivery.

God sends the Son by the human flesh of a woman: Jesus's mother grounds his humanity (Matt. 1:18; Luke 2:5). The Gospels usually refer to the woman who births the Son by her name, Mary. But in Gal. 4:4, this earliest reference to Mary in the New Testament, Paul leaves her name unspoken. Instead, he identifies her by her biological and christological roles: she is the woman

---

17. "Then Mary said, 'Here am I, the servant of the Lord; let it be with me according to your word.' Then the angel departed from her" (Luke 1:38).

18. The earliest Christology is of divine identity; Gal. 4:4 is just one example of this. See Bauckham, *Jesus and the God of Israel*.

19. Barth, *CD* II/1, 622, citing John 8:58; Eph. 1:4–6; 1 Pet. 1:18–20.

who bears the Son. In grounding Jesus's humanity, Mary is mother of God.[20] Any statement about this woman must therefore be a properly christological statement.

The preposition "of" preceding the noun "woman" came to pose a christological problem specifically with regard to its implications for understanding Christ's humanity. In the second century, Irenaeus of Lyon pointed to "some" who impugned the humanity of Jesus by saying that Jesus "passed through Mary just as water [passes] through a tube."[21] According to Irenaeus, Jesus could not have been truly human if he had not been truly born of a woman, so he must have received something from his mother's flesh. He had to come not just "through" her but "from" her. Just as Jesus was born of woman, he came for all woman-born, all humanity.[22] He is in solidarity with the entire human race, Jews and Gentiles alike, including even Paul's foolish Galatians (3:1).

Even though Mary's role is not independent of the Father's act of sending or of her Son's coming, nevertheless it is she alone who truly conceives, gestates, births, nurtures. The Father sent the Son, but the mother delivered him. That her delivery was from a womb untouched by male sperm is basic to the tradition and remains uncontested in the creeds. This virgin-birthing of her son finds its type in the Old Testament. The church has traditionally heard in the prophecy of Isa. 7:14 the virgin birth announced, "Behold, a virgin shall conceive, and bear a son, and shall call his name Immanuel" (KJV). If we look only at the Hebrew text, this use of Isa. 7:14 may seem odd; the Hebrew word here, *almah*, can mean simply an unmarried woman. The Septuagint, however, gives us *parthenos*, a word indicating someone who has never engaged in sexual intercourse. Because Paul and the earliest church read the Septuagint, interpreting the young woman from Isa. 7:14 as referring to a physically chaste young woman, or a "virgin," is entirely reasonable.[23] The Vulgate gives us *virgo*, also expressing the sense of chastity.

Mary is an antitype of John the Baptist, and he is her type; both point away from themselves to Christ. John the Baptist plays the role of Elijah, preparing

---

20. Literally, "God-bearer," *theotokos*; Council of Ephesus (AD 431).
21. *Ek:* "from." *Dia:* "through." Irenaeus, *Against Heresies* 3.11.3 (*ANF* 1:427).
22. See Job 14:1; 15:14; 25:4.
23. The pre-Christian Greek Septuagint predates the earliest texts of the Hebrew Bible, but not the earliest traditions.

for and announcing the Messiah.[24] Mary bears the Messiah, the seed of the promise; she is thus the antitype of Eve.[25] Whereas John the Baptist is a hinge figure between the two covenants, Mary is God's instrument precisely for the inauguration of the eschatological age itself (Gal. 6:15).

When we think of Mary, our imaginations are often drawn to the nativity stories in Luke and Matthew. But there is also a rich correspondence between Gal. 4:4 and John 1:14, "And the Word became flesh and dwelt among us" (RSV). Both verses point to the sacramentality of Christ's presence among the elect people as well as the role of this people in the incarnation. The image of Mary as tabernacle takes its inspiration in part from the interplay between these two verses. While the echo is lost in many English translations, the Greek verb in John 1:14 (*eskēnōsen*) evokes the tabernacle.[26] In gestating the Son of God under the law, Mary's womb is the antitype of the tabernacle, where the law of God was kept safe during Israel's wilderness journeys.[27] Just as the tabernacle contained the law, the word of God, and bore the presence of God among the people in the desert, so Mary's womb bears the presence of God, the Son sent in the fullness of time (Rev. 21:3). The image of Mary as tabernacle is a version of the christological claim that Jesus is the antitype of the law (Gal. 5:14).

The Jewishness of Jesus's body is not accidental to the gospel message.[28] He is of the house and lineage of David (Luke 1:27). He knew Abraham, and Abraham rejoiced to greet him (John 8:56). Born under the law, Jesus fulfills the law and embodies the law (Gal. 6:2; Rom. 10:4). Circumcised on the eighth day, Jesus receives the rite of the covenant (Luke 2:21). Paul knows that Jesus's Jewish flesh is a sacred blessing, and Paul himself takes pride in his own Jewish flesh (Rom. 11:1; Phil. 3:4–5). God's election of the Jewish people in the covenant of Abraham stands fast and is not annulled (Gal. 3:15;

24. "And if you are willing to accept it, he is Elijah who is to come" (Matt. 11:14).
25. Gen. 3:15; Gal. 3:16; →3:13 on the protoevangelium. Irenaeus, *Against Heresies* 3.22.4 (PG 7/1:959A); Epiphanius, *Refutation of All Heresies* 78, 18 (PG 42:728CD–729AB), in *Catechism of the Catholic Church*, #494.
26. Some of the major options for translation are "dwelt" (e.g., RSV, KJV, Douay, Geneva, ASV, ESV), "lived" (NRSV, CJB, WEB, JANT), "made his dwelling" (NIV), "took up residence" (NET), and "took a place" (BBE).
27. This ancient typology of Mary as the tabernacle also reads Luke 1:35 in light of many Old Testament texts, just some of which are Exod. 40:35, Num. 10:34, and Deut. 33:12. See Athanasius, *Homily of the Papyrus of Turin*; Gregory Thaumaturgos, *Homily on the Annunciation to the Holy Virgin Mary*, in *Catechism of the Catholic Church*, #2676.
28. In this at the very least, Paul corresponds to the Gospels. See also my comments at Gal. 3:13 on its coherence with the passion narrative in Luke. For a comprehensive study of the relationship between Paul's writings and the Synoptic Gospels, see Hiestermann, *Paul and the Synoptic Jesus Tradition*.

Rom. 11:29). Paul has shown that the gospel itself is the foundation of the particular covenant and that the universal covenant knows its election in this Jewish seed. Rejecting the Jewishness of Jesus ruptures the relationship of the Gentile church with the church of Jerusalem; this is at the heart of the pastoral and doctrinal problem in Galatia. Ignoring (or far worse, despising) Jesus's religious and ethnic specificity promotes a fundamental misunderstanding not only of Jesus but also the gospel.[29]

It follows that part of Mary's function in the Gospels, as here in Gal. 4:4, is to pin Jesus to the family of God's election. This is identified in the genealogies of Matthew and Luke. Matthew sketches Jesus's line beginning with Abraham, proceeding chronologically through the generations up to the apex, Mary herself.[30] The genealogy in Luke reverses that order, moving from Joseph, Mary's husband, backward through David and the patriarchs and finally to the universal father of all: Adam, "son of God."[31] The fact that Mary's womb is the point of reference for Jesus's genealogies corresponds to the Jewish tradition that traces family lineage through the mother, regardless of the religious/ ethnic identity of the father, a tradition that continues to this day among many Jews.[32] The fact that matrilineage will be key in Paul's allegory is all the more remarkable in light of the Galatians' having taken on circumcision, the rite that marks covenantal identity on the anatomical site of the fathering of a child. Paul shows that the Galatians find their lineage and access to Christ not through Abraham's circumcised penis but through Mary's Jewish womb.

under the law—Mary's own adherence to the law would have included the religious privileges and responsibilities attending any Jewish woman with children. She and Joseph fulfill the Levitical statutes surrounding the birth of her baby, traveling to Jerusalem to present Jesus in the temple (Luke 2:22–27; Lev. 12:4). At the temple, the devout Simeon directs his prophecy about Jesus directly to Mary (Luke 2:34). The infant is named Jesus, as the angel had

29. "Making Jesus more of a Jew seems still to entail making him less of a Christian—or at any rate less palatable as a figure of Western Protestantism" (Bockmuehl, "God's Life as a Jew," 64, 66). Bockmuehl links Western Protestantism's rejection of the Jewishness of Jesus with gnosticism. I find an analogous move in our theological distaste for the gendered specificity of the incarnation: e.g., Jesus had a penis that was circumcised on the eighth day. See Luke 2:27.
30. Matt. 1:1, 16, "of whom Jesus was born."
31. Jesus "was the son (as was thought) of Joseph son of Heli" (Luke 3:23; see also 3:28). Joseph is identified not as father but as "the husband of Mary, of whom Jesus was born" (Matt. 1:16).
32. See Cohen, "Origins of the Matrilineal Principle."

instructed Mary (Luke 1:31). The naming is specifically linked to the story of his circumcision, the name itself rooted in Mary's womb.[33] Mary oversees the sacramental wine at Jesus's first sign at the Cana wedding feast, fulfilling a statute under the law pertaining to women for the care and feeding of their household (John 2:1–5).

While it is true that in Mary the Son is fixed to a specific people, culture, and place, his reach is not limited to these. His ethnicity and gender generate as well as complicate a mission of "enculturation."[34] The religious and ethnic specificity of the particular covenant is also universal: Jesus is a light to the Gentiles *and* the glory of his people Israel (Luke 2:32; Isa. 42:6; 51:4). In Christ, the God of Israel has brought the pagan Galatians, who are properly descendants of Ishmael, to join with Isaac in the promise to Abraham. The Galatians live apart from the law, yet in Christ they are privileged to dwell in obedience to the law of Christ (Gal. 5:14; 6:2). The Galatian churches are types of the church universal dwelling among the nations throughout the world and across time.

Jesus was born under (*hypo*) the law but not according to (*kata*) the law. The Gospel stories illustrate Jesus's complex relationship to the law: at times he observes it, but at other times he does not. He accuses the Pharisees of hypocrisy when they observe what he deems to be inconsequential tithes yet neglect "the weightier matters of the law" (Matt. 23:23; cf. Luke 11:42). However, we do not find Jesus actually observing the statutes that might represent those "weightier matters," with the possible exception of a muted detail in Mark 6 and Matt. 9 where Jesus is described as wearing the fringed prayer shawl of the observant Jew.[35] The fringes on the shawl serve to remind the wearer to observe the commandments in daily life. The narrator in the Gospel story adds the comment that all who touched the fringes of Jesus's shawl were healed (Mark 5:27).[36] His prayer shawl, an outward and visible sign of the law, heals by the inward and spiritual grace of the one who wears it, the one who is the law.

33. "After eight days had passed, it was time to circumcise the child; and he was called Jesus, the name given by the angel before he was conceived in the womb" (Luke 2:21; cf. Gen. 17:10–14).
34. On the concept of enculturation in missions, see Sanneh, *Translating the Message.* Paul's evangelization of the Galatians might be seen as a first-century version of a missions of enculturation.
35. "Speak to the Israelites, and tell them to make fringes on the corners of their garments throughout their generations and to put a blue cord on the fringe at each corner. You have the fringe so that, when you see it, you will remember all the commandments of the LORD and do them, and not follow the lust of your own heart and your own eyes. So you shall remember and do all my commandments, and you shall be holy to your God" (Num. 15:39–40).
36. See also Matt. 9:20–22; Mark 6:56; Luke 8:44.

Even more, his prayer shawl is a sign of the prophetic vision of the last days:
a *minyan* of Gentiles who acknowledge that God is with the people of Israel
will ascend to Zion, all ten grabbing the prayer shawl of a single Jew.[37] Jesus is
that Jew who, in the fullness of time, brings the Gentiles of Galatia to Zion,
the heavenly Jerusalem (4:26).

"Born under the law" is also a statement about Mary's typological relationship to Eve. This type begins in the universal covenant, in the garden where
Eve is both referred to and named. Eve's husband pronounces her "woman"
in accordance with her created relation to him, punning: "This one shall be
called Woman [*ishah*], / for out of Man [*ish*] this one was taken" (Gen. 2:23).
It is only after the disobedience and ensuing curse that she receives her proper
name. Eve, *Chavah*, is the "mother of all living" (*em kol khay*; Gen. 3:20).[38]
Even so, in the story Eve births the dying; Mary bears the living (Gal. 2:19–20;
3:10–13, 16; 6:14–15). Eve is the mother of curse; Mary is the mother of
blessing. Eve receives the promise of the seed; Mary births its fruit (Gen. 3:15;
Luke 1:31–33). Eve is the promissory mother of the seed, Mary's son, who
will himself bring life in his death (Gal. 2:19–20; 6:14–15).

The unnamed Eve plays a veiled role in Gal. 3:16. Nevertheless, this is
no cameo: Eve is an implicit linchpin to Paul's larger argument in Galatians
(→3:16). Her seed is the substance of the promise. It bears repeating: the
protoevangelium is the tradition of reading Gen. 3:15 that notes a detail in the
narrative: even before God curses, he announces the good news.[39] The gospel of
Jesus Christ precedes even the curse on Eve and Adam. The unnamed mothers
Eve (the universal covenant) and Mary (the particular covenant) both play a
role in the drama of the divine sending.

The unnamed Sarah will play a role throughout Galatians mostly offstage;
referred to as the Jerusalem above, she will come into the spotlight toward
the end of the allegory in 4:28. The barren-turned-fertile mother Sarah is an
antitype of her predecessor, the once-fertile Eve. Each woman stands in the line
of childbearing from creation to incarnation; without both there would have
been no delivery of the Son. While the tradition of Christian interpretation

---

37. "Thus says the LORD of hosts: In those days ten men from nations of every language shall
take hold of a Jew, grasping his garment and saying, 'Let us go with you, for we have heard that God
is with you'" (Zech. 8:23).

38. The name is related to the Hebrew word for "life."

39. "I will put enmity between you and the woman, and between your seed and hers; *he will strike
your head, and you will strike his heel*" (Gen. 3:15 AT; →3:13, 16).

reads Mary as Eve's antitype, in Gal. 4 Sarah herself functions as a mediating type between both of them. Just as Isaac, the son of the promise, cannot be born of any mother but Sarah (Hagar will not do), neither can the Son of God be born but of this woman who is commissioned with, and accepts, the task (Gen. 15:4; 17:19; Luke 1:26–38). While Mary is the only one of these three women to have a function in the economy of redemption independent of a husband, none of them has a function independent of the Father's will.

The typology of Eve and Mary brings us full circle back to the humanity of Christ. The Father wills to redeem creation through sending the Son into human history according to the biological processes of birthing. Born of a Jewish mother, Jesus is subject to the law and is the law. He brings life to the Gentiles, the dying children of Eve. Born of woman, Jesus is subject to mortality and all the infirmities of human life.[40] If Jesus is not human, he is not subject to death; if he is not subject to death, he cannot actually die; if he does not die, he cannot be raised from the dead. And if he is not raised from the dead, we are found to be liars, we are still in our sins, and "we are of all people most to be pitied" (1 Cor. 15:12–19).[41]

4:5 so that we might receive adoption as children—God redeems "those under the law" (*hina tous hypo nomon exagorasē*) with the purpose that "we" might receive adoption (*hina tēn huiothesian apolabōmen*). These clauses set up a contrast: those who are "under the law" seem to be different from the "we" who are receiving adoption. The first, those "under the law," would logically be Jews; the others, those receiving "adoption," would logically be Gentiles. But by shifting the pronoun from the third-person plural ("those") to the first-person plural ("we"), Paul includes himself among his addressees.

4:6 And because you are children, God has sent the Spirit of his Son into our hearts, crying, "Abba! Father!"—The Aramaic word *abba* is followed by its Greek translation *patēr* (father).[42] This Semiticism (a word in Aramaic followed by its Greek equivalent) indicates that the writer would have known

---

40. "A mortal, born of woman, few of days and full of trouble, / comes up like a flower and withers, / flees like a shadow and does not last" (Job 14:1–2).

41. A modern expression of this logic can be found in John Updike's poem, "Seven Stanzas at Easter."

42. Paul uses the phrase *abba ho patēr* also in Rom. 8:15; see also its use on Jesus's lips in Mark 14:36.

Aramaic but that some of the addressees would have needed a translation. The New Testament contains many Semiticisms, most of which are in the Gospels.[43] The phrase *abba ho patēr* seems to be a liturgical formula that Paul has received from the oral history of the earliest church and is not his own invention.[44] The address to the Father corresponds to the prayer that Jesus taught his disciples.[45] Some of the petitions are eschatological, especially the petition for "daily bread" (Matt. 6:11; Luke 11:3).[46] The doxology that closes the Matthean version of the prayer also includes eschatological elements: in its bidding of rescue from the evil one, it declares the surety of God's coming kingdom, power, and glory (Matt. 6:13). Because the coda of the prayer in Matthew has been contested in the text tradition, the NRSV has chosen to put it in a note, explaining, "Other ancient authorities add . . ." But because of its eschatological coherence with the prayer itself, the coda fits theologically. It is not beyond the bounds of possibility that Paul has even heard the prayer and that he may have heard it this specific way, because his eschatological horizon corresponds to it.[47] The words of Jesus himself may be a purposeful eschatological allusion to God's provision of manna in the desert.[48] Because on the Sabbath no work is permitted, God provides on the previous day twice the amount needed for the following (Exod. 16:5). The Sabbath is the prime eschatological sign of the fullness of time. The Galatians, even as Gentiles, are privileged to address God as *abba* in the fullness of time, the end-time Sabbath of God's self-giving in the incarnation. God sends the Spirit of his Son into the hearts of even his Gentile children as they are invited to pray to God: *abba ho patēr*.

43. For example, Mark 5:41. These constructions often appear in translation of names: e.g., Mark 10:46. See also Acts 9:36.
44. For the concept of oral history as distinguished from oral tradition, see Bauckham, *Jesus and the Eyewitnesses*, esp. 30–38, 240–90.
45. Note: with the Greek *patēr*, not the Aramaic *abba*; see Matt. 6:9–13; Luke 11:2–4 omits "our."
46. There are many suggestions for the meaning of the phrase "daily bread," but because it is exceedingly rare in the Greek literature of the era, "daily bread" likely reflects the Aramaic "bread for tomorrow." E.g., Levine and Brettler, *Jewish Annotated New Testament*, 13n11, 125n3.
47. Paul certainly would have been familiar with the eschatological doxology in 1 Chr. 29, which itself may have influenced the dominical prayer: "Yours, O LORD, are the greatness, the power, the glory, the victory, and the majesty; for all that is in the heavens and on the earth is yours; yours is the kingdom, O LORD, and you are exalted as head above all. Riches and honor come from you, and you rule over all. In your hand are power and might; and it is in your hand to make great and to give strength to all" (1 Chr. 29:11–12).
48. "Morning by morning they gathered it, as much as each needed; but when the sun grew hot, it melted" (Exod. 16:21).

4:7 So you are no longer a slave but a child, and if a child then also an heir, through God—Here is the goal of the fullness of time: to redeem and to adopt.[49] The incarnation is God's eternal plan from before all time, executed in and as history. Jesus's humanity is from and through and of his mother, yet it is eternally his. The Son is eternally in the bosom of the Father, not "created" at the incarnation. He makes the Father known, or "exegetes" (*exēgēsato*) him (John 1:18). The Father sends the Son and, through the power of the Spirit, frees those in Christ who are now heirs according to the promise.

As we saw, the only occurrence in Galatians of the noun "heir" in the plural was at 3:29: "And if you belong to Christ, then you are Abraham's offspring [singular: "seed," *sperma*], heirs [plural: *klēronomoi*] according to the promise." There the noun is ecclesial. But because the unit at 4:1–7 begins and ends with the singular noun "heir" (*ho klēronomos*; 4:1, 7), the material inside the inclusio is set off as richly christological, even incarnational.[50]

4:8–11 Formerly, when you did not know God, you were enslaved to beings that by nature are not gods—Paul returns to his personal address: the Galatians have reverted to their former pagan identity. Previously they were in bondage to idols, to that which is not-God. This corresponds to Paul's sermon in Acts 17, where he preaches to the pagans in Athens.[51] In the sermon, he describes pagans according to their distinguishing feature: ignorance of the God of Israel. As worshipers of non-gods, they are idolaters.[52] But the pagans in Galatia are in an even more serious state of degradation; they do know God, because Paul has taught them, and they are indeed known by God. How can they then turn back to their former paganism?

49. We find a similar movement in Eph. 1:9–10.
50. Even the scribal textual variants indicate this: the heir "through God" is also read "through Christ" and "through Jesus Christ" and "of God through Jesus Christ." See the apparatus to NA[28], p. 584; and Silva, "Text of Galatians." Many thanks to Peter Rodgers for pointing this out to me.
51. "For as I went through the city and looked carefully at the objects of your worship, I found among them an altar with the inscription, 'To an unknown god.' What therefore you worship as unknown, this I proclaim to you. The God who made the world and everything in it, he who is Lord of heaven and earth, does not live in shrines made by human hands, nor is he served by human hands, as though he needed anything, since he himself gives to all mortals life and breath and all things" (Acts 17:23–25).
52. "Pour out your wrath on the nations that do not know you, / and on the peoples that do not call on your name" (Jer. 10:25; cf. Ps. 79:6). "They exchanged the truth about God for a lie and worshiped and served the creature rather than the Creator" (Rom. 1:25). "You know that when you were pagans, you were enticed and led astray to idols that could not speak" (1 Cor. 12:2). "Control your own body in holiness and honor, not with lustful passion, like the Gentiles who do not know God" (1 Thess. 4:4–5; see also 2 Thess. 1:8).

4:9 how can you turn back again to the weak and beggarly elemental spirits? How can you want to be enslaved to them again?—The elemental spirits are the enslaving beings from which, as Paul has already said, the Galatians have been freed (4:3). The rupture between the Galatians and Abba, Father, the one whom they are privileged to address in prayer (4:6), has now cut them off from knowing God, and from God's knowing them.

4:10 special days, and months, and seasons, and years—These "special days" may be the feasts of Jewish law: the Sabbath, Shavuoth (Pentecost), Succoth (Feast of Booths), Passover, and/or the Year of Jubilee.[53] Paul suggests that these have been imposed on the Galatians by the Third Party. By observing the law's feasts and fasts, in their theological confusion the Galatians might as well be returning to their pagan past.[54] Ambrosiaster suggests that in these pagan elemental spirits linked to Jewish observances lies the clue to Paul's "mediator" from 3:19–20. Christ mediates between the Gentile pagan feasts and the Jewish feasts and rites.[55] In 4:11 Paul reiterates his earlier worry from 2:2 that his work was in vain.[56] It is as if he were telling them, "You have deviated from my teaching, and I myself have failed." His own success at catechizing the Galatians would have resulted in their properly following his teaching in the gospel: he feels he must not have taught them well.

4:12–20 In this section we move to an increasing pastoral concern first expressed in 1:6–10 and again in 3:1–5. This pastoral concern will become intensified after the allegory and will occupy the remainder of the letter in chapters 5 and 6. Whereas in 1:6–9 Paul's tone is scolding, in 3:1–5 his reprimand

53. See Exod. 23, 34; Lev. 23, 25; Deut. 15–16.
54. While in Gal. 4:8–10 Paul equates the feasts and fasts of the law with pagan elements, in Colossians these law observances are types of Christ: "Therefore do not let anyone condemn you in matters of food and drink or of observing festivals, new moons, or Sabbaths. These are only a shadow of what is to come, but the substance belongs to Christ" (Col. 2:16–17).
55. According to Ambrosiaster, it is Christ's mediation that brought the Gentile Galatians out of slavery: "Without a doubt, a mediator, that is, arbiter is not of one but two. . . . So he took from the Gentiles the plurality of gods and from the Jews the works of the law, that is, new moons, circumcision, the keeping of the sabbath, the distinction of foods and other things that the Gentiles abhorred. And thus those who were formerly enemies came to be at peace. If this is the case, how could the Gentiles be so dull-witted as to violate this reconciliation by conversion back to Judaism?" Ambrosiaster, *Epistle to the Galatians* 3.20.1–2 (CSEL 81.3:38–39), translation in Edwards, *Galatians, Ephesians, Philippians*, 47.
56. See also Phil. 2:16: "It is by your holding fast to the word of life that I can boast on the day of Christ that I did not run in vain or labor in vain."

begins to modulate, and here in 4:12–20 his tone becomes intimate. He emphasizes the former quality of their relationship that has now changed: the bonds of affection have been strained, but as far as Paul is concerned, they are not beyond repair.

4:12 Friends, I beg you, become as I am, for I also have become as you are. You have done me no wrong—Paul sets himself up as a pastoral example of piety and ethics: when the Galatians imitate him, he will be with them in their witness to the gospel even if he is not physically present. They will be like a letter of recommendation, as he says explicitly of the Corinthians (2 Cor. 3:2).[57] Here at Gal. 4:12, Paul's plea has softened and is even conciliatory in tone: they have done him no wrong.

The verb in the phrase "you have done me no wrong" (*ēdikēsate*) is the same verb that appears in Gen. 16:5 (*adikoumai*, LXX) on the lips of Sarai as she upbraids Abram after Hagar conceives Ishmael, Abram's first son.[58] This is one of the moments that generates a potential threat to the promise and undergirds the narrative logic of the allegory. The narrator of Gen. 16 shows that in fact Abram had done no harm to Sarai but had simply followed her request that he impregnate Hagar. Just as Abram has in fact done Sarai no wrong, Paul in his work among the Galatians has done them no wrong. Unlike Sarai with Abram, Paul is gentle with the Galatians: "You have done me no wrong."

4:13 You know that it was because of a physical infirmity that I first announced the gospel to you—We learn in Paul's letters and in Acts that he faces much suffering on account of his missionary work: beatings, floggings, shipwrecks, deprivations, and imprisonments (2 Cor. 11:23–27). He acknowledges that he has a reputation for being weak, unengaging, even contemptible.[59] He counts his powerlessness as a mark of authenticity of his ministry.[60] In his

57. See also Gal. 4:19–20; 1 Cor. 11:1; 4:16; Phil. 3:17; 4:9; 2 Thess. 1:6–7; 2:14; 3:7–9.

58. "Then Sarai said to Abram, 'May the *wrong* done to me be on you! I gave my slave-girl to your embrace, and when she saw that she had conceived, she looked on me with contempt. May the LORD judge between you and me!'" (Gen. 16:5). The word translated into English as "wrong" (NRSV) is in Hebrew *hamas*, literally "wrongdoing" or even "violence." This Hebrew word shares the Semitic root underlying the Arabic noun *Hamas*.

59. "For they say, 'His letters are weighty and strong, but his bodily presence is weak, and his speech contemptible'" (2 Cor. 10:10). "And I came to you in weakness and in fear and in much trembling" (1 Cor. 2:3).

60. "[The Lord] said to me, 'My grace is sufficient for you, for power is made perfect in weakness'" (2 Cor. 12:9). "If I must boast, I will boast of the things that show my weakness" (2 Cor.

weakness, Paul says, he manifests the power of God in Jesus Christ.[61] He speaks
of a recurring thorn in his flesh that, despite his continuous prayers for relief,
causes him anguish (2 Cor. 12:7–10). Jerome reflects an early tradition that
credited this thorn in the flesh to migraines, while others suggest the thorn was
the general opposition he faced.[62] Another suggests the possibility that Paul
may have had malaria.[63] This physical infirmity may have been the reason for
Paul's change of itinerary that landed him in the backwater of Galatia.[64] While
we have no direct evidence as to the exact nature of this physical infirmity,
we do know its results: Paul's condition has caused ill will on the part of the
Galatians. This remark in Gal. 4:13 hints at what he will say in 6:17 about
the marks of Jesus being branded on his body. As Paul sees it, his physical
infirmity identifies him as Christ's own, the sacramental presence of the Lord
among the Galatians.

**4:14 though my condition put you to the test, you did not scorn or de-
spise me, but welcomed me as an angel of God, as Christ Jesus**—They first
received him as a messenger (*angelos*) of God, even welcoming him as Christ
himself (*hōs Christon Iēsoun*). Paul reminds the Galatians that even this unidentified weakness did not originally make them reject him, his friendship, or his
preaching. Why has this changed? Paul has scolded them for accepting a false
gospel taught by outsiders and contrasts himself with them by underscoring
his own faithfulness (1:8–10).

**4:15 What has become of the goodwill you felt? For I testify that, had
it been possible, you would have torn out your eyes and given them to
me**—As with the earlier reference to Paul's "physical infirmity," his remark
about the Galatians' eyes (and by implication his own) gives us little concrete
information. With his "double literal sense" that embraces hyperbole within
the plain sense, Nicholas of Lyra is able to read this detail literally: the fact

11:30). "So, I will boast all the more gladly of my weaknesses, so that the power of Christ may
dwell in me" (2 Cor. 12:9).
    61. "For he was crucified in weakness, but lives by the power of God. For we are weak in him,
but in dealing with you we will live with him by the power of God" (2 Cor. 13:4).
    62. Jerome, *Commentary on Galatians*, 171n224, and Lightfoot, *Epistle of St. Paul*, 186–91. For
this tradition, Lightfoot points to Tertullian, *Modesty* 13.16; Chrysostom, *Homily 26 on 2 Corinthians* (*NPNF*[1] 12:400).
    63. Ramsay, *Historical Commentary*, 417–22.
    64. Martyn, *Galatians*, 420.

that the Galatians could have torn out their eyes indicates more than just a gruesome gift. Lyra says that they never would have done such a thing because it would have been "unsuitable."[65] In other words, for Lyra, Paul's statement is no metaphor. More importantly, Paul's hyperbolic remark underscores his formerly close relationship with the Galatians and tells us something significant about Paul's preaching and the Galatians' reception of the gospel through it. Their eyes are the physical organs that have beheld Jesus "publicly exhibited as crucified" (3:1). Their eyes witnessed the marks of Jesus branded on Paul's body (6:17), signs of the truth of the gospel (2:5, 14). Their eyes are reliable witnesses, bearing sacramental testimony. Paul knows that at one point the Galatians would have given to him even their sense of sight with which they gazed on the glorious scars of Jesus on Paul's body, so deep was their mutual love.[66]

4:16 Have I now become your enemy by telling you the truth?—This question reflects Paul's earlier recounting of the narrative of his second trip to Jerusalem in chapter 2, with his support for Titus's refusal of circumcision (2:3–5) and his scolding words to Peter (2:11–15). Circumcision of Gentile converts to Christ must be refused. Unlike Titus, and in spite of Paul's earlier teaching, the Galatians have not had the strength to resist the Third Party's demand of circumcision for conversion to Christ. And yet Paul himself has maintained "the truth of the gospel" on behalf of Titus and the Galatians.

At 4:16, Paul asks whether his insistence on the truth of a circumcision-free gospel for the Gentiles is now creating hostility on their part toward him. In accepting the rite of circumcision, the Galatians have put both their fidelity to the gospel and their loyalty to Paul in jeopardy. They have denied the truth of the gospel: Gentile Christians are heirs to the promise of Abraham through Christ alone apart from law observance. They have rejected Paul's preaching and scorned his friendship. They now bear hostility toward their former friend and missionary whom they had once held in great affection. Because he has told them the truth, and because they have rejected it, they now perceive him as the enemy. He does not, however, perceive them this way.

65. Levy, *Letter to the Galatians*, 250.
66. "Those dear tokens of his passion, still his dazzling body bears / Cause of endless exultation to his ransomed worshippers / With what rapture, with what rapture, with what rapture / Gaze we on those glorious scars!" Charles Wesley, "Lo! He Comes with Clouds Descending," in Episcopal Church, *The Hymnal 1982*, #57, verse 3.

4:17 They make much of you, but for no good purpose—The pastoral motivations of the Third Party are different from Paul's: they are not interested in the well-being of the Galatians at all, but in seeking their own reputation and status. This recalls Paul's earlier scolding of Peter over his hypocrisy in chapter 2 in his implicit approval of Gentile Christian circumcision. Paul warns the Galatians that the Third Party's motives are malignant and their intentions are not in the Galatians' own best interests. They are deceiving the Galatians.

4:19 My little children, for whom I am again in the pain of childbirth until Christ is formed in you—Labor and delivery, to state the obvious, are women's work. There is a cluster of terms around the topic of labor in the prophets and in the New Testament that use this imagery to speak of the Day of the Lord.[67] In Galatians, the pains of the laboring mother reflect the delivery of God's son (4:4), when the fullness of time will be finally and completely revealed. Whereas there is an apocalyptic sense to Paul's motherhood imagery, Paul's concern here has more to do with election, Sarah's bearing of the seed, and Christology.[68] While that birthing imagery is in the context of apocalyptic, Paul bears Eve's cursed labor pains that disfigured humanity's reproduction from the disobedience in the garden but that will be relieved in the eschatological delivery of the Son.[69]

Paul describes his pastoral care of the Galatians in this motherly vocabulary: he participates in the formation of Christ in his "little children."[70] While the Third Party preaches that the foreskin is the site of the sign of election, Paul teaches that the essential organ in election is the quickened uterus: Eve's, Sarah's, and Mary's.

Paul is not the only figure in scripture whose task is illustrated in imagery of motherhood. Moses also is described as mothering: he complains that the

---

67. Isa. 13:6, 8; Jer. 6:24; Mic. 4:10; see also *1 Enoch* 62:4; *2 Baruch* 56:6; *4 Ezra* 4:42; 1QH^a (Thanksgiving Hymns) 3.7–10. In the New Testament, see Matt. 24:8 // Mark 13:8; Rom. 8:22; 1 Thess. 5:3; Rev. 12:2.

68. *Pace* Gaventa, "Maternity of St. Paul," esp. 193–94. I take apocalyptic and eschatology to be overlapping but not identical categories: eschatology is not always apocalyptic, nor apocalyptic always eschatology. In classical Christian eschatology, what is unveiled is not fundamentally unknown but is typologically present in creation. This is the nexus of Paul's allegory in particular.

69. See my comments on the protoevangelium at 3:13, 16.

70. Elsewhere he also describes himself as a father to his children, but in admonishment, example, and discipline. See 1 Thess. 2:11; 1 Cor. 4:14–17; 2 Cor. 6:11–13.

Lord has burdened him with the nurture of an ungrateful people.[71] For Moses the lawgiver, motherhood imagery includes conceiving, birthing, and nursing; for Paul the evangelist, motherhood imagery includes the pains of labor and delivery. But even so, Paul's christological mothering does not "deliver"; he fears that it has failed as a tool for the formation of Christ the seed in the Galatians. The birth pangs Paul speaks of are types that point to the entry of Christ into the world that, in and through Mary's womb, transforms time into its fullness (Gal. 4:4).

4:20 I wish I were present with you now and could change my tone—In his absence after his first preaching among them, the Galatians have fallen into theological and spiritual confusion. Paul is angry but emphasizes his desire to modulate his tone. If he could be with them now, he would be comforted, as also would they. He has exhorted the Galatians to imitate him (4:12). He wishes that he could speak to them with the fondness and goodwill they had once shared (4:15). Pastoral persuasions will return in chapters 5 and 6. But before he focuses more tightly on the pastoral problems in the Gentile Galatian churches, he now turns to explore the nature of Gentile identity and election in Christ by offering his interpretation of some of the Abraham stories in what he describes as an "allegory."

4:21 will you not listen to the law?—Paul pivots from his earlier alternating pastoral scolding and nurture back to his teaching mode. He has quoted, referred to, and interpreted scripture for the Galatians. Now he turns directly to them: they should listen for themselves.[72] Paul suggests that the Galatians cannot observe the law if they do not know it, and they certainly can't know it if they don't read it. And they can't read it if they are not taught, just as the Ethiopian eunuch knew intuitively (Acts 8:31). And while the Third Party has taught the Galatians to observe the Torah, they have not taught them to read it carefully. Paul intends to remedy the situation by reading the Torah to them aright. The Galatians have heard about Abraham's son Isaac, yes, but they

---

71. "Did I conceive all this people? Did I give birth to them, that you should say to me, 'Carry them in your bosom, as a nurse carries a sucking child, to the land that you promised on oath to their ancestors'?" (Num. 11:11–12).

72. The verb is *akouō*, which can mean "to listen," "to hear," "to obey," or "to heed." It is the verb in the LXX that translates the Hebrew *shema* of Deut. 5:1 (→1:13, 23; 3:2, 5 on the role of hearing in the confession of belief).

have overlooked the important detail in the story that Abraham in fact has *two* sons, not just one; even more importantly, these two sons are from different mothers. The identity of the two mothers forms the engine of the allegory.

4:22 For it is written that Abraham had two sons—Paul has already introduced the sons, showing the Galatians that they themselves are also "descendants [sons, *huioi*] of Abraham" (3:7; cf. 3:26). But membership in the family of Abraham is not the point.[73] Paul reads the Torah and Prophets in order to show that the Galatians are not sons of Hagar, as they might have thought; Paul wants to show them that through Sarah, the free mother, they are sons according to the promise (4:26).

When Paul introduces a quotation of scripture, he usually uses the conventional formula, "It is written." But here at 4:22 he says, "It is written *that*"; in other words, he is offering a teaching *based on* the story. His interpretation thus recalls the episode in Nehemiah where the reading of the long-lost Torah is given along with its explanation ("the sense") so the people could understand.[74] Paul's allegory recounts the Genesis stories about Sarah and Hagar but "gives the sense" so the Galatians can understand.

In chapter 3 Paul used Abram as the key player in the story; here at chapter 4 he gets more specific. The question is not "Who is our father?" but "Who is our mother?" (4:26). Thus enters the first tangle in the plot: Abram's wife Sarai is barren.[75] But the promise is to come only through Sarai's initially infertile womb, a detail that plays a crucial role in the allegory just as it has throughout the story of Israel. As firstborn, Ishmael should be the heir, but he is born of Hagar and as such he is not the son of the promise. As secondborn, Isaac should not be the heir, but he is born of Sarah, and as such he is indeed the son of the promise.

This is an example of the biblical pattern of reversal where the younger usurps the birthright of the elder. The story of Israel's genealogy of election

---

73. For another opinion: "According to Galatians 4:21–31, insofar as Abraham has two families, they can be characterized as the slave family and the free; and it is the multiethnic people defined by faith, the people formed through Christ and the Spirit, who are the Isaac children, the free people of God." Wright, *Pauline Perspectives*, 212.

74. "So they read from the book, from the law of God, with interpretation. They gave the sense, so that the people understood the reading" (Neh. 8:8).

75. God changes the protagonists' names, first Abram's at Gen. 17:5 and then Sarai's at 17:15. To repeat: I refer to these characters by the names they bear in the episode cited as I talk about the stories. When I read Paul's interpretation of them, I will follow his own usage.

is shot through with these reversals. The pattern appears first in the universal covenant, where the younger son, Abel, and not his brother, Cain, is favored by God for his sacrifice. This pattern continues into and throughout the particular covenant: it is Isaac and not Ishmael who is elect to bear the promise. It is Jacob, not Esau, who receives Isaac's blessing. It is Joseph, not his older brothers, who is favored by Jacob. It is Ephraim, not Manasseh, who receives Jacob's blessing.

The internal movement of many of Jesus's parables follows a disruptive logic that mirrors this reversal pattern. One example is the parable of the laborers in the vineyard (Matt. 20:1–16), in which the landowner gives equal pay for the day laborers' unequal time worked: those who began in the morning earn the same as do those who began later in the day. In the parable of the good Samaritan (Luke 10:29–37), the righteous person is not a law-observant Jew (of the particular covenant) but a Gentile (of the universal covenant). This points to the astoundingly unexpected, even unjust, nature of God's grace. To revisit the idea, in the New Testament this pattern is broken in Jesus, the firstborn who opens the womb of Mary (Exod. 13:2; Gal. 4:4; Heb. 1:2, 4). Jesus is the first and only son of his mother, the heir of all things.[76] There is no younger to usurp the place of the elder. The pattern of reversal funds Paul's allegory, not with regard to the sons but primarily the mothers. Sarah, chronologically secondary, is theologically primary; Hagar, chronologically primary, is theologically secondary.

The identities of Sarah and Hagar thus govern the allegory. In the biblical narrative, Sarah is the first mother of the people of Israel.[77] However, out of desperation over her infertility, she takes Hagar as her surrogate. The risk ensues that this Egyptian woman herself will usurp Sarah's place. This is theologically significant in part because of the role Egypt plays in the story of the people of Israel: Egypt is its oppressor and a threat to its very existence (Gen. 16:1, 3; 21:9; 25:12). Another difference between the mothers we might overlook is that surrogacy arrangements in the ancient world had the opposite impact on the birth mother than is often the case in the contemporary world. In the twenty-first century, the practice often benefits the surrogate mother economically while the adoptive mother hopes for emotional benefit. But in the ancient world, the surrogate mother would have been left economically deprived, for

76. See my comments at 1:19 on Jesus's brothers and the doctrine of perpetual virginity.
77. Zucker, "Sarah," 221.

her future material security and physical well-being depended, in the event of the death of her husband, on a son. This would have been the case with Hagar; but God provided Isaac to replace Ishmael in the family. Hagar is thus able to keep her own son, Ishmael; through Isaac, God preserves Hagar.

4:23 **His son by the slave woman was born in an ordinary way; but his son by the free woman was born as the result of the promise**[78]—The sons are mentioned in chronological order, not in order of theological importance. Ishmael is conceived in the usual way, but Isaac is conceived against all odds. Ishmael is born in the ordinary way, but Isaac is born as the result of the promise. The stock Pauline contrast between "flesh" and "spirit" that emerges elsewhere in Galatians is not at play here.[79] The juxtaposition between the sons' conception and birth hints at the way the mothers and their children function in the logic of the allegory. The difference between the two births results in two pairs of terms that contrast: the first son and mother (ordinary birth, slavery) and the second son and mother (promise, freedom).

4:24 **Now this is an allegory**—Here properly begins the typological correspondence of the two mothers, the two churches of Gentiles and Jews. There are those who say that Paul's writings are hard to understand (2 Cor. 10:10; 2 Pet. 3:16). The allegory in Gal. 4 may be one example. Luther, having begun with the assumption that the letter is about the doctrine of justification by faith, finds that the allegory does not fit the letter's intended goal. He suggests that Paul was about to end the letter at 4:20 but then added an illustration, the "allegory."[80] Luther finds this section theologically extraneous, complaining about allegorical interpretation in general as useless.[81] Because I myself find that the doctrine of justification by faith takes up a relatively small amount

---

78. Translation from Sacks, *Not in God's Name*, 95. The NRSV's rendering of *kata sarka* is the literal "according to the flesh" and, to be sure, is not unjustified. However, it is unhelpful within the context of the allegory.

79. Gal. 3:3; 4:29; 5:16–17; 6:8; see also Rom. 7:13–25; 8:4–6, 9.

80. Luther, *LW* 26:432. In modern scholarship this allegory has been read in many ways: about freedom from slavery (Oakes, *Galatians*, 32); a reprise of 3:1–27 (Bedford, *Galatians*); the expulsion of the slave woman (Matera, *Galatians*). Some find it, as do I, to be the climax of the entire letter (e.g., Boyarin, *Radical Jew*, 32).

81. "Allegories do not provide solid proofs in theology, but, like pictures, they adorn and illustrate a subject. . . . Now, at the end of his argument, he adds an allegory as a kind of ornament. . . . An allegory is a kind of illumination of an oration or of a case that has already been established on other grounds." Luther, *LW* 26:435–36.

of energy in the letter, I do not find the allegory to be a randomly tacked-on illustration; it shows in a new way that election is in the seed born of Sarah and specifically not of Hagar. The allegory is essentially ecclesiological.

In the fifth century, the monk and exegete John Cassian applied Paul's allegory to the practice of reading biblical texts. Carrying forward a tradition born before him, most especially from Origen of Alexandria, Cassian developed a vision for biblical interpretation that was inspired by his attention to the two Jerusalems in Paul's allegory: "One and the same Jerusalem can be understood in a fourfold way: historically as the city of the Jews, allegorically as the church of Christ, anagogically as the heavenly city, and tropologically as the human soul."[82] Cassian saw that Paul's allegory points to the roles of the mothers in election and in the coming of Christ. Building on these two figures of Jerusalem, Sarah and Hagar, Cassian discerned four "senses" of reading scripture that are often (although not consistently) listed as the literal, the typological, the allegorical, and the anagogical. Augustine of Dacia in the thirteenth century wove Cassian's scheme into a memorable quatrain: *Littera gesta docet, quid credas allegoria, moralis quid agas, quo tendas anagogia.* "The letter teaches the deeds, the allegory what you are to believe, the moral what you are to do, and the anagogy what you are to strive for."[83] Biblical texts were read according to these different lenses, often with little attention to any precise ordering of the levels. While the fourfold schema was not a method per se, it fueled Christian biblical interpretation until the sixteenth century in the Protestant West.

The overlapping concepts of allegory, typology, and figure all apply here as ways of reading the biblical story at face value in order to hear it speak of a substantial, broader, and deeper subject matter.[84] They all seek to "prolong the author's meaning in a direction congenial to the text."[85] Paul uses the term "allegory" to describe his reading of the Genesis stories. But I myself prefer the term "typology" because, more so than the figure of allegory, it acknowledges the temporal nature of story via its categories of type and antitype; it recognizes the crucial role of chronological ordering in Paul's reading of the Genesis stories in his allegory.

82. John Cassian, *Conferences* 14.8.4 (CSEL 13:405), quoting Abbot Nestoros, translated in Edwards, *Galatians*, 70.

83. Translation in Levy, *Letter to the Galatians*, 256, 252n18.

84. Even the names given to Cassian's senses and their ordering are fluid in the later tradition.

85. I borrow this observation from C. S. Lewis in his description of the literary function of allegory in particular. Lewis, *Reflections on the Psalms*, 102–3.

Typology, like allegory, is itself a form of prolonging the author's meaning in a direction congenial to the text. It is a version of multivalent interpretative strategies that saturate not only Christian interpretation but also other religious traditions. Remarking on the Genesis stories, Jonathan Sacks gives a contemporary example of a rabbinic hermeneutic of multivalence when he asks: "But what if [the Genesis stories] do not mean what people have thought them to mean? What if there is another way of reading them? What if this alternative reading turned out, on close analysis, to be how they were written to be read? *What if the narratives of Genesis are deliberately constructed to seem to mean one thing on the surface, but then, in the light of cues or clues within the text, reveal a second level of meaning beneath?*"[86]

As with Lewis and Sacks, Paul seeks to prolong the sense of the text, gathering clues on the surface of the Genesis stories of the election of Israel; he finds that same election to be in Christ. While this may seem like he is importing from another theological framework, Paul assumes that he is leaving the story unencumbered.[87] He is not adding meaning, or embroidering, or illustrating; he claims to give the divine sense with interpretation so the faithful can understand. In the context of Paul's argument in Galatians, the two Jerusalems are not only the two mothers; they are the two churches: the Gentile Christian mission and the Jewish Christian mission. The teaching of the Third Party among the Galatians is a fundamental misappropriation of the relationship between these two Jerusalems. Both covenants are in fact grounded in Christ.

In 4:24–5:1 we find a number of characters whose identity is veiled: some are named; others are only mentioned. Abraham is named first (4:22). Hagar is named second (4:24). The last to be named is Isaac (4:28). This reflects what Paul has been trying to teach the Galatians: Hagar (a Gentile, named) bears the first child, Ishmael (a Gentile, unnamed). Sarah (a Jew, unnamed) bears the second son, Isaac (a Jew, named). The mother of the first son is a slave; the mother of the second son is a free woman.

Hagar is first introduced into the Abram/Sarai story at Gen. 16:1 immediately after we hear that Sarai has borne Abram no children. There Hagar is identified only as Sarai's Egyptian slave girl. She is not the mother of the seed

86. Sacks, *Not in God's Name*, 103 (emphasis added). Sacks makes his plea for an acknowledgment of Genesis's multivalent meanings specifically to counter readings that "on the surface" promote religious violence. That is, his hermeneutical concerns are ethical.
87. Hans Frei uses the phrase "to leave the story itself as unencumbered as possible" to speak of literal (or "plain sense") reading. Frei, *Identity of Jesus Christ*, xv.

but will become the mother of the elder son, the first turned last, Ishmael.[88] It bears repeating: whereas God changes the name of Abram (and Sarai) in Gen. 17 to reflect the change in Abram's identity at his election, Hagar's name remains static throughout the narrative. However, even though she is not the mother of the promise, she and the child in her womb are not abandoned by the God of the promise. The angel of the Lord has mercy on them in the desert at Beer-lahai-roi and blesses both mother and her unborn son (Gen. 16:11). The angelic promise to Hagar about her son echoes the messianic prophecy from Isaiah that the New Testament hears as prophecy of the birth of Jesus.[89]

Hagar, the mother of this boy whose cries for help God will hear, becomes the first character in the Bible to name God, acclaiming him "the God who sees" (*El-Roi*; Gen. 16:13). And in doing so, she herself sees, becoming one of the few characters in the Bible who sees God and actually lives.[90] The detail that this Gentile slave sees (and names) God yet lives to tell about it is a remarkable statement about her role in the two covenants. Even though she belongs to the universal covenant, she is given the grace to see the Lord of the particular covenant. The name that Hagar gives God identifies the way in which the Lord blesses her, specifically through the blessing on her son. Hagar's faith is the well from which springs the Reformers' slogan: *To know Christ is to know his benefits*.[91] Christ's benefits for Hagar and Ishmael are that in the desert God hears her son's cry. They are not left to die; they are spared. Even while Hagar sees and names God, and is rescued through the cries of her son, she and Ishmael do not function in election apart from serving as a hinge between the two covenants.

4:25 Now Hagar is Mount Sinai in Arabia and corresponds to the present Jerusalem, for she is in slavery with her children—In 4:22–23 Paul

---

88. Islam understands its own identity and inheritance of the promises to Abraham through Hagar's son Ishmael, Abraham's firstborn. For the figure of Keturah, see Gen. 25:1–6.

89. "Therefore the Lord himself will give you a sign. Look, the young woman is with child and shall bear a son, and shall name him Immanuel" (Isa. 7:14). The Isaiah passage is cited in the messianic prophecy of the angel to Mary's betrothed, Joseph, with the translation of the name Emmanuel added: "God is with us" (Matt. 1:23).

90. Moses speaks with God and lives: "Today we have seen that God may speak to someone and the person may still live" (Deut. 5:24). Jacob sees God and lives: "I have seen God face to face, and yet my life is preserved" (Gen. 32:30).

91. Philipp Melanchthon, *Loci communes* 1521 (trans. Pauck, 21). Hagar knows God's graciousness to her through the blessings on her son Ishmael. While he will have his own land and descendants, they are not the blessings of Isaac (Gen. 17:20; 21:13; 25:12–18). See my discussion of Perkins at 2:16.

has laid out the problem: Abraham had two sons, not just one, through two different mothers, one a slave and one a free woman. The son of the slave was born in the ordinary way, and the son of the free woman was born according to a miraculous promise. In 4:24–25, Paul lays out the terms of the allegory.

The detail that Hagar bears children for slavery makes sense: Hagar is of the slave class. But what does this Gentile slave have to do with Sinai? Two articles of different genders are used in reference to Hagar. In 4:24, the feminine article (*hētis*) precedes Hagar's name as is grammatically correct and to be expected. But in 4:25 the neuter article "it" (*to*) precedes her name that itself is sandwiched between the article *to* and the word *horos*, "mountain."[92] This strengthens the theological bond between Hagar and the place of the giving of the law, Mount Sinai. The "present Jerusalem" (*tē nyn Ierousalēm*; the "now Jerusalem") is the city we find on a map, the Jerusalem of sounds and smells, of children playing and mothers giving birth. This is the Jerusalem to which Paul says that Hagar corresponds: the "present" ("now") Jerusalem. She is also drawn into the orbit of Gentile Christianity, Arabia (→1:17). She is Mount Sinai; she is Arabia; she is Jerusalem; she has slave children. Sarah is less thickly described. She is free, the "upward" Jerusalem, "our mother" (that is, the Galatians' mother).

We might have expected these mothers and their Jerusalems to correspond in some way, either in likeness or dissimilarity. After all, in the Genesis story the mothers correspond insofar as they compete for status within the family. But for Paul, Hagar and Sarah are not comparables.[93] Otherwise, since the first Jerusalem is "present," the other would be "future."[94] But the other is not the "future" Jerusalem; it is the "heavenly" (*anō*, literally "upward"). And again, since the second is the "heavenly" Jerusalem, the first should be the "earthly" Jerusalem. But this is not the case; the cities are not binaries. They are simply in different categories: chronological ("now") and spatial ("up"). In much the same way, Hagar and Sarah do not correspond to each other in significant ways, apart from being mothers. Their identities are incommensurable.

But why Jerusalem at all? The present Jerusalem is the geographical city that Paul visited after his mission among the Gentiles: he goes to *Hierosolyma*

---

92. *To de Hagar Sina* (4:25), untranslated in English. Lightfoot, *Epistle of St. Paul*, 193.

93. "Comparables" in the context of real estate appraisals, in which the value of a dwelling is used to determine the value of another.

94. The image of the "Jerusalem above" was not uncommon in the Second Temple period; there are allusions in Isa. 65:17; 66:22; *Jubilees* 1:29; 4:26; *1 Enoch* 91:16; and Ps. 87:5 with its "Mother Zion." In the New Testament, see Heb. 11:10; 12:22; Rev. 3:12; 21:2, 9–27.

(Gal. 1:18; 2:1). However, here in chapter 4 he calls the city *Ierusalēm*. This may seem an insignificant matter and may simply reflect the manuscript tradition.[95] But, following this curious detail down its potential rabbit hole points out something that should be obvious: the name "Jerusalem" does not appear at all in the Genesis story of Hagar and Sarah.[96] While the Jebusite city that preceded Jerusalem appears in the stories of the Torah, it is not mentioned in the Abraham stories at all. The holy city of Jerusalem itself does not figure into the narrative until many generations after Hagar, Sarah, and Abraham have all gone to their reward. The geographic locators in the narrative of Gen. 16–21 do not set the scenes in relation to Jerusalem but to other places: "the spring on the way to Shur" (Gen. 16:7), "the oaks of Mamre" (Gen. 18:1), and "the wilderness of Beer-sheba" (Gen. 21:14).

Why then does Paul bring the figures of Sarah and Hagar into the geographic orbit of Jerusalem? To be sure, Jerusalem is the holy city of the people of Israel, but there must be more. In lining up these women with Jerusalem, Paul has already stepped beyond the narrative setting of the Abraham/Sarah story. Even before he introduces the words "present Jerusalem" or "above Jerusalem," the narrative framework of the stories about Sarah and Hagar has been deconstructed. That is, the two cities correspond directly neither to Hagar nor Sarah. There is no literal city to be canceled by a spiritual city. There is no subsuming: Hagar does not "replace" Sarah, nor does Ishmael "replace" Isaac, because there is no direct correspondence that can be negated. The fact that the two mothers have been plucked from their own geographical/narrative context and given incommensurable descriptors of the city far beyond their own plot setting indicates that there is something far more complex here than simple correspondences and negations. Both Jerusalems, "present" and "above," are eschatologized from the outset.

While Cassian does not say this explicitly, his multilevel schema rests on the profound hermeneutical significance in these small qualifiers "now" and "above": they themselves force the reader to see that there is no single meaning to Paul's interpretation. Because the identities of the Jerusalems are not mutually canceling, the levels of interpretation built on them can potentially embrace different readings simultaneously without contradiction. They can be read in a multitude of ways without distorting the verbal meaning of any

95. See BDAG 470; Wright, *Galatians*, 298n32.
96. Another pun is appropriate: sometimes following a rabbit hole can be productive.

text interpreted; they mutually enrich, rather than exclusively prescribe, any single meaning. Within the allegory itself, the literal and spiritual levels by definition overlap. Paul's allegory becomes for Cassian not so much a literary device as a prophetic oracle.

4:26 But the other woman corresponds to the Jerusalem above; she is free, and she is our mother—As the first book of the Torah, Genesis functions hermeneutically within the canon as promise rather than fulfillment.[97] Paul therefore does not distort the Abraham stories when he reads them as indicators of hope. For Paul, Sarah points to the reality of the heavenly city, the church of Jews and Gentiles, the eschatological blessing. Within the Hebrew Bible itself, the Gentiles' relationship to Zion represents an oracle of hope: "I remember Rahab and Babylon among those who know me; and Philistia and Tyre and the people of Ethiopia, 'They were born there,' they say. And of Mother Zion, they will say, 'This one and that one were born in her'; for the Most High himself will establish her. The LORD registers the peoples and the rulers, 'These ones were born in her'" (Ps. 86:4–6 LXX, AT). The nations stream up to Jerusalem, but not to destroy her. They stream for a blessing.[98]

4:27 For it is written, "Rejoice, you childless one"—While he paraphrases the Genesis stories at 4:22 ("it is written *that*"), here Paul quotes directly from the prophet Isaiah: "It is written." The prophetic text links the two mothers:

> Rejoice, you childless one, you who bear no children,
>> burst into song and shout, you who endure no birth pangs;
> for the children of the desolate woman are more numerous
>> than the children of the one who is married. (Gal. 4:27; Isa. 54:1)

In the quotation from Isaiah we hear some of the most important details that Paul shares about the two mothers. It verbally links Sarah's barrenness to the infertility of the mother in Isaiah.[99] The quotation emphasizes the future expectation inherent in the allegorical reading. It announces the eschatological

97. Sacks, *Not in God's Name*, 185.
98. Deut. 16:16; Pss. 120–134; Isa. 66:20; Zech. 8:20–23.
99. Paul's linking texts of Torah with Prophets may point to an awareness of the Palestinian triennial liturgical cycle of Torah/Haftorah reading. "Even post-70 texts, notably Acts 13.13–15 and Luke 4.16–21, lend themselves to the conclusion that a Torah–Prophet reading was practiced prior to the destruction of the Temple in 70 CE ([Schiffman] 47–48)." DiMattei, "Paul's Allegory," 114,

hope and rejoicing at the fulfillment of the promise, the reversal of the painful bearing of children (Gen. 3:16). Astoundingly, the barren woman will rejoice and will "enlarge the site of [her] tent . . . and [her] descendants will possess the nations" (Isa. 54:1, 3). With this quotation Paul gathers together the allegory's (and the letter's!) themes: barrenness and fertility, birth pangs and delivery, the present and the heavenly. The particular covenant embraces the universal.

4:28 Now you, my friends, are children of the promise, like Isaac—Paul turns from exposition and interpretation of the Genesis stories to direct discourse: "now you, my brothers and sisters."[100] Family relationships have been key throughout the letter: childhood, coming of age, inheritance, and the promise of a biological son for Abraham and Sarah. Family relationships also saturate the allegory: fatherhood and sonship, motherhood and childbearing. The Galatians belong to this family nexus and, like Hagar and Ishmael, function as a theological link between the two covenants. The fact that they are *like Isaac* will be decisive for the allegory, a detail that will become clearer at Sarah's command to Abraham in 4:30.

4:29 But just as at that time the child who was born according to the flesh persecuted the child who was born according to the Spirit, so it is now also—Paul described himself at the beginning of the letter as one who, before his conversion, had persecuted the church that he once saw as a threat to his people Israel, to its covenant election, and to its law (1:14; see also Phil. 3:4–6). But a puzzling detail complicates Paul's reading of Genesis here at Gal. 4:29. He interprets the story such that Ishmael persecutes Isaac, a detail not present in Gen. 21:9. Not until Gen. 21:10 do we hear hostile tones, where Sarah angrily berates Abraham about Hagar and her son Ishmael. Paul's account of Sarah's acrimonious order seems overblown; it does not fit the plot of Gen. 21.

The interaction between the sons in Gen. 21:9 is translated in the NRSV as "playing." In Hebrew, the verb is *tsakhaq*, "to laugh," etymologically related to

citing Schiffman, "Early History of Public Reading," 44–56. See also Fishbane, "Introduction," xxi. If this is the case, here Paul would be extending rather than breaking from his liturgical tradition.

100. The NRSV renders the Greek word *adelphoi* (lit., "brothers") as "friends." While it could also be translated "brothers and sisters," rendering it as "friends" is a stretch. The problem of gendered language remains stubbornly with us as we try to read the text closely. There may be no other way to address this other than to do our best in reading the text in the original languages, making our own translations and interpretive decisions.

Isaac's name.[101] The postmenopausal Sarah hears the promise that she will have a son and responds with delighted laughter (Gen. 17:17; 18:12–13, 15; 21:6), a detail pointing to the joy that comes from God's providence and promises in election. Even the name Isaac, *Yitskhaq*, points to the eschatological promise of God. It appears seven times in the narrative of Gen. 17–21, seven being the number of eschatological perfection, a detail not missed by the rabbis and church fathers.[102]

While the Septuagint at Gen. 21:9 gives the verb *paizō*, "to play" or "to amuse," Paul gives *diōkō*, "to persecute," a verb completely foreign to the context of the Genesis story. If Ishmael were being violent toward Isaac, Sarah's harsh words directed to Abraham might be justified.[103] While it is not clear just what Ishmael has done to incur Sarah's wrath in the story at Gen. 21, it seems to be related to Isaac's identity as expressed in his punned name. The boys are simply playing (*paizonta/metzakheq*). The reason Paul makes the conceptual leap from playing to persecuting may simply be that it makes better sense out of Sarah's behavior in Gen. 21:10. Galatians 4:29 provides this justification. However, it may be based on Paul's sense of pastoral care for the Galatians. Ishmael's persecuting of Isaac illustrates the behavior of the Third Party's misconstrual of the Galatians' identity in Christ. Paul uses the concept of persecution here to point to the contrast between himself and the Third Party. He is willing to suffer as he defends the Galatians' life in Christ (5:11); but the Third Party refuses to suffer for the name of Christ on behalf of the Galatians (6:12).

The focus now shifts from a familial context to the theological reality undergirding the relationships between the mothers and their sons: the promise. Sacks's translation of *kata sarka* is helpful at this point: "At that time the son born in the ordinary way persecuted the son born of the Spirit" (4:29). The juxtaposition of "ordinary" birth with "promised" birth is exactly what Paul has been trying to emphasize. Paul is not contrasting material and spiritual reality but the everyday (physical) and the promised (miraculous). This is election: completely laughable, miraculously unpredictable, and astoundingly grace-filled.

---

101. Here we have the *qal*; in the *piel*, the verb means "to joke" or "to make fun of." The NIV translates this as "mocking." Many thanks to Michelle Knight for the clarification.

102. Sacks, *Not in God's Name*, 276n3.

103. There is a similar rabbinic story where Ishmael shoots arrows at Isaac, apparently pretending it is all in fun. Sarah accuses Hagar's son of "persecuting" Isaac. Paul may have known about this story (Levy, *Letter to the Galatians*, 254n24, citing Ginzberg, *Legends of the Jews*, 1:263–64; 5:246n211). See also Josephus, *Jewish Antiquities* 1.215; Betz, *Galatians*, 250; Wright, *Galatians*, 302n40.

**4:30 But what does the scripture say? "Drive out the slave and her child;
for the child of the slave will not share the inheritance with the child of
the free woman"**—While the principal voice we hear in Galatians is Paul's,
there are others who join him. Some speak indirectly: the Gentile churches of
Judea (1:23) and the Jerusalem pillars (2:10). We overhear the God of Israel
address the Galatians through scripture: in Abraham's story (3:8), through the
law (3:10–13, 16; 4:4; 5:14), and through the prophets (3:11; 4:27). But only
one person in addition to Paul addresses the Galatians: Sarah. Her words form
the climax to the entire letter (4:30).

Sarah now orders Abraham to "drive out" the other mother. This has at
various times in the Christian tradition been used as a justification for anti-
Semitism over the centuries. This is unjustifiable for (at least) two reasons: it
fails to read the text closely, and it violates the rule of love.[104] An anti-Jewish
reading logically depends on the assumption that Sarah's words on Paul's lips
are voiced in fact by Hagar, who commands Abraham to cast out Sarah and
her son Isaac. This is the inverse of the plot in Gen. 21. But the Galatians have
been declared to be children of Sarah and not of the slave (4:26). Sarah would
not be bidding rejection of herself and her son; that makes no sense of the
narrative as Paul has told it. Hagar remains Sarah's slave and is never declared
a "free woman" as is Sarah (4:23–25, 30). Like Ishmael, the Galatians neither
replace Isaac nor do they cast out his mother who is now their own adoptive
mother, Sarah.

Continuing to mine scripture, Paul turns from his earlier conventional
formula, "It is written" (*gegraptai gar*; Gal. 3:10, 13; 4:27), to a rhetorical
question: "But what does the scripture say?" (*alla ti legei hē graphē*; Gal. 4:30).
The question itself replaces the narrator's words in Gen. 21:10 that set up
Sarah's bitter command. Her words are introduced by the clause: "*So she said to
Abraham.*" This is important: omitting the narrator's introduction and replac-
ing it with his own rhetorical question, Paul takes Sarah's command directly
on his own lips: "Drive out the slave and her child." While in the Genesis
narrative, Sarah's words are addressed to Abraham, here in Galatians Sarah's
words are addressed to the Galatians. But their father in the faith, Paul, has

104. Here Augustine's rule of love, the functional twin of the rule of faith, should come into
play: "Whoever, then, thinks that he understands the Holy Scriptures, or any part of them, but puts
such an interpretation upon them as does not tend to build up this twofold love of God and our
neighbor, does not yet understand them as he ought." Augustine, *On Christian Doctrine* 1.36.40.
→2:2, 5; 5:6; 6:16.

done everything *not* to drive out Hagar's (Galatian) children. In Christ they, too, are children of the promise, and they are his own children. The Galatians, born in the "ordinary way," would deserve to be driven out because they have listened to the Third Party, the ones who are specifically *not like* Isaac. However, in Christ the Galatian children are born according to the promise, *like* Isaac; their mother is in fact the free woman Sarah (4:31). The allegory closes with Paul's own counternarrative for the Galatians: in Christ they themselves are not to be cast out of the people of Israel.[105]

Paul then alters the final sentence. Where in Gen. 21:10 Sarah says, "for the son of this slave woman shall not inherit along *with my son Isaac*" (Gen. 21:10 LXX, AT), Paul instead writes, "The son of the slave woman will not inherit *with the son of the free woman*" (Gal. 4:30 NA[28], AT). Sarah refers to herself in the third person. The emphasis is not on her son Isaac but on Sarah herself, the free woman, the mother of the Galatians. The Galatian Gentile Christians do not replace Sarah's son; they join him. Sarah "our mother" replaces her surrogate, Hagar. This is Paul's purpose in his choice of altering this verse. He is not talking about throwing anyone out but drawing the Gentiles into Sarah's fold. Sarah is now the Galatians' mother "according to the promise," in Christ. Sarah has replaced Hagar, their mother "in the ordinary way." A female tour jeté of the pattern of reversal results.

4:31 So then, brothers and sisters, we are not children of the slave woman but of the free woman (AT)—Paul now returns to the first-person plural, including himself among the Galatians as children of Sarah, the free mother in whom they are liberated from their former slavery. And even though they were born in an ordinary way, in Christ they are born according to the promise, *like Isaac*. Paul sets the allegory as the capstone of the whole letter to show the Galatians that, by their faith in Christ, they are members of the particular covenant; through Christ they are children of Sarah apart from the law. They are *like* Isaac, but they do not subsume or replace Isaac. Remaining uncircumcised, they are to remain steadfast in the freedom of the Jerusalem above, their free mother, the church.

5:1 For freedom Christ has set us free. Stand strong, therefore, and do not submit again to a yoke of slavery (AT)—Here we reach the hinge between

---

105. The term "counternarrative" is Sacks's; the application of it to Gal. 4:30 is mine.

the rather lopsided first and second halves of the letter. Chapters 1–4 laid out a theology of Gentile identity in Christ, while chapters 5–6 will take up its implications in the ongoing life of the church. It will become clear that the freedom Paul declares is not simply a repudiation of the efforts to earn God's favor through law observance but is wrought through the cross of Christ.

GALATIANS 5

In the first four chapters of the letter, Paul sets out the nature of the promise and the relation of the Gentile Galatians to it. As they believe in Christ, so they share the faith of Abraham. They are no longer outsiders to the covenant. The free mother, Sarah, now steps into the role of their own mother, the slave Hagar. The Galatians now join Isaac as heirs to the faith of Abraham through the promise. Paul now reminds the Galatians that, even though they are "like Isaac," they are and must remain free from law observance. They are to be led by the Spirit and live in its fruit, being built up in love of God and neighbor.

5:1 For freedom Christ has set us free. Stand strong, therefore, and do not submit again to a yoke of slavery (AT)—Moving from the storied allegory in Gal. 4 to the exhortation in Gal. 5, Paul brings his teaching mode to a close in a pastoral tone. Here we find what has been implicit all along: justification by faith is election in Christ, the inner basis of sanctification in the power of the Spirit.

Paul bids the Galatians to stand fast and not to submit to the slavery of law observance. This foreshadows 5:9, with its allusion to the story of the people's flight from Egypt. Their disobedience is the leaven that has made the Galatians fall away from grace (5:4, 7, 9; see also 1 Cor. 5:6). The same God who set the people of Israel free from the bondage of Egypt has in Christ set the Galatians free as well (5:1). As Israel is freed in the exodus from their bondage to pagan Egypt, so the Galatians are freed from their own pagan past (5:7, 13; 4:8–11). They are to be strong in Christ as they flee from their former slavery (4:8–10). Like an army, they are given a military command: stand fast and do not submit.

What Paul means by the word "yoke" is informed by its use in the Hebrew Bible, where it functions in both literal and figurative senses. When it appears figuratively, it is often in a negative context: unjust punishment, pagan power, slavery in Egypt, idolatry.[1] In these examples, the yoke that enslaves is broken as God liberates.

The word "yoke" here in Galatians clearly has a figurative sense, pointing back to Paul's earlier discussion of the enslaving imposition of law, particularly circumcision (4:8–10). This echoes for the reader Peter's assessment at the Jerusalem Council as reported in Acts: "Now therefore why are you putting God to the test by placing on the neck of the disciples a yoke that neither our ancestors nor we have been able to bear?" (Acts 15:10). Paul agrees: the law condemns the Galatians who attempt to observe it, because observing it completely is impossible, and observing it incompletely condemns (3:10–13).

While Paul's use of the word "yoke" here is negative, the rabbis understand the yoke of the law as a blessing.[2] The law was given precisely as God liberates the people of Israel from their slavery in Egypt, and as such it is a gift that opposes slavery. Jesus himself presents his own life as a yoke, a summing up of the law. "Take my yoke upon you, and learn from me; for I am gentle and humble in heart, and you will find rest for your souls. For my yoke is easy, and my burden is light" (Matt. 11:29–30). Paul will present the yoke of Christ (5:13–14) as offering the Galatians freedom from their pagan past as well as from their law-observant present; it also points them to their ecclesial service in the eschatological promise of the Jerusalem above.

5:2 Listen! I, Paul, am telling you that if you let yourselves be circumcised, Christ will be of no benefit to you—This is one of the few places since his initial address at the opening of the letter where Paul speaks to the Galatians personally and insistently, using his own name. It is almost as though, beginning afresh, he says, "Now, I, Paul, remind you what I have been saying all along, that circumcision takes from you Christ's benefits, because it is only through faith in him that you Gentile Christians are children of the free woman." Whether Paul thought Peter's Jewish converts should continue to follow the law upon conversion to Christ we cannot know, but it is certainly possible. Irenaeus assumes this is the case:

1. Lev. 26:13; Num. 25; 1 Kgs. 12; 2 Chr. 10; Isa. 9:4; 10:27.
2. See *m. Avot* 3.5; *m. Berakhot* 2.2; *Sifra* 11.43. Levine and Brettler, *Jewish Annotated New Testament*, 341.

And the apostles who were with James allowed the Gentiles to act freely, yielding us up to the Spirit of God. But they themselves, while knowing the same God, continued in the ancient observances.[3]

If Paul thought that Jewish Christians were specifically not to observe the law, it is unlikely that he would have approved of Peter's mission, but at Antioch he does just that. We can safely assume that in the earliest generations, all Jewish Christian males would have been circumcised on the eighth day. This is simply an acknowledgment of the situation in the first generation of the church; whether or not Paul himself would have circumcised his own son (if he had one) on the eighth day is a separate question.[4] Paul's situation in Galatia is the inverse: he warns his Gentile converts against taking on the yoke of circumcision, which would cause the Galatians to be cut off from Christ.[5]

5:3 Once again I testify to every man who lets himself be circumcised that he is obliged to obey the entire law—This verse restates what Paul said about law observance in 3:10. By nature the law demands consistent observance: it is a complete package and does not come in optional modules.[6] If the Galatians take on circumcision but do not observe all of the law, they are opening themselves up to God's judgment.

5:4 You who want to be justified by the law have cut yourselves off from Christ; you have fallen away from grace—This sentence is difficult to render in English while honoring its structure, because the Greek is governed by a nest of inclusios. A literal translation reflecting the Greek sentence structure, although awkward in English, would be as follows: "Cut off from Christ, you whoever by law observance want to be justified, from grace have fallen away." Standing in first place in the sentence is the verb *katērgēthēte*, "you have cut yourselves off"; at the end of the sentence is the verb *exepesate*, "you have fallen

3. Irenaeus, *Against Heresies* 3.12.15 (*ANF* 1:436). See also Justin Martyr, *Dialogue with Trypho* 57; →2:11–14.
4. Michael Wyschogrod answers this question in the affirmative, that if he were to have a son, Paul would indeed have had him circumcised on the eighth day according to the law. Wyschogrod reports that Roman Catholic New Testament scholar Raymond Brown agrees, but he provides no reference. Wyschogrod, "Christianity and Mosaic Law," 456.
5. "Christ will be no benefit to you" is literally "Christ will gain you nothing" (*Christos hymas ouden ōphelēsei*; 5:2; →2:16). There is no Christ apart from the Christ *pro nobis*, for us (→2:21).
6. See Luther, *LW* 27:12–13.

away." Between these two verbs is another inclusio: "from Christ" follows the first verb, and "from grace" precedes the final verb. At the center of this double inclusio is the governing idea of the sentence: *en nomō dikaiousthe* ("you who want to be justified by law"). The placement of these clauses draws our attention to the fact that the words "Christ" and "grace" surround the "law," highlighting the results of seeking justification by law observance: being cut off from Christ and falling away from grace. The subject matter of the sentence is neither law nor justification by faith but law observance itself that marks the threat to the Galatians' identity in Christ. The Galatians are to reject law observance and to choose the grace of Christ. If they are presented with any binaries at all, this is it: the grace of Christ versus law observance (→3:28).

5:5 For we through the Spirit by faith await the hope of righteousness (ASV, revised)—Paul now moves from speaking of Christ to the Spirit and Christian hope, in terms that are similar to his words in Romans: "For in hope we were saved. Now hope that is seen is not hope. For who hopes for what is seen? But if we hope for what we do not see, we wait for it with patience" (Rom. 8:24–25).

But what is the Spirit? It is not identical to Jesus Christ but is of him and from him and through him. The Spirit is not a chronological addition but a continuing revelation of Christ, sowing and bearing fruit in the life of the church. The risen Jesus breathes his Spirit on the disciples gathered in the upper room (John 20:22). The Spirit is the true teacher, and the teacher of truth,[7] the first installment of God's declaration of yes in Christ (2 Cor. 1:22), the pledge of our inheritance (Eph. 1:14). The Spirit comforts us and prays in us, makes Christ real through the church; it declares both the prophetic authorization and the apostolic command. The Spirit empowers the church as a whole and makes its individual members agents of mercy through its fruit. The Holy Spirit sanctifies and frees the church for communion with the Father through the Son.

The Spirit given to the church is the love of the Father for the Son and the Son for the Father.[8] This is the love shed abroad in our hearts so that we cry "Abba, Father" (Rom. 8:15). The Spirit's presence is the identifying mark

7. Tertullian, *Prescription against Heretics* 28.
8. Augustine, *On Faith and the Creed* 9.19–20; *On the Trinity* 9.14; 10.2–3, 8; 15.17. Thanks to Phil Cary for pointing me here.

of the church.[9] The embrace of Mother church (4:25–26) and confession of God as Abba Father (4:6) pour on us the Spirit's love.[10] The Spirit is the arena where Creator and creature meet.[11] In the Spirit's fruit the church is sanctified.

The American Standard Version's translation is helpful at this point because it follows closely the Greek word order, which is key to understanding the sentence.[12] As in chapters 2 and 3, again now we encounter the phrase "by faith" (*ek pisteōs*). The context is different here, in part because another inclusio is formed by the words "Spirit" and "await." Between these two words we read in this order the clauses "by faith," "[in the] hope," and "of righteousness." The first term of the inclusio ("Spirit") makes clear that, whatever faith and hope and righteousness are and however they are related one to the other, they are directly related to the Spirit. The final term of the inclusio ("await") indicates the eschatological context of waiting (*apekdechometha*). Despite our having fallen away from grace (5:4), the Spirit is the agent of our captivity to hope by faith. Through this inclusio Paul shows us that in Christ righteousness by faith is an eschatological reality.

Here we have a genitive construct similar to the one at 2:16: *ek pisteōs Christou*, "by faith in Christ." But the genitive construct in this verse is *elpida diakosynēs*, literally "hope of righteousness." If we read the word "righteousness" as an objective genitive, the phrase would indicate the righteousness for which we hope. Both meanings are important: we hope for righteousness, and righteousness supplies hope. The righteousness that gives us hope points to the fruit of the Spirit later in chapter 5: love, joy, peace, patience, kindness, generosity, faithfulness, gentleness, self-control (5:22–23). Given the overall context of the discussion, the righteousness of which Paul speaks in 5:5 is primarily sanctifying. He is preparing us for his statement in the following verse about the sanctifying force of faith and love.

5:6 For in Christ Jesus neither circumcision nor uncircumcision counts for anything; the only thing that counts is faith working through

---

9. Irenaeus, *Against Heresies* 3.21.1.

10. About the relationship between confessing the Father and having the church as Mother, see Cyprian, *The Unity of the Catholic Church* 6; Calvin, *Institutes* 4.1.1.

11. Barth, *CD* III/2, 356.

12. I alter the ASV slightly: "await." There is one word in the Greek for the two English words "wait for."

love—We now hear that faith corrects and heals lives, orienting the believer toward love of God and neighbor. The question about the role of circumcision among Gentile Christians returns. While this role was implicit in the first couplet at 3:28 with its distinction between Jew and Gentile, here in 5:6 it becomes explicit. The binary it creates, Jew ("circumcised") versus Gentile ("uncircumcised"), is overturned. Paul says that what counts is the rite's internal substance, election in Christ, in which faith works through love. The overall context of 5:6 points us not only back to 3:28 with the Jew/Gentile binary and with the implied rite of circumcision, but more precisely further back to 3:16, with its promises to Abraham. Neither circumcision nor uncircumcision counts, not simply because circumcision is adiaphoron but because it came after the election of Abraham. Thus it points forward to the new creation of 6:17.

Paul showed throughout chapter 3 that, given this chronology, it is clear that Abraham's election to the particular covenant is in Christ. Law observance for the Galatians, especially the rite of circumcision, followed God's promise of Christ; therefore the Galatians are not responsible for fulfilling it. Because election was given in the promise of Christ before the covenant rite, circumcision neither benefits nor alters the Gentiles' status in election. This is why in Gal. 3 Paul prefers the episodes of Abraham's promises in Gen. 15 and Gen. 17 over the others.[13] The Galatians must not observe the law, because to do so would confound Paul's teaching about God's providential ordering of election: the Spirit of Christ himself fulfills the law in those who trust, precisely as faith working through love (6:2; 5:6, 14). Our faith in Christ is itself sanctifying love.

As I showed earlier (→2:7–9), in English, the opposite of the term "circumcision" is indicated simply by adding the negative prefix "un-" to make the word "*un*circumcision." In the majority of the Greek and in all the Hebrew occurrences of these terms in the Bible, however, the words are etymologically unrelated. The word "circumcision" in Greek is *peritomē*, literally "cut around" (Hebrew, *himmol*, referring to the covenant rite), while "uncircumcision," literally "foreskin," in Greek is *akrobystia* (Hebrew, *arel*).[14] While the words "circumcision" and "uncircumcision" in English form a semantic binary, in

---

13. See my discussion of the promises at Gal. 3:16.
14. BDAG 33. This is a verbal form as per Gen. 17:10, the first time the covenant rite is mentioned in the Hebrew Bible. Here at Gal. 5:6, Paul uses the nominal form. In Gal. 2:3; 5:2–3; 6:12–13, he uses the verbal form. Cf. 1 Cor. 7:18 and Col. 2:11, where he also uses the verbal form.

Greek and Hebrew they do not.[15] A Gentile penis retains what the Jewish penis would have had culticly removed: the foreskin. The concept "Gentile" is itself a Jewish construct; Gentiles themselves have no category of "Gentile" identity. The terms and the cultic realities these words represent are simply incommensurate. This conceptual relationship, an applesauce-to-orange-juice, is formally similar to that between Sarah and Hagar and their two (noncorresponding) Jerusalems (→4:25–26).

The question then becomes this: What is the nature of the incommensurability of the cultic status of Jew and Gentile with regard to law observance in particular? Whereas in Rom. 2:25–27 the term "law" (*ho nomos*) appears in conjunction with "circumcision," and in 1 Cor. 7:19 the term "commandments" (*hē entolē*) takes the place of the term "law," in Gal. 5:6 both terms, "law" and "commandments," are absent. While the terms "circumcision" and "law" appeared together at Gal. 5:3 and will again at 6:13, the phrase that substitutes for circumcision here at 5:6 becomes "faith working through love."[16] Faith is neither cognitive nor emotive; it is intention coupled with action. Faith is sanctifying; it increases the believer's love of God and neighbor. Faith working through love is a medicine with "the greatest corrective effect on every life, fulfill[ing] the whole force of the Law, and contain[ing] all those things which are precepts in the Decalogue."[17]

Paul's "faith working through love" comes to us from the Septuagint Greek (*pistis di' agapēs energoumenē*) into the Latin Vulgate as *fides quae per caritatem operator*. In the later interpretive debate the phrase becomes *fides caritate formata*: "faith formed by love." Galatians 5:6 becomes important for Augustine particularly in *The Spirit and the Letter* (412). Reading Gal. 5:6 in light of other verses, most importantly Rom. 5:5, Augustine focuses on the second half of Gal. 5:6, "faith working through love," setting the stage for the tradition of interpretation to follow. Augustine understands Paul's focus to fall not on justification but on sanctification.[18]

---

15. Interestingly, Exod. 12:48 (the Passover story) is one of the few places in the LXX where the usual word for "uncircumcised," *akrobystia*, is replaced by *aperitmētos*, the etymological opposite of the word "circumcised" (→2:7–9; 6:15).

16. Gal. 5:14; 6:2; see also Phil. 2:12; Jas. 2:18.

17. Marius Victorinus, in Cooper, *Victorinus's Commentary*, 330–31.

18. Augustine's focus on the second half of Gal. 5:6 is the driving force behind Luther's re-reading. For an overview of Augustine on this verse, see Bochet and Fédou, *L'exégèse patristique*, 155–80.

Luther rejects Augustine's interpretation, instead emphasizing that love is the tool through which faith works.[19] His concern is to avoid patristic and medieval teaching that he took to mean that love is an agent in justification: "Since Paul does not even give love the credit for works, how would he give it credit for justification? . . . But this is what happens to lazy readers and to those who superimpose their own ideas on the reading of Sacred Scripture."[20] Commenting on Gal. 5:6, Luther says that one of the problems with the teaching of his scholastic opponents is that it reads the second half of the verse as a distortion: "In this manner they completely transfer justification from faith and attribute it to love."[21]

But for Paul, justification by faith is indeed tightly bound to sanctification: it produces acts of love (5:14) and mercy (6:1–2). In being justified, the Galatians are loved into loving (5:14). In their sanctification, Christians are built into the body of righteousness through slavery to one another (5:13). In Christ, the Galatians are given the two hands that receive and give love (so Perkins, →2:16). This cooperation between faith and love also appears in Jesus's parable of the good Samaritan, where the enacting of love and mercy fulfills the law (Luke 10:29–37; Matt. 22:40). In their own acts of charity the Galatians fulfill the law of Christ (Gal. 6:2). They do not need to be circumcised in order to fulfill the law and be righteous, because the Holy Spirit works righteousness in them.

As an action and not an emotion, love is a determination, a decision empowered by faith. It bears all things, believes all things, hopes all things, endures all things (1 Cor. 13:7). It bears the unbearable even to the edge of doom (Shakespeare, Sonnet 116).[22] It is not for nothing that these words from Paul and Shakespeare are often read at Christian weddings: just as marriage is a sacrament of the church, so marital love is a type of ecclesial love, christologically formed. The love of God is borne out to the edge of doom on the cross.

5:7–8 You were running well; who prevented you from obeying the truth? Such persuasion does not come from the one who calls you—The imagery

---

19. This marks a development from Luther's earlier Galatians lectures of 1519, where the verse plays a relatively small role. See Wilken, "*Fides Caritate Formata*," 1089.

20. Luther, *LW* 27:29.

21. Luther, *LW* 27:28.

22. "Love alters not with his brief hours and weeks, But bears it out even to the edge of doom." Shakespeare, Sonnet 116.

of athletic competition in running a race opens the verse. Paul's question "Who prevented you?" can be translated literally as "Who cut you off?" The Galatians have allowed someone to cut them off in their race toward the goal of the upward (*anō*) calling of the heavenly city (4:26; Phil. 3:14). Paul may be making a play on words to link those who circumcise to interfering with the Galatians' obedience to Christ. The Galatians have been "cut off" (*enekopsen*) from the truth. The verb comes from the same root of the verb that Paul will use at 5:12 to suggest that the Third Party should castrate themselves (*apokapsontai*). Here his cry of dismay echoes his concern about his own work among them: that he had run in vain (2:2). Those who prevented the Galatians from obeying the truth have bewitched them (3:1) and have alienated the Galatians quickly from Christ (1:6).

5:9 A little yeast leavens the whole batch of dough—The word "yeast" or "leaven" recalls the flight from slavery in Egypt (Exod. 12) and the festival celebrating it.[23] The imagery of unleavened bread indicates the haste with which the people are to flee Egypt (Exod. 12:34, 39). While Paul's aphorism may reflect a secular proverb current in the day, given his own specifically religious context it is impossible to think that he would have used the word "leaven" without intending at some level an allusion to the Passover story and its feast. He taught the Galatians about baptism (Gal. 3:27); surely he would also have taught them the Passover stories so central to the early church's understanding of Christ's death and the celebration of the Lord's Supper (1 Cor. 5:6–8).[24]

Even more compelling is the detail tying Gal. 5:8 to Exod. 12: foreigners could eat the Passover meal among the people of Israel, provided they first undergo the covenant rite of circumcision.[25] "If an alien [*proselthē . . . prosēlytos*, LXX; *yagur . . . ger*, MT] who resides with you wants to celebrate the Passover to the LORD, all his males shall be circumcised [*peritemeis*, LXX; *himmol*, MT]; then he may draw near to celebrate it; he shall be regarded as a native of the

---

23. The word is best translated "leaven," since "yeast" itself may not have been a common ingredient in ancient baking production (BDAG 340). First Corinthians 5:7 points to Paul's use of the imagery of unleavened Passover bread and eucharistic bread of the Christian pascha: "Purge out therefore the old leaven, that ye may be a new lump, as ye are unleavened. For even Christ our passover is sacrificed for us" (KJV).

24. Jesus uses the imagery of leaven to speak of the hypocrisy of the religious authorities (Matt. 16:11; Mark 8:15).

25. Even though women are not specifically mentioned by personal name, they are present in the stories in the traditional gender roles and activity of women: families, households, children, cooking, feeding.

land. But no uncircumcised person [*arel,* MT; *aperitmētos,* LXX] shall eat of it; there shall be one law [*nomos,* LXX; *torah,* MT] for the native and for the alien who resides among you" (Exod. 12:48–49). The tipping point for the Galatians' submitting to circumcision may then have been in the context of the celebration of the Passover. Cultic distinctions in table fellowship, such as that of the Passover meal and the Lord's Supper, may be reflected in the disruptions within the Gentile community at Antioch in chapter 2. The fact that attendance at the sacred Passover meal is limited to circumcised males and foreigners who are cultically circumcised may hint at what Paul means by the Third Party's "persuasion" (Gal. 5:8). The Galatians who have succumbed to circumcision may be in a similar situation: the Third Party may have required the rite in order to permit the Galatians to join in their sacred feasts.

Paul also incorporates imagery from the Passover story elsewhere in his correspondence. The transgressions in Corinth are likened to the leaven that must be removed before the Christian Passover meal can be eaten.[26] In 1 Corinthians, the Passover lamb is a type of Jesus, and the Passover meal is a type of the Lord's Supper, itself a type of Jesus's eschatological return and presence. Just as the Israelites must cleanse their homes of all leaven before the Passover celebration, so the Corinthians must cleanse themselves of sin before the Lord's Supper lest they bring guilt on themselves.[27] Reading the Passover meal as a type of the Lord's Supper and the Lord's Supper as a type of the heavenly banquet, Paul gives us implicit evidence that the Passover narratives are understood christologically even in the first generation of Christian worship and interpretation of scripture. This typology even predates Paul's missionary journeys of the mid-first century; he says that he does not invent but receives this typological interpretation of the Passover celebration from the Lord himself (1 Cor. 11:23). We find just one example of the continued use of this typology in the eucharistic liturgies of the 1979 Episcopal *Book of Common Prayer:* in both Rite One and Rite Two, the presider declares at the fraction, "[Alleluia.] Christ our Passover is sacrificed for us," to which the people respond, "Therefore let us keep the feast. [Alleluia]."[28]

26. "Your boasting is not a good thing. Do you not know that a little yeast leavens the whole batch of dough? Clean out the old yeast so that you may be a new batch, as you really are unleavened. For our paschal lamb, Christ, has been sacrificed. Therefore, let us celebrate the festival, not with the old yeast, the yeast of malice and evil, but with the unleavened bread of sincerity and truth" (1 Cor. 5:6–8).

27. "For as often as you eat this bread and drink the cup, you proclaim the Lord's death until he comes. Whoever, therefore, eats the bread or drinks the cup of the Lord in an unworthy manner will be answerable for the body and blood of the Lord" (1 Cor. 11:26–27).

28. *Book of Common Prayer,* 337, 364.

5:10 **I am confident about you in the Lord that you will not think otherwise. But whoever it is that is confusing you will pay the penalty**—The Galatians receive pastoral encouragement even in the midst of their confusion (see also 2 Thess. 3:4). At this point, Paul does not scold them for straying from the gospel, but instead points to the guilt of the ones who have misled them: the Third Party will pay the penalty. Peter and his associates are not the ones who are confusing them. In chapter 1 Paul mentions some who are confusing the Galatians and distorting the gospel (1:7), but does not identify them with the Jerusalem church. Paul acknowledges Peter as one of the pillars of the church (2:8–9). He accepts that Peter, James, and John bear the same grace that he himself preached among the Gentiles, and he acknowledges that he receives from them recognition of this same grace (2:9). This means that the "whoever" Paul refers to in 5:10 cannot be the Jerusalem pillars (see also 1:9).

5:11 **But my friends, why am I still being persecuted if I am still preaching circumcision? In that case the offense of the cross has been removed**—The persecution of which Paul speaks is likely over his preaching. His message is proof that along with his former law-observant religious identity, Paul has left behind "preaching circumcision." His current ministry is now to welcome Gentiles into the body of Christ without imposing the rite of circumcision, a welcome that may have drawn controversy among Jewish Christians resulting in his persecution and suffering (2 Cor. 11:24–29). The persecutions that he mentions here in Gal. 5:11 (and 6:12) also result from his circumcision-free ministry among the Gentiles. If he had converted his Gentile churches by first imposing conversion to Judaism, the Galatians could potentially have benefited from the imperially granted protection of the Jewish people. But Paul's own persecution is a direct result of preaching the good news of the foreskin, the gospel to the Gentiles (→2:7).[29] Paul's references to the cross, having begun explicitly at 2:19, increase from that point to the end of the letter (2:21; 5:24; 6:12, 14, 17).

5:12 **I wish those who unsettle you would castrate themselves!**—Here Paul makes a pun: religious circumcision for the Galatians is a form of castration.[30]

---

29. Again, for the translation "good news of the foreskin," see Kahl, *Galatians Re-imagined*, 275. See Gal. 2:12; Acts 15:1, 5.

30. Lou Martyn suggested translating this "I wish their own knife would slip" (personal conversation, 1998). Some take this figuratively: "'Castrated' means cut off from Christ" (Ambrosiaster, *Epistle*

Paul may have intended an allusion to the Third Party and the pagan priests of Cybele, whose religious rites included castrating themselves.[31] Paul's statement would have, at the very least, shocked the Galatians and strengthened his implicit suggestion that circumcision and pagan observances are ontologically similar.

The same law that demands circumcision also prohibits other alterations to the body: damaging, wounding, scarring, or tattooing the body will bring curse (Lev. 19:28; 21:16–24).[32] Those who are "blemished" or otherwise "mutilated," even if by no fault of their own, profane the holy altar of God and are prohibited from making the requisite sacrifices.[33] Castrating themselves (as Paul indicates they should), the Third Party would bring further defilement on themselves under the law. They have already brought on themselves their own penalty for confusing the Galatians (5:10). The Third Party should castrate themselves, imposing on themselves a greater curse than they have cast on the Galatians.

5:13 For you were called to freedom, brothers and sisters; only do not use your freedom as an opportunity for self-indulgence, but through love become slaves to one another—The little word that begins this verse, "for" (*gar*), indicates that Paul moves on to the logical outworking of what he has just stated; he now explains that the freedom in which the Galatians must stand fast (5:1) must be lived out in slavery to the body of Christ. There is no morally neutral freedom; it can either build up or tear down the church (1:3–4; 4:26; 4:31–5:1). It can either devour their community (5:15) or sow among them the fruit of the Spirit (5:22–24). The freedom in which the Galatians must stand is ecclesial: it is not meant for individual satisfaction (NRSV, "self-indulgence") but for service within the body of Christ.

---

to the Galatians 5.12, translation in Edwards, *Galatians, Ephesians, Philippians*, 80). Augustine suggests that by castrating themselves, the Third Party would become "eunuchs for the sake of the kingdom of heaven" (*Augustine's Commentary on Galatians*, 203). Like Augustine, Jerome links Gal. 5:12 to Matt. 19:12, suggesting that "Paul did not so much curse them as he prayed for them to dispense with the parts of their body that made them go astray" (*Commentary on Galatians*, 215). N. T. Wright points out that castration would be a cultic abomination for Jews (*Galatians*, 323).

31. Martyn points to the presence of a prominent temple of the cult of Cybele in Pessinus, in the region of Galatia where one of Paul's churches may have been located. Martyn, *Galatians*, 478. See also Wright, *Galatians*, 324; Keener, *Galatians*, 241–42.

32. This same statute in Leviticus prohibiting the marking of the body undergirds Paul's discussion of the curse of the cross in Gal. 3:10–13.

33. This was also the case for those with wounded testicles (Lev. 21:20).

The NRSV uses a very loose hand in giving us "self-indulgence" as the counterpart to freedom, obscuring the specifically ecclesial form of freedom in servitude that Paul teaches. The Greek word is *sarx*, literally translated "flesh." Paul uses the word *sarx* in Galatians to refer to many things: human beings (1:16; 2:16), bodily life (2:20; 4:13–14), anything opposed to Spirit (3:3; 4:23–29; 5:17; 6:8), the defiling desires of the human heart (5:16, 19, 24), and even the circumcised penis (6:12–13; 3:3). Here in 5:13, *sarx* is the opposite of neighbor love that can fracture the church.

The distinction between individual freedom and communal responsibility for the upbuilding of the church becomes central in the letter from here as it moves toward its close (see also 1 Cor. 8:9–11; 1 Pet. 2:16). The slavery Paul commands of the Galatians flows from this specifically ecclesial freedom: a slavery not to the law but to love for each other. It is the concrete outworking of his earlier statement in 5:6 regarding the relationship between faith and love. Their choices are not free unless they are bound in the servitude of love for each other. Freedom in the Spirit is "the finger of God that sanctifies us in its fruit."[34] This freedom reframes the earlier hierarchical binary of slave and free: slavery in the body of Christ is a form of servitude where Christ is both master and slave, where no one suffers at the hand of another (see Phil. 2:7).

5:14 For the whole law is summed up in a single commandment, "You shall love your neighbor as yourself"—In the commandment Paul quotes that embraces and sums up all of the law, we find a reformulation of his earlier phrase at 5:6, "faith working through love" (see also Rom. 13:9–10; Lev. 19:18). The teaching in 5:6 is reflected in the words drawn from Jesus's lips: "In everything do to others as you would have them do to you; for this is the law and the prophets" (Matt. 7:12; see also Matt. 22:36–40).[35] The double phrase "the law and the prophets" appears in both Jesus's teachings and apostolic preaching.[36]

---

34. Augustine, *The Spirit and the Letter* 16, 28. The reference is to the episode at Sinai when the finger of God engraves the two tablets of the law (Exod. 31:18). That same finger of God sanctifies in the fruit of the Spirit.

35. Rabbi Hillel, roughly contemporary to Jesus, says something very similar: "That which is hateful to you, do not do to your fellow. That is the whole Torah; the rest is interpretation; go and learn." Talmud *Shab.* 31.a.

36. In addition to Matt. 7:12; 22:40, see John 1:45; Acts 13:15; 28:23. We find the phrase "law, prophets, and writings" referring to the three portions of the Tanak (Torah, Nevi'im, Ketuvim) in Luke 24:26–27, 44.

Jesus gives his summary of the Law and the Prophets in response to a question from a scribe who asks which commandment is the most important (Matt. 22:34; Mark 12:28). Jesus begins his response to the question with the Shema from Deut. 6:4–5, Israel's central prayer that declares the identity and demand of God: "Hear, O Israel: The LORD is our God, the LORD alone. You shall love the LORD your God with all your heart, and with all your soul, and with all your might." He then adds the command from Lev. 19:18: "Love your neighbor as yourself." Paul, however, chooses to summarize the law for the Galatians with the single command from Leviticus: love your neighbor.[37]

Here we find that the law is more than simply a text with statutes of covenant obligation. Paul's teaching that the summary of the law is in neighbor love will find its twin in his later exhortation to bear one another's burdens (6:2). The summary informs the remainder of chapter 5, with its characteristics of the nature and vocation of the church.[38] The fact that the law of Christ establishes the vocation of the Christian shows just how tightly justification and sanctification, faith and love, are bound to each other.

But what of love of self? Even the secular world tells us that if we do not love ourselves, we cannot love others, for we are our own neighbor. Luther warns that, while some of the fathers find the idea that neighbor love begins with the self, we must not conflate the two: if Paul had meant this, he would have said so, but does not expressly communicate this.[39] While love of oneself is inherently part of love for others, the claim that neighbor love extends to the self is at the same time both true and misleading. First, the truth: there is no stronger affirmation of our infinite value before the God of heaven and earth than to declare and defend human worth as judged completely apart from family, wealth, social class, race, ethnicity, or wholeness of body or mind. Rather, human dignity is grounded in our being created in the image of God (Gen. 1:26–27; 2:7). This image is perfected in Jesus Christ, and we will bear it in the resurrection (1 Cor. 15:49). Second, the inverse is its falsehood: there is no stronger degradation of

37. Whereas in Rom. 3:21 Paul uses the double phrase "law and prophets," here in Gal. 5:14 he uses a single term, "the whole law."

38. Once integral to Episcopal eucharistic liturgies, the prayer known as the Summary of the Law has almost entirely fallen out of use. In the 1979 Episcopal *Book of Common Prayer* Holy Eucharist Rite One, which is based on older liturgies, the Summary of the Law follows immediately the Collect for Purity. The summary does not appear at all in the more contemporary Holy Eucharist Rite Two. The reasons for and results of this shift away from opening the Mass with the summary of the law are worth our reflection, something for another project.

39. Luther, *LW* 27:290n12, 355; Peter Lombard, *Sententia* 3.29.

human worth than to deny that the human is created in the image of God. This can result in a purely utilitarian view of human worth. This sows hatred toward the self and others. I am reminded of how in the late twentieth century Jesse Jackson inspired Black audiences with the corporate refrain "I am somebody," encouraging them to contradict the lies of past centuries to the contrary. Self-esteem, as a form of neighbor love, can in fact be one fruit of the Spirit even if, as Luther notes, Paul does not explicitly list it here.

In the Christian tradition the notion that the human creature is intrinsically valued by God is pinned not to a general anthropology but specifically to Christology. The gospel declares that we have value insofar as we are the Lord's, completely without regard to our utility to society. This insistence on human worth as rooted in our belonging to the Lord is basic to Christian anthropology. We are not our own; we are the Lord's; we are bought with a price and called to glorify God in our body (1 Cor. 6:19–20). It is this grace that assures us that we are to love ourselves and our neighbor as having infinite value in the one who bought us with a price. But when the claim to human dignity is loosed from its basis in Christology, the value of a human life can be diminished when deemed inconvenient to society. This is evident in how society treats the vulnerable: its children, poor, sick, and elderly. The body of Christ has a unique word to speak to a culture that dishonors its "little ones" (Matt. 18:10) and instead assesses the value of human life according to consumerist criteria. The Galatians are to follow the love of neighbor demanded in the law of Christ. Love of self and neighbor are complementary, and both are inseparable from love of God. To honor the law of Christ and to love our neighbor, the least we need to do is to look to our own hearts.[40]

5:15 If, however, you bite and devour one another, take care that you are not consumed by one another—Christian traditions have historically parsed the law into different categories: eternal, natural, human, divine, ceremonial, judicial, moral, and so on.[41] The moral law is generally understood to be normative for the church's understanding of ethics and is traditionally divided into

---

40. In his later lectures on Galatians (1535), Luther says, "You do not need any professor to tell you about this matter; merely consult your own heart, and it will give you abundant instruction that you should love your neighbor as yourself" (Luther, *LW* 27:57); and "You will not lack for people to help, for the world is full of people who need the help of others. This is the perfect doctrine of both faith and love." Luther, *LW* 27:59.

41. See, e.g., Aquinas, *Summa Theologiae* I-II.98–108; Calvin, *Institutes* 4.20.15. The Talmud counts 613 commandments. See *Berakhot* 12a.

two parts, corresponding to the two tablets given to Moses on Sinai.[42] The first tablet delineates duties to God, and the second tablet contains precepts for behavior toward neighbor.

Most of the commandments of the two tablets are prohibitions. Two, however, are positive commands: Sabbath observance and honoring parents. The Sabbath command is the longest of all ten, and it is expressed in the context of creation: "Remember the sabbath day, and keep it holy. Six days you shall labor and do all your work. But the seventh day is a sabbath to the LORD your God; you shall not do any work—you, your son or your daughter, your male or female slave, your livestock, or the alien resident in your towns. For in six days the LORD made heaven and earth, the sea, and all that is in them, but rested the seventh day; therefore the LORD blessed the sabbath day and consecrated it" (Exod. 20:8–11). Immediately following the Sabbath command comes the honoring of parents. This command is linked to the gift of the land: "Honor your father and your mother, so that your days may be long in the land that the LORD your God is giving you" (Exod. 20:12). Both of the positive commandments are therefore in the context of eschatology.

In Gal. 5:15 Paul's summary of the law for moral formation uses a positive command that references neither of these from the Decalogue but instead gives a verse from Leviticus: "You shall love your neighbor as yourself" (Lev. 19:18). He then gives his own pastoral corollary and admonishment that is neither in the Decalogue nor elsewhere in the Hebrew Bible: "Take care that you are not consumed by one another" (5:15). His teaching does not come from the categories of the moral, civil, or ceremonial at all: the summary of the law for Paul is not itself a text or genre at all and therefore shares with the positive commands of the Decalogue their eschatological quality. The law is a human person who became a slave for all: Christ Jesus. He is its content, and obedience to this law is the sum of righteousness (6:2). If the Galatians do not obey the law of Christ, no matter how strictly they may observe the law of Moses, they run the risk of tearing asunder the body of Christ.

While in his summary of the law in 5:14, Paul omits the first tablet of the law (love of God) and focuses only on the second tablet (love of neighbor),[43]

42. Sometimes referred to as the Decalogue, the Ten Commandments, or the Ten Words in the Hebrew Bible, they are found in Exod. 20:1–17 and Deut. 5:6–21; see also Exod. 31:18. Christian communions differ in their numbering of the commandments.

43. James 2:8–13 extends the sum of the law in neighbor love to other commands of the second table. "For whoever keeps the whole law but fails in one point has become accountable for all of it. For

in Rom. 13:9–10 Paul quotes pieces of the Decalogue and then turns to the command for neighbor love.[44] The positive command, neighbor love, when disobeyed has its negative effects: if you fail to love each other, you will destroy each other. The building up or the tearing down of the church results from either following or abandoning the summary of the law of Christ; this is an ecclesial rather than a merely personal failure. Paul's later warning against the "works of the flesh" furthers this admonition. He warns the Galatians that their behavior toward each other, not their observance of the rite of circumcision, fulfills the law of Christ. By works of compassion and mercy will the church be known (Matt. 25:31–46; Jas. 2:18; 3:13).

5:16 **Live by the Spirit, I say, and do not gratify the desires of the flesh—** While the NRSV gives us "live by the Spirit," the KJV gives a closer translation of the Greek verb "to walk" (*peripateite*). Its corresponding Hebrew verb, *halak*, is used in the context of law observance. It is etymologically related to the Hebrew noun *halakah*, a form of ethics of rabbinic prescription for observance of the law in matters of daily life. Translating this Greek verb as "walk" alludes to its Hebrew roots and renders the performatory sense that Paul intends: through the power of the Spirit we *walk* in the law of Christ, substance of the law of Sinai. The Spirit does not override or cancel the law but is itself promised as the energizing grace enabling us to follow (*walk in*) the law in love of God and neighbor. The Spirit observes the law of Christ in us (5:18, 23), fulfilling the prophecy of Ezekiel: "I will put my spirit within you, and make you follow ["walk," *telekhu*, from the verb *halak*] my statutes and be careful to observe my ordinances" (Ezek. 36:27). Paul is a pastor and commands what he knows is possible for the Galatians in the power of the Spirit. He does not demand the impossible; he knows that, being led by the Spirit, they can resist the desires of the flesh.

5:17 **For what the flesh desires is opposed to the Spirit, and what the Spirit desires is opposed to the flesh; for these are opposed to each other,**

---

the one who said, 'You shall not commit adultery,' also said, 'You shall not murder.' Now if you do not commit adultery but if you murder, you have become a transgressor of the law. So speak and so act as those who are to be judged by the law of liberty" (Jas. 2:10–12).

44. "The commandments, 'You shall not commit adultery; You shall not murder; You shall not steal; You shall not covet'; and any other commandment, are summed up in this word, 'Love your neighbor as yourself.' Love does no wrong to a neighbor; therefore, love is the fulfilling of the law" (Rom. 13:9–10).

to prevent you from doing what you want—The subject of the first clause is "the flesh," and the subject of the second is "the Spirit." The main verb of each clause is "to desire." The flesh and the Spirit both desire, and they each do so over against the other in a struggle. There are (at least) three ways of understanding these desires of the flesh and the desires of the Spirit in their mutual opposition: they could be two fundamentally competing *ways* of desiring, or two different *objects* of desire, or even two types of *behavior* resulting from these desires. Paul intends all three. The desires of the flesh are not limited simply to physical passions; they are what threaten the ability to love the law of Christ.

5:18 But if you are led by the Spirit, you are not subject to the law—The word "law" at this point no longer means the law of Christ, the "whole law" of 5:14, but the rite of circumcision for Gentile Galatians. The Galatians are released from circumcision but not from the love of neighbor.

5:19 the works of the flesh are obvious—In the ancient world, lists of behaviors either to be avoided or taken on were used for moral instruction. These are known as vice and virtue lists; they bear a resemblance to the teaching in the Gospels and the Epistles, as well as in parts of the Apocrypha.[45] In Gal. 5, Paul may possibly be adapting this genre for his own pastoral teaching.[46] But for Paul and the Galatians, these vices are not merely categories of improper behavior; they are "works of the flesh" that correspond to the Gentile taproot of idolatry, habits that oppose the Spirit (5:17). These works of the flesh are relational, damaging the well-being of both the individual who engages in them and the community at large. The works of the flesh have the effect of animals that tear apart their prey (5:15). They are deadly and dying, murderous and murdering. But as with the breath of the Spirit in creation (Gen 1:2), the fruit of the Spirit is life that provides abundant nourishment (5:22). It is an eschatological food that satiates the hunger of the desires and works of the flesh.

This is the only time the phrase "works of the flesh" appears in Paul's letters.[47] Earlier in Galatians, Paul spoke of "works of the law" (*ex ergōn nomou*; 2:16;

---

45. See, e.g., Matt. 15:19–20; Mark 7:21–22. Other vice lists are in Eph. 4:31; 5:3–5; Col. 3:5–8; 1 Tim. 1:9–10; 6:4–5; 2 Tim. 3:2–4; Titus 3:3; 1 Pet. 4:3; Rev. 21:8; 22:15. In the intertestamental period, 2 Macc. 6:3–6; 4 Macc. 1:26–27; 2:15–16.

46. See also Rom. 1:29–31; 1 Cor. 5:9–13; 6:9–10; 2 Cor. 12:20.

47. A functionally similar expression, "the works of darkness," *ta erga tou skotous*, appears in Rom. 13:12, where it is opposed to "the armor of light."

3:2, 5, 10) in the larger context of justification. Here, sanctification rather than justification is at the heart of Paul's concern, listed in the behaviors that tear down the church. These "works of the flesh" introduce the context of sanctification: how we are made holy. We hear echoes of 5:6.

Paul says that these behaviors "are obvious" (*phanera estin*) to God and to the world. While not challenges specific to the Christian life alone, the fact that they are obvious means they are public witnesses for the Christian. This is true especially of the physical works Paul mentions. The first term, *porneia*, translated as "fornication," generally refers to sexual offenses resulting in a violation of relationality.[48] The word may refer to having sex with a cult prostitute, which would be a transgression of the first commandment and, as such, a relapse to the Galatians' pre-Christian pagan life. The noun could refer to other extramarital sexual liaisons. *Akatharsia* points to behavior that renders one impure or corrupt especially with regard to morally vile sexual behavior.[49] The more general "licentiousness" (*aselgeia*) refers to unboundaried behavior, especially with regard to sexual excesses.[50]

5:20 idolatry, sorcery, enmities, strife, jealousy, anger, quarrels, dissensions, factions, envy, drunkenness, carousing, and things like these—Idol worship and sorcery denote corrupt behaviors stereotypical of Gentiles as viewed from the standards of Jewish morality: these behaviors violate the commandments. The larger context of the laws is service to the one God who redeemed Israel out of Egypt: "I am the LORD your God, who brought you out of the land of Egypt, out of the house of slavery; you shall have no other gods before me" (Exod. 20:2–3). Practicing idolatry and sorcery in effect sends God's redeemed back to their bondage in Egypt with its pagan spells and plagues. While idolatry and sorcery are transgressions against the first tablet of the law and are therefore sins against God, the sins that follow are transgressions against the second tablet as behaviors that break fellowship and fracture the church.

5:21 I am warning you, as I warned you before: those who do such things will not inherit the kingdom of God—The concepts of inheritance and family that run throughout the second half of Gal. 3 and into chapter 4 (3:15–18; 3:29–4:7) appear here under the form of warning. The works of flesh oppose

48. BDAG 693.
49. BDAG 28.
50. BDAG 114.

the Spirit and therefore also the inheritance of God's kingdom.[51] The promised inheritance of the kingdom is linked to the Galatians' control of the works of the flesh (Gen. 21:10; Gal. 4:30). Being led by the Spirit results in behavior that conforms to the law of Christ (6:2) and thus grants the inheritance of the kingdom.

5:22–23 By contrast, the fruit of the Spirit is love, joy, peace, patience, kindness, generosity, faithfulness, gentleness, and self-control. There is no law against such things—In baptism we are clothed with Christ (3:27); the fruit of the Spirit is this clothing, the blessing and counterpart to the curse with its ensuing works of the flesh (→3:27). The prohibitions against fornication and idolatry are warnings to the Galatians lest they fall into the sins that beset pagans (5:19–20; Gen. 3:14–19).

Just as the works of the flesh correspond to pagan vice lists, Paul's list of fruit (singular!) of the Spirit corresponds to virtue lists. This section of his epistle became foundational for rich development in the history of Christian moral theology.[52] As flowing from the presence of the Spirit of the Son in the church, this fruit may reflect the purity demands set out in the apostolic decree of Acts 15. While halakic moral codes for Gentiles prohibit the "works of the flesh" listed earlier, Paul insists that "there is no law" against the fruit of the Spirit (5:23).[53]

Verses 22–23 form an inclusio around Paul's entire discussion of the works of the flesh and the fruit of the Spirit. The works and the fruit are not simply secular vices and virtues; because they are surrounded by references to the law of Christ, they thus are defined by it. The Spirit and its fruit conform to the law of Christ, and the law of Christ grounds the Spirit's fruit. The Spirit is identified as the Spirit of God's Son in 4:6. The Spirit gave life to the world at creation (Gen. 1:2); filled John the Baptist to bear witness to Jesus (Luke 1:15); and quickened the womb of Mary (Luke 1:35). The Spirit gives life to the Galatians (5:16, 25), frees them from circumcision (5:18, 23), and builds up the church in its fruit (5:24). The fruit of the Spirit is displayed not in positive character traits but in qualities exhibited in behaviors that contribute concrete gifts that build up the church. The Spirit is not an interior experience

---

51. See also the lists in 1 Cor. 6:9–10; 15:50; Eph. 5:5; Matt. 5:5; 25:34; and Rev. 21:7.
52. Jerome, *Commentary on Galatians*, 229.
53. See Bockmuehl, *Jewish Law in Gentile Churches*, 168.

but instead is to be embodied, exhibited by the Galatians in the life of Christ as publicly as was Paul's preaching among them (3:1).

Christ is the seed sown; the fruit is reaped in the church by the power of the Holy Spirit. The first of the Spirit's fruit is love: "Faith, hope, and love abide . . . and the greatest of these is love" (1 Cor. 13:13).[54] This fruit follows immediately after the works of the flesh; it covers a multitude of sins (1 Pet. 4:8). Love is the sum and goal of the law (Gal. 5:14), fulfilling the law of Christ (6:2). Love is the fruit of the new creation tied specifically to the law of Christ and his body, the church. The elect Israel of God (Gal. 6:16) bears the prophetic eschatological fruit:

> In days to come Jacob shall take root,
>   Israel shall blossom and put forth shoots,
>   and fill the whole world with fruit. (Isa. 27:6)

In the age to come the fruit of Israel will bless the nations (Gal. 3:8; see also Gen. 12:3; 18:18; 22:18). Even now the Gentile churches of Galatia are blessed with the eschatological fruit of the Spirit of Christ; as such, they are children of Sarah, the heavenly Jerusalem made present among the Gentile churches (Gal. 4:26). This fruit of the Spirit, love, is thus a sign of the fullness of time and marks the identity of the church. It is grace bestowed specifically for the purpose of being lived out (5:25) in blessing; "faith working through love" is a practiced habit (5:6).

Joy logically follows love in the catalog of fruit of the Spirit. Walking in Jesus's own command to love God and neighbor fills the believer with the joy of the Lord (John 15:11–12). It produces a quality in the soul that is firmly tied to knowledge and love of Christ. Joy attends the news of Jesus's birth (Luke 1:14, 44; 2:10) and the reports of his resurrection (Luke 24:41, 52). Despite not having known Jesus in his earthly life, the Galatians, like Paul, share "indescribable and glorious joy" (1 Pet. 1:8).

Following joy comes the peace of God. While in secular terms, peace is often understood as freedom from conflict, the peace of God in Christ comes directly from Jesus's cross and resurrection: it is "strife closed in the sod."[55] Patience is

---

54. On Perkins's inversion of the theological virtues, see my comments at 2:18.
55. The phrase is from the final stanza of William Alexander Percy's hymn *They Cast Their Nets in Galilee*: "The peace of God, it is no peace / but strife closed in the sod." Episcopal Church, *Hymnal 1982*, #661.

that peace lived out in the course of our own lives. The patient endurance of Job is an example: in his deep personal suffering, Job trusts in God's goodness and faithfulness despite all evidence to the contrary that would otherwise cause him to give up hope (Jas. 5:11). Patience itself is faith lived forward, itself a form of hope. Jerome suggests that faith follows patience because of its numbering; as seventh on the list, faith occupies the place of the number of perfection. Yet hope, which accompanies faith and love in 1 Cor. 13, is absent among the fruit of the Spirit in Gal. 5.[56] Gentleness opposes hardships, quarrels, and bullying; it reaps the peace of God. Self-control takes the final position, and yet in some ways it should come immediately after love; without the fruit of self-control the other fruit may not follow at all. But none of these are harvested except by the Spirit.

5:24 And those who belong to Christ Jesus have crucified the flesh with its passions and desires—Paul's own life and vocation are cruciform: "We are treated . . . as dying, and see—we are alive" (see 2 Cor. 6:4–10; Rom. 6:5–11). His own ministry is formed by the cross of Christ.[57] Belonging to Christ means participating in his death and resurrection, itself a participation in the life of the Spirit, and the law of Christ. The marks on Jesus's body are engraved also on Paul's, written by the finger of God that inscribed the law on the stone tablets at Sinai (Gal. 3:1; 6:17).[58] The seed in whom all are made righteous before God and through whom the Gentiles enter the elect people of Israel is Christ himself, the one who sums up the law (6:2; Rom. 10:4). Living in Christ, Paul lays the desires of the flesh at the foot of the cross, handing them over to the power of the Spirit of Christ.

5:25 If we live by the Spirit let us also be guided by the Spirit—The sentence in Greek is structured in such a way that the focus is not on the verbs "living" or "being guided," as we might have expected from the English translation. In the Greek sentence we find another inclusio. The verbs bookend two occurrences of the noun Spirit, giving us something like this: "If we live by the Spirit, by the Spirit let us be guided." The sentence structure itself

---

56. Jerome finds the logic here: "The object of hope is already included as part of faith." Jerome, *Commentary on Galatians*, 238.

57. Gal. 2:19–20; 4:12; 6:14–15; see also 1 Cor. 11:1; 1 Thess. 1:6.

58. "When God finished speaking with Moses on Mount Sinai, he gave him the two tablets of the covenant, tablets of stone, written with the finger of God" (Exod. 31:18).

emphasizes the Spirit, not the behavior of the believer. Living by the Spirit involves both our conduct and our will as we are sanctified in the Spirit's guidance. The Spirit is then a known quantity: while the unknown can coerce, it cannot guide. Being guided entails making the decision to follow, and one rarely follows a leader whom one neither knows nor trusts. Living by the Spirit is both a passive and an active pursuit; it involves simultaneously exercising and abandoning one's agency, and is an intention lived out in both the active and passive forms of following.

Living by the Spirit is a mark of the new creation (6:15). This life in the Spirit is the fullness of the Christian's life before God. The Spirit lives in, prays through (4:6; Rom. 8:15), and produces in the church the fruit of the new creation. This eschatological victory demands the Galatians' choice to be guided by the Spirit with the Spirit's publicly manifested fruit.

5:26 Let us not become conceited, competing against one another, envying one another—The besetting conflict between the works of the flesh and the fruit of the Spirit exists not only within the individual but more properly within the body of Christ. Paul's earlier discussion of works and desires of the flesh now returns to the works of the flesh: conceit, competition, and envy, all of which attack the body of Christ itself. Even the sanctified live in the midst of struggle against the works of the flesh, as dogs returning to their vomit (Prov. 26:11; 2 Pet. 2:22).

GALATIANS 6

Paul opens the chapter with direct discourse ("my friends"), offering pastoral encouragement, advice, and admonition. He speaks of the internal spiritual affairs of the churches in Galatia in the discipline of the body of Christ. He then gives wisdom in the form of proverbs and touches on some of the earlier key points of the letter as he draws it to a close. The Galatian churches have a new identity in Christ apart from the law of Sinai: in the new creation they are, like Isaac, the Israel of God by the power of the cross.

6:1 My friends, if anyone is detected in a transgression, you who have received the Spirit should restore such a one in a spirit of gentleness. Take care that you yourselves are not tempted—It is often the case that those who know themselves to be transgressors are able to display gentleness in restoring another transgressor, recognizing the condition in themselves. This kind of restoration demands generosity, a fruit supplied by the Spirit (5:22). This one seemingly small fruit opposes all the works of the flesh listed in 5:20; generosity is in part the fulfillment of Jesus's command that we not judge others so that we ourselves may not be judged (Matt. 7:1). "Now nothing proves that a man is spiritual like his handling of another's sin."[1]

Here we come upon a significant difference from Paul's counsel to the Corinthians, where he tells them to give a transgressor over to his own sin.[2] Unlike them, the Galatians are to restore the transgressor to the community, being guided by the Spirit (Gal. 5:25). Whereas in Corinth the goal in handling the situation with a transgressor was the protection of the community

1. Augustine, *Augustine's Commentary on Galatians*, 221.
2. "You are to hand this man over to Satan for the destruction of the flesh, so that his spirit may be saved in the day of the Lord" (1 Cor. 5:5).

from Satan, in Gal. 6:1 Paul is concerned with the manner of the church's response to a transgressor in their midst. The fruit of the Spirit necessary for restoring the transgressor is gentleness, the mirror opposite of the Third Party (1:8–9; 5:23; 6:1). But because the Third Party is not and never properly was part of the Galatian churches, there can be no restoration of that relationship: it was never established in the first place. The Third Party is not welcome in the Galatian churches.

6:2 Bear one another's burdens, and in this way you will fulfill the law of Christ—As a pastor, Paul crafts terms, illustrations, and analogies to address the theological challenges his churches face. The phrase "the law of Christ" points back to 5:14.[3] Paul has said that Christ is the substance of the promise (3:16) and that the law of Christ is observed by being led by the Spirit (4:6; 5:25).

Bearing one another's burdens is tied specifically to this law of Christ and his redeeming work. "We who are strong ought to put up with the failings of the weak, and not to please ourselves. Each of us must please our neighbor for the good purpose of building up the neighbor. For Christ did not please himself; but, as it is written, 'The insults of those who insult you have fallen on me'" (Rom. 15:1–3; see also Gal. 3:13). This echoes the words of Jesus when he teaches his own disciples to pray, "Forgive us our debts, as we also have forgiven our debtors" (Matt. 6:12). Jesus's parable of the unforgiving slave is a storied teaching of this gift of forgiveness (Matt. 18:23–35). Jesus's instructions on adjudicating intracommunal disputes and restoring the integrity and wholeness of the community in Matt. 18:15–20 are formally similar to Paul's command in Gal. 6:2; both express christological and ecclesial discipline.[4]

Neglecting to share in each other's burdens tears at the church (1 Cor. 1:10; Phil. 2:2), but building up concord nurtures mutual sharing of both joy and sorrow (Rom. 12:15; see also 1 Cor. 9:22). The bearing of burdens is a christological act: Jesus bears our burdens by laying down his life (Gal. 1:4; 3:10–13; John 15:12–13). Bearing one another's burdens is therefore obedience to Christ's command to love one another as he has loved the church (Gal. 1:4;

3. See also Rom. 7:22, 25. A similar phrase, "Christ's law," appears in 1 Cor. 9:21 (NRSV). But there the translation masks a Greek play on words: "To those outside the law [*anomois*] I became as one outside the law [*anomos*] (though I am not free from God's law [*anomos theou*] but am under Christ's law [*ennomos Christou*]), so that I might win those outside the law [*tous anomous*]." In Rom. 3:27, in the larger context of justification, Paul uses the phrase "the law of faith [*dia nomou pisteōs*]."
4. For the correspondence between Paul and Matt. 18 in particular, see my comments at 1:8–9, 16, 20; 2:11–14.

3:10–13). "I give you a new commandment, that you love one another. Just as I have loved you, you also should love one another" (John 13:34; cf. 15:12).

Because chapters 5 and 6 are more pastoral in tone than the earlier more doctrinal chapters, they invite different modes of interpretation, even imaginative and playful approaches. Augustine illustrates one such interpretation of what it means to bear one another's burdens by means of an observation from the natural world: how deer swim in a group. As one for whom friendship was as cherished as it was elusive, Augustine is drawn to this image of a herd of deer fording a river as he turns to Gal. 6:2; he speaks of the bearing of burdens as friendship in Christ. No individual deer gives itself completely self-sacrificially to the progress of the whole herd; rather, one deer leads the group until it becomes tired, returning to the rear of the line to rest its antlers on the one it now follows. Here is Augustine:

> Certain experts in this sort of area have written that stags when they cross a ford to get to an island for pasture organise themselves so that they support each other's heavy antlers, with the one behind stretching out its neck and resting its head on the one in front. Since one of them has to go in front of the others, and not have anyone in front to rest its head on, they take it in turns. When the one at the front gets tired from the weight of his head, he goes to the back, and the one whose head he was supporting when he was first then takes over. In this way, carrying each other's burdens, they cross the ford until they reach solid ground. Solomon might have been referring to this characteristic of stags when he said, "May the stag of friendship and the hind of your graces speak with you" [Prov. 5:19 LXX]. For there is no better proof of friendship than bearing a friend's burdens.[5]

Augustine's deer analogy illustrates the ecclesial nature of life in Christ and the sense that attaining to the life to come (in this case, crossing the river without drowning!) is not a solitary endeavor. In this delightful image, bearing one another's burdens becomes an ecclesial act of friendship. Augustine's example here does not include any overtly christological imagery.[6] The grace by which

---

5. Augustine, *On 83 Diverse Questions* 71.1, trans. Margaret Atkins, available at http://www.augnet.org/en/works-of-augustine/writings-of-augustine/2121b-question-71.

6. For a more theological understanding of friendship, see one of his letters to Jerome: "Upon the love of such friends I readily cast myself without reservation, especially when chafed and wearied by the scandals of this world; and in their love I rest without any disturbing care: for I perceive that God is there, on whom I confidingly cast myself, and in whom I confidingly rest. Nor in this confidence am I disturbed by any fear of that uncertainty as to the morrow which must be present when we lean upon human weakness, and which I have in a former paragraph bewailed. For when I

the deer cross to the island is in his illustration not overtly linked to the cross
and resurrection but to the swimming as a herd. As Paul has stated earlier and
will state again, fulfilling the law of Christ means being conformed to the cross
of Christ (6:14; 5:11), being formed in the fruit of the Spirit (5:24), recognizing the cross even in the midst of deception (3:1). While Augustine's playful
example neglects the detail that, in fulfilling the law of Christ, Paul displays on
his own body the love of Christ (6:17), it shares with 6:2 the ecclesial sense.
The law of Christ, love substituted for us from Jesus's own love of the Father, is
manifest in restoring the lost to the body of Christ in a spirit of gentleness (6:1).

**6:3 For if those who are nothing think they are something, they deceive
themselves**—The positive injunction of bearing one another's burdens yields
now to a warning against those who behave in the opposite manner. Individuals who think more of themselves than of the well-being of the church deceive
themselves and impose extra burdens on others. They are like Theudas and
Judas the Galilean, messianic pretenders who had convinced many to follow
them (Acts 5:36–37). Gamaliel warns the Sanhedrin about them, saying that
in setting themselves up as "something," these two men deceived not only
themselves but also the community. The integrity of Christian discipleship
is displayed publicly in the fruit of one's witness to Christ. Gamaliel tells the
Sanhedrin that the judgment of the disciples' preaching will be God's alone.
"I tell you, keep away from these men and let them alone; because if this plan
or this undertaking is of human origin, it will fail; but if it is of God, you will
not be able to overthrow them—in that case you may even be found fighting
against God!" (Acts 5:38–39). Both personal integrity and self-deception are
revealed on the public stage. Those who think more of themselves than of
others have an inflated sense of self-importance that is corrosive to the church.

**6:4 All must test their own work; then that work, rather than their
neighbor's work, will become a cause for pride**—While pride is not directly
mentioned among the works of the flesh in 5:19–20, it is implied especially
in the following items: conceit, competition, and envy (5:26). While boasting

---

perceive that a man is burning with Christian love, and feel that thereby he has been made a faithful
friend to me, whatever plans or thoughts of mine I entrust to him I regard as entrusted not to the
man, but to Him in whom his character makes it evident that he dwells: for God is love, and he that
dwells in love dwells in God, and God in him (1 John 4:16)." Augustine, *Letter* 73.10, from Augustine
to Jerome (AD 404), available at https://www.newadvent.org/fathers/1102073.htm.

in Christ can build up the church (6:14; see also 2 Cor. 10:17), pride does the opposite. Paul's words reflect Jesus's teaching in his parable of the Pharisee and the tax collector (Luke 18:9–14). The Pharisee who fancies himself righteous with his tithing and fasting is proud, thinking that he is superior to the tax collector. Presumably a Roman collaborator, the tax collector nevertheless performs the righteous deed of testing his own work: he acknowledges his sin, prays for God's mercy, and is declared justified. "All who exalt themselves will be humbled, but all who humble themselves will be exalted" (Luke 18:14). Paul tells the Galatians to look to their own sanctification, the fruit of the Spirit manifest in their lives. In this way, their own fruit will become a cause for proper boasting, building up and restoring the church.

6:5 For all must carry their own loads—On the surface, this sounds completely contradictory to what Paul said earlier in 6:2 about living out the law in bearing one another's burdens. The verbs in 6:2, 5, and 17 are the same (*bastazō*), but used in different contexts they are translated differently. The NRSV translates the verb in 6:2 as "to bear," and in 6:5 and 6:17 as "to carry." The objects of the verbs are different in each verse. In 6:2 we have "bear one another's burdens [*ta barē*]"; in 6:5 "bear their own load [*phortion*]"; in 6:17 "bear the marks [*stigmata*] of Christ Jesus." Bearing one another's burdens is ultimately defined by imitating Paul as he bears the marks of Christ (3:1; 4:12; 6:17). The Third Party is unwilling to undergo this kind of suffering on behalf of the cross; they are even unwilling to bear the marks of circumcision (Gal. 4:17; 6:12–14). Paul says that because of their unwillingness to bear the marks of suffering, to die and to rise with and in Christ, their apostleship is not a true witness to Christ (2:19–20). But most importantly, the Third Party does not carry their own loads; rather, they impose heavy burdens on the Galatians. Like Jesus's hypocritical interlocutors in the Gospels (Matt. 23:4), the Third Party binds unnecessary burdens for conversion: specifically, circumcision. But here, the fact that each must carry their own load means that all must render account at the judgment throne. "This passage shows us, albeit covertly, a new and inconspicuous teaching. While we are in the present age, we are able to be helped by one another's prayers and counsel. When we come before the judgment seat of Christ, however, neither Job nor Daniel nor Noah will be able to intercede on behalf of anyone, but each person will carry his own burden."[7]

7. Jerome, *Commentary on Galatians*, 253.

6:6 Those who are taught the word must share in all good things with their teacher—These next verses take the genre of Wisdom proverbs. The nouns for "the one who is taught" (*katēchoumenos*) and "teacher" (*katēchounti*) share the same root from which comes our English word "catechesis." Being taught in the true gospel, not the false one (1:6–9), involves a mutual sharing of both spiritual and material benefits. While in this verse Paul himself is the teacher, he may also be preparing the way for future evangelists. In some respects Gal. 6:6 resembles 1 Cor. 9:14, where he also speaks of the support owed to a teacher: "In the same way, the Lord commanded that those who proclaim the gospel should get their living by the gospel." This is an oblique reference to Jesus's instructions to the seventy as they go out to preach: "Remain in the same house, eating and drinking whatever they provide, for the laborer deserves to be paid" (Luke 10:7). With an instruction like Jesus's in Luke 10, Paul turns to the Corinthians and adds a quotation from the Torah: "For it is written in the law of Moses, 'You shall not muzzle an ox while it is treading out the grain'" (1 Cor. 9:9, quoting Deut. 25:4). Even though Paul himself has relinquished this apostolic right for material support (1 Cor. 9:12), he insists that the command to support the evangelist itself abides because it is based on the authority of Christ's teaching of the seventy drawn from the Torah.

The exhortation to share (Gal. 6:6) includes both material well-being and spiritual health (see Phil. 4:15–18). Gathering the collection for the saints in Jerusalem, Paul commands that all are to share materially with brothers and sisters in need (→2:10). Generous sharing in ministry is the churches' privilege and responsibility; it flows from the confession of faith, the spread of the gospel, and the unity of the body (2 Cor. 9:11–15). The support itself is evidence of the commitment that the Gentile Christian churches have to the Jewish Christian churches (Rom. 15:27). The sharing of material support among the churches, and between them and their evangelist, is for the well-being of the whole church. The main verb is "to share," not "to give." As the Galatians support Paul's ministry, they benefit from the opportunity and privilege to fulfill the law of Christ and share in the gospel.[8]

6:7–10 Do not be deceived; God is not mocked, for whatever a person sows, so shall they harvest. Whoever sows to their own flesh will from the flesh harvest corruption. But the one who sows to the spirit will from the

---

8. *Koinōneō*, "contribute a share." BDAG 438.

spirit harvest eternal life. So let us not grow weary in doing the good, for we will reap at harvest time, if we do not grow weak. So then, whenever we have the time, let us work for the good of all, most of all for those of the household of faith (AT)—From here to the end of the letter, the focus turns to eschatological hope.[9] We are again drawn to the image of the seed, but, rather than in its nominal form, the word now appears in its verbal form: to sow. A cluster of phrases plays with the images of sowing and harvesting at the end time. With pithy illustrations from the natural world, these phrases resemble Wisdom literature and point to existential human reality.[10] Employing the parallel structure characteristic of Wisdom proverbs, Gal. 6:6 speaks of spiritual reality through images of farming. Translating the sentence closely, we have "For whatever a person sows, so shall they harvest."[11] This honors the integrity of the Greek sentence structure, gives voice to the aphoristic style of Wisdom literature, and avoids gendered language. But most importantly, it lands the word "harvest" exactly where it belongs in the sentence: at the end. This allows us to hear the overall context of 6:7–10: the eschatological working of the Spirit in the harvest of the new creation (6:15). These images of sowing and reaping continue, echoing Paul's frequent use in Galatians of imagery of new life: germination, generation, conceiving, and birthing. All of these point to the central concern of the letter: God's fulfillment of the promise to Abraham in Christ the son and seed.

The harvest time exposes our "works," the realities that oppose the Spirit's gift of eternal life. The word "rot" (*phthora*; NRSV: "corruption") here can be taken in a physical as well as moral sense. First, a germinating seed grows, brings life, and generates new plants.[12] The promise to Abraham itself depends on biological reproduction and birthing, the opposite of which is *phthora*, rot. The Spirit brings eternal life even in this material, biological context.

---

9. The themes in these verses overlap with 2 Cor. 4.

10. Sowing sin and harvesting disaster are also found in aphoristic sayings in Proverbs and Job. "Whoever sows injustice will reap calamity, / and the rod of anger will fail. / Those who are generous are blessed, / for they share their bread with the poor" (Prov. 22:8–9; see also 2 Cor. 9:6). A saying less like Gal. 6:7 in structure but similar in content appears on the lips of Job's friend, who speaks of God's righteous anger at Job: "As I have seen, those who plow iniquity and sow trouble reap the same" (Job 4:8).

11. The NRSV curiously transposes the verbs: "You reap whatever you sow." The RSV gives "Whatever a man sows, that he will also reap."

12. "Then God said, 'Let the earth put forth vegetation: plants yielding seed, and fruit trees of every kind on earth that bear fruit with the seed in it.' And it was so" (Gen. 1:11).

Second, just as agricultural harvest requires human toil as well as the grace of good weather, spiritual sowing and harvesting require work, skill, and patience. The Spirit's sowing requires the grace and power of the Spirit's presence. The Spirit brings forth from the thorns and thistles of Eden the fruit of sanctification for those in Christ. This harvest of the Spirit is free of the sweat of our brow (Gen. 3:19).

We might think that Paul has a dualistic anthropology at this point if we read the primary juxtaposition in 6:7–9 as flesh versus spirit. However, the prepositional clauses show that this disjunction is not present here. Paul's contrast between "to the flesh" and "from the flesh" points to the disjunction between "harvest" and "rot," not between "spirit" and "flesh." The sentence structure moves the reader through the clauses "to the spirit" and "from the spirit" to the final clause, "harvest eternal life." Paul is saying that harvesting to the spirit does not oppose flesh but leads to everlasting life; the spirit opposes not flesh but rot. Landing as it does on the phrase "eternal life," the sentence also reflects Sarah's role in the story of Abraham: she does not remain infertile. She does conceive; she does not miscarry; she does give birth. The story of Abraham and Sarah is the story of a birth that generates the promise, a promise that generates a birth, the harvest of which is eternal life in the Spirit of Christ. This all points to the fact that Paul's understanding of "Spirit" in Galatians, even as the third person of the Trinity, is not divorced from material, biological, physical life. The gospel Paul preaches to the Galatians is about the God who sent his Son who is not a disembodied spirit, not a cyborg, but a Jewish baby boy. The Spirit's harvest of everlasting life is itself a fleshly eschatological promise.

In 1 Cor. 15 Paul's words on the general resurrection give us parallel vocabulary in a similarly eschatological context, but there the subject is the resurrection of the dead. There Paul says that "what is sown is perishable [*phthora*, "rotting"], what is raised is imperishable [*aphtharsia*, its lexical opposite]" (1 Cor. 15:42). The image of Christ ("the man of heaven," 15:49) governs the eschatological hope.[13] The imagery of reaping everlasting life at the harvest time furthers Paul's encouragement for persistence (Gal. 6:9), restoring the transgressor (6:1), bearing one another's burdens (6:2), sharing with the teacher (6:6), and working

---

13. Note the difference: the juxtaposition in Gal. 6:8 is a nonbinary between "corruption" (*phthora*) and "eternal life" (*zōēn aiōnion*); in 1 Cor. 15:42 the distinction is indeed a binary between "rot" (*phthora*) and "nonrotting" (*aphtharsia*). The meaning of the word "perishable" is filled out in 1 Cor. 15 with the words "dishonor" (*atimia*) and "weakness" (*astheneia*; 1 Cor. 15:43).

for the good of all (6:10). Even Paul's pastoral teaching directs our attention to eschatological hope.

As any gardener knows, the results of agricultural sowing and reaping are not immediate. They take place over time and rely on the passage of days and seasons. Patient hope is needed for the time between the sowing and the harvest at the end (e.g., Luke 18:1; 2 Cor. 4:1, 16; 2 Thess. 3:13). The fullness of time came about in Jesus's conception and birth, life and death, resurrection and ascension, and yet we await the final consummation with endurance. Time in its fullness is the arena in which the Spirit is active; the church is the Spirit's home, where seed is sown and fruit is harvested at the close of the age. This is precisely what Paul means in 1:4 where he speaks of Christ's death as freeing us from the present evil age: the church dwells in this age, possessing now the sure and certain hope of the promised redemption yet to come.[14] One conclusion we can draw is that, because the eschatological harvest is not itself disengaged from Christian life in the present, we cannot properly call Paul's eschatology "apocalyptic" in that it is not discontinuous with the created, physical, biological order. Another is related, but even more obvious: Paul does not neglect pastoral care.

This household of faith, the church, is defined not primarily by the believers' relationships among themselves but first by their relationship to Jesus Christ and his law (6:2; cf. 5:15, 26). Living as the household of faith demands the nurture of healthy relationships in the church, Christ's counterpart and bride.[15] Here, as elsewhere in the New Testament and the Christian tradition, the church appears in feminine personae: the church is Sarah, the free mother, the type of Mary. Like Paul, the church boasts in the cross alone, and the church gathers to herself those who, crucified with Christ, live in him (2:20; 6:14). The household of faith is Jesus's earthly presence in the "now Jerusalem" (4:25). And yet this household lives not only for herself: "Let us work for the good of all" (6:10).

6:11 See what large letters I make when I am writing in my own hand!— The nominal plural form of the verbal root *graphō*, "to write," is the word for "scriptures": *hē graphē*, literally, "the writings." For the earliest Christians,

14. Endurance is the twin of patience (5:22) and hope (6:9–10; see Rom. 5:3).
15. That the image of the church as the bride of Christ appears explicitly in the final and uniquely eschatological book of the New Testament is instructive: the marriage of the Lamb and the church is an eschatological event (Rev. 18:23; 19:7, 9; 21:2, 9; 22:17).

and thus for Paul, "the writings" refer to what we call the Old Testament, or more precisely for Paul, the Septuagint. While it is highly unlikely that Paul thought himself to be writing "scripture," it is certain that from the very fact that the churches collected and read his letters aloud together in worship, his letters were deemed to some extent uniquely authoritative and even revelatory of the gospel.

Paul takes the stylus from the scribe and closes the letter with his own handwriting. This practice is not unique to Galatians; Paul's other letters, both authentic and disputed, follow this convention.[16] In antiquity, the orthographic postscript identified the author, providing a mark of authenticity. This corresponds to Pilate's unknowing act of dictating the authoritative claim to be posted above the cross, declaring the identity of the crucified criminal: "Jesus of Nazareth, the King of the Jews" (John 19:19). When the chief priests ask Pilate to rewrite this declaration, Pilate refuses, sealing by his own authority the publicly announced identity of Jesus: "What I have written I have written" (John 19:22). Even though the message was dictated and not written in his own hand, Pilate's insistence that the message remain as he had authorized functions in the narrative as an ironic and implicit confession of Jesus. While Pilate unwittingly authorizes Jesus's identity, Paul's large handwriting explicitly identifies him as Christ-bearer: he is willing to be conformed to the cross, bearing persecution on behalf of this King of the Jews.

There have been many suggestions to account for Paul's remarks about his large handwriting, everything from his poor eyesight or his wounded hands or his attempt to instruct the illiterate Galatians how to write, or simply to emphasize his message.[17] The only thing we can be sure of is this: what he had announced as his final remark falls eight verses before the end of the letter, where we would have expected it. Paul does not bring the letter to a close at 6:11; rather, he continues his theological, ethical, and spiritual teaching, summarizing the letter's overall message and pointing to his own vocation of conforming to the cross of Christ. The final verses of the letter will serve as a prophecy of Paul's own martyrdom (6:14, 17).

---

16. "I, Paul, write this greeting with my own hand" (1 Cor. 16:21); "I, Paul, write this greeting with my own hand. Remember my chains. Grace be with you" (Col. 4:18); "I, Paul, write this greeting with my own hand. This is the mark in every letter of mine; it is the way I write" (2 Thess. 3:17); "I, Paul, am writing this with my own hand" (Phlm. 19).

17. Keener, *Galatians*, 281.

6:12 It is those who want to make a good showing in the flesh that try to compel you to be circumcised—only that they may not be persecuted for the cross of Christ—While Paul is ready to be persecuted for the cross (see also 6:14, 17), the Third Party is not willing. They evangelize out of a desire for self-aggrandizement. They want to avoid persecution on behalf of Christ (4:17); they are cowards and hypocrites. From the second half of 6:12 moving forward, as we approach the end of the letter, the references to the cross increase.

6:13 Even the circumcised do not themselves obey the law, but they want you to be circumcised so that they may boast about your flesh—The Third Party preaches a gospel that is based on a lie. Like the false prophets in Corinth whose hypocrisy is manifest in disguising themselves as angels (2 Cor. 11:12–15), the Third Party practices deceit. Even though they impose the law on the Galatians, they do not observe it themselves. The Third Party should boast in the cross, not in circumcising Gentile converts to Christ. They have eviscerated the meaning of circumcision itself, for the substance of the promise is and has always been Christ (Gal. 3:16; Rom. 10:4). In coercing the Gentiles to take on a halakic practice that by definition is not required of Gentiles (Gal. 2:3), the Third Party splits the church (4:17) through a false proclamation of the cross (1:6–9; 5:10–11).

Theodoret of Cyrus points out that, on a simply practical level, keeping the whole law would have been a logistical challenge for the Galatians given their isolated location in Asia Minor. Particularly with regard to the pilgrimage feasts and temple sacrifices, Theodoret asks, "How is it possible for them to keep the Law, living far from Jerusalem as they do? How do they celebrate the festivals? How do they offer sacrifices? How do they keep themselves pure when touching impure things?"[18] But Paul's point is theological, not logistical: the Third Party preaches the law but does not observe it. The Galatians must not succumb to their hypocrisy.

6:14 May I never boast of anything except the cross of our Lord Jesus Christ, by which the world has been crucified to me, and I to the world—For Paul, conforming to the cross is his pride.[19] Boasting is, in itself, not the problem; the danger lies in the object of the boasting: "Let the one who boasts,

---

18. Theodoret of Cyrus, *Commentary on the Letters of St. Paul* (trans. Hill, 2:23).
19. See also 1 Cor. 1:23; 9:14; et passim.

boast in the Lord" (1 Cor. 1:31).[20] Even the places where Paul might seem to boast in his own ministry, he makes clear that his pride is in the power of God working through him. Paul speaks of boasting in Christ and in his converts, especially among the Corinthians. Here in Galatians, Paul boasts specifically in the cross, the instrument of execution that, through the power of Christ's resurrection, brings life (2:19–21; 5:24).

While the NRSV translates the verb *kauchasthai* as "to boast," the RSV and the KJV give "to glory" and Tyndale translates as "to rejoice." The verb can also be translated as "to brag."[21] At Mary's visitation by the angel, she sings her Magnificat, "My soul magnifies [*megalunei*] the Lord." This is in a sense what Paul is doing when he "boasts." Just as she points to the greatness of what God will do through her in the incarnation (Luke 1:46), so Paul magnifies neither himself nor his Galatians, only God. Paul magnifies in his boasting what God has already done in his own evangelization among the Galatians through the cross. As Mary sings her Magnificat, she has not yet heard Simeon's prophecy of her suffering: "A sword will pierce your own soul too" (Luke 2:35). Mary does not yet know the full contours of her son's life and death. She nevertheless trusts God's promise (Luke 1:30–33) and praises God's name (Luke 1:46–55). But while Mary looks ahead, Paul looks back. He sees the promise fulfilled that Mary trusts without seeing. Because Paul himself has witnessed in Jesus's revelation to him (1:12, 16) the fulfillment of the promise to Mary, he boasts of the "greatness of the Lord," not of his own.

6:15 For neither circumcision nor uncircumcision is anything; but a new creation is everything!—The explicit juxtaposition of circumcision and uncircumcision entered Paul's discussion twice earlier in Galatians (2:7–9; 5:2–6; see also Rom. 2:25–27; 1 Cor. 7:18). While circumcision may have seemed to be a matter of indifference in 5:6, this was in fact not the case; the substance and meaning of the rite of circumcision is precisely "faith working through love" (5:6). In 6:15 the phrase "a new creation" nests within references to the cross (6:12, 14, 17). This is not primarily a statement about circumcision,

20. This is a loose quotation of Jer. 9:23–24, where the content of righteous boasting is the knowledge of God: "Thus says the LORD: Do not let the wise boast in their wisdom, do not let the mighty boast in their might, do not let the wealthy boast in their wealth; but let those who boast boast in this, that they understand and know me, that I am the LORD; I act with steadfast love, justice, and righteousness in the earth, for in these things I delight, says the LORD."
21. BDAG 536.

nor about the relationship between Jews and Gentiles but, as Jerome notes, about the nature of the glorified body: "We will have a body that neither the Jew can circumcise nor the Gentile can keep uncircumcised."[22] Paul speaks here of eschatology, not of the rite of circumcision or even how it affects the relationship between Jewish and Gentile Christians within the church.

As I said at 3:28, circumcision made the physical distinction between Jewish and Gentile males obvious, particularly at the public baths. Jewish males, whether Christian or non-Christian, who wanted not to be identifiable as Jews could have the marks of circumcision removed. This procedure was not unheard of among Jews of antiquity, even though it was seen as a gross betrayal of religious identity.[23] As far as Paul is concerned, with the election of Israel in Christ, the marks of circumcision are neither to be imposed nor removed.[24] As Paul has taught the Galatians, the flesh of election is the body of Jesus on the cross, the new creation.

The fruit of the Spirit manifests this new creation where the present Jerusalem (*tē nyn*; 4:25) and the heavenly Jerusalem (*hē de anō*; 4:26) are united: "For I am about to create new heavens and a new earth; the former things shall not be remembered or come to mind" (Isa. 65:17). The new creation manifests itself in the fruit of the Spirit, the sacramental presence of Christ in the church.[25] One sign of this new creation will be the increase and flourishing of Israel: "They shall build houses and inhabit them; they shall plant vineyards and eat their fruit" (Isa. 65:21). The church of Jews and Gentiles participates in this eschatological typology. The new creation is neither like a kernel extracted from its husk, nor a butterfly leaving its chrysalis. It is precisely the first creation perfected in the consummation of the fullness of time.

6:16 As for those who will follow this rule—peace be upon them, and mercy, and upon the Israel of God—For the Third Party and for Paul's

22. Jerome, *Commentary on Galatians*, 265.

23. For example, "In those days certain renegades came out from Israel and misled many, saying, 'Let us go and make a covenant with the Gentiles around us, for since we separated from them many disasters have come upon us.' This proposal pleased them, and some of the people eagerly went to the king, who authorized them to observe the ordinances of the Gentiles. So they built a gymnasium in Jerusalem, according to Gentile custom, and removed the marks of circumcision, and abandoned the holy covenant. They joined with the Gentiles and sold themselves to do evil" (1 Macc. 1:11–15; →3:28).

24. "Was anyone at the time of his call already circumcised? Let him not seek to remove the marks of circumcision. Was anyone at the time of his call uncircumcised? Let him not seek circumcision" (1 Cor. 7:18–19).

25. Gal. 3:2, 5, 14; 4:3, 6, 9, 29; 5:16, 22, 25; 6:1, 8, 18.

churches there are competing sets of criteria to discern what counts as the gospel of Jesus Christ. One is this "rule," which blesses with peace and mercy. Paul does not tell us here what the precise content of this rule is, but according to its placement in the letter, it seems to be linked to the dual crucifixion of the world to Paul and Paul to the world. "This rule" means at the very least being led by the Spirit, in which the Spirit manifests its fruit and restrains the works of the flesh (5:16–21).[26] The rule therefore includes bearing one another's burdens (6:2), fulfilling the law of Christ (5:14), boasting in the cross alone (6:14), and enduring with patience until the harvest time (6:9).

As such, Paul's rule is the whole shape and norm of the gospel that safeguards the Galatians' faith in their struggle against the Third Party. The fact that the rule was being jeopardized is evident in Paul's passionate scolding of the Galatians over their untrustworthiness. To underscore from earlier, the Third Party does not understand the gospel because they have not been properly taught the rule that norms it and that it norms. Even the Ethiopian eunuch knows what the Third Party does not: understanding the scriptures demands being catechized by those who know how to read it according to the rule (Acts 8:26–40). From this rule that undergirds all of Paul's writings germinates the seed from which will grow the rule of faith.[27]

Beginning in the decades immediately following Paul, a recognition of the coherence of the gospel's norming norm began to emerge.[28] As early as the second century, the *regula fidei* began to develop in oral form, with only slight variations from one local church to another. These oral forms became codified over the following generations into written forms, eventually undergirding the ecumenical creeds. Even pre-creedal forms of the rule functioned in early Christian biblical interpretation to proscribe interpretations that violated christological and trinitarian norms while not prescribing any single interpretation.[29] The rule permitted a wide range of valid interpretations but "ruled out" readings that violated the content of the gospel. This provided an elasticity of reading

26. Paul uses the term "rule" also in 1 Cor. 7:17, where it refers more to a manner of living than to a form of belief: "However that may be, let each of you lead the life that the Lord has assigned, to which God called you. This is my rule in all the churches."

27. See Rom. 12:6: *analogian tēs pisteōs* (→2:2, 5; 5:6).

28. The discussion of the relationship between the *norma normans* and the *norma normata* emerges explicitly in the Formula of Concord, epitome 1 (1584). There the context likewise is discerning how the rule functions, not its content.

29. For example, Ignatius warns: "Stop your ears, therefore, when anyone speaks at variance with Jesus Christ." *Epistle of Ignatius to the Trallians* 9:1–2 (ANF 1:69). Tertullian says, "To know nothing in opposition to the rule (of faith) is to know all things." *Prescription against the Heretics* 14 (*ANF* 3:250).

while setting limits to the normed and norming truth of the gospel. The rule was the implicit foundation of canonicity, shaping the way in which the two Testaments were read in tandem as a holistic, living witness to the triune God.

The logic undergirding this rule of faith is present here in the shape of Paul's proclamation in the context of catechesis and pastoral care. The function of the rule is formally similar to the lifeboats on the deck of a cruise ship, which are deployed only in the event of an emergency. Paul's flock in Galatia is in such an emergency.

The rule safeguards both the *fides quae creditur* (the doctrinal content of the faith) and the *fides qua creditor* (the believer's trust in and experience of Christ).[30] In norming the *fides quae,* the rule of faith undergirds Paul's interpretation of scripture in the first four chapters of Galatians.[31] In norming the *fides qua,* the rule is the engine of the moral exhortation that we find in the final two chapters of Galatians as Paul tries to distinguish the behavior of those who follow the rule from those who don't. The Third Party has taught the Galatians about Abraham's story, but they do not understand the story themselves; they do not have the rule by which appeal is made to and from scripture. They do not understand the law because they have not read it according to the rule (Gal. 4:21–22).

The phrase "Israel of God" occurs only here in the New Testament; even in other Jewish literature of the day the phrase is relatively rare.[32] The term evokes the blessings that close Pss. 125 and 128; in Gal. 6:17 "the Israel of God" may be the earliest indicator of the church's self-understanding as Israel.[33] For Paul, this Israel of God is the one people of the universal and the particular covenants, joined in the seed, the Christ (Gal. 3:16) from the beginning of creation (Gen. 3:15). The "all Israel" of Rom. 11:26 and the "Israel of God" of Gal. 6:16 point as one to this eschatological body, the heavenly Jerusalem (Gal. 4:26).

---

30. Augustine, *On the Trinity* 13.2, where he links the *fides quae* with the faith that works through love (Gal. 5:6) and living in the Spirit (Gal. 5:22–25). For the development of the distinction between the *fides qua* and the *fides quae,* see Barth, CD I/1, 209, 236, and my comments at 5:6.

31. "The church has handed down from the apostles, the apostles from Christ, and Christ from God. . . . The reason of our position is clear, when it determines that heretics ought not to be allowed to challenge an appeal to the Scriptures, since we, without the Scriptures, prove that they have nothing to do with the Scriptures." Tertullian, *Prescription against Heretics* 37 (*ANF* 3:261). For what I suggest is a contemporary formal (if not material) version of the hermeneutical norming function of the rule, see Frei, "Literal Reading," 68–69.

32. Eastman, "Israel and the Mercy of God," 374n26. See also Goodrich, "Until the Fulness."

33. "But those who turn aside to their own crooked ways the Lᴏʀᴅ will lead away with evildoers. Peace be upon Israel!" (Ps. 125:5). "May you see your children's children. Peace be upon Israel!" (Ps. 128:6).

6:17 From now on, let no one make trouble for me; for I carry the marks of Jesus branded on my body—The scars that Paul bears on his body are proof of his apostolic integrity, for in these wounds he shares in the cross of Christ (1:4; 3:1). His reference to these marks corresponds to his earlier rhetorical question in 1:10, "Am I now seeking human approval, or God's approval? Or am I trying to please people? If I were still pleasing people, I would not be a servant of Christ." The marks that Paul bears point to his grief over his having persecuted the church prior to his encounter with the risen Lord. The marks of Jesus are also evidence of Paul's life as he participates in Christ's death (2:20; 2 Cor. 4:10; Phil. 3:10). As such, they certify that Paul is Jesus's chattel property, his trustworthy apostle, his faithful pastor.[34]

The Greek word translated here as "marks" is *stigmata*; in its singular it is *stigma*. This is the only occurrence of the word in the New Testament. In Luke's stories of the resurrection appearances, Jesus's wounds are implied: "Look at my hands and my feet; see that it is I myself" (Luke 24:39). In John, Jesus's wounds (*typoi*) serve to identify for Thomas the risen Lord as the same man with whom he had lived, the same one who had been crucified (John 20:24–29). Another word, *charagma*, also appears in the Bible and refers to the branding on a slave's body that identifies their owner or the god whom they serve. It also can be translated "marks."[35] Paul's marks identify him as both Jesus's slave and his supplicant. They also make him ritually unclean; for the observant Jew, tattoos or markings on the flesh are prohibited (Lev. 19:28; →3:1). But Paul's own wounds preach healing from the curse of Eden that Christ has overcome (Gal. 3:10–12).[36] They also foreshadow his own martyrdom and link him to Peter in their mutual suffering for the name of Jesus (Acts 5:41).[37] The Galatians of all people should know that Paul's marks are precious, reflecting not the deformity they once perceived them to be but the fair beauty of the Lord (Gal. 4:13–14; Ps. 27:4).

6:18 May the grace of our Lord Jesus Christ be with your spirit, brothers and sisters. Amen—This final blessing invokes the name of Jesus and blesses

34. See also Acts 14:19; 17:5–6; 23:6; 1 Cor. 4:11–13; 2 Cor. 6:4–10; 11:22–29; Col. 1:24; 1 Thess. 2:14; 1 Tim. 3:11.
35. Rev. 13:16; 14:9, 11; 16:2; 19:20; 20:4; see Isa. 44:5; 3 Macc. 2:29.
36. "With his stripes we are healed" (Isa. 53:5 KJV).
37. See my comments in 2:11–14 on the relationship between Paul and Peter.

with the same grace that opened the letter (1:3).[38] The "Amen" of 1:5 and the "Amen" of 6:18 bookend even Paul's harshest remarks in Galatians, embracing them in the context of an extended and agonized pastoral prayer that his churches not be swayed from the truth of the gospel.

38. Paul uses this blessing also to close Phil. 4:23; cf. 2 Tim. 4:22; Phlm. 25.

EPILOGUE

I opened this commentary with two observations about the content of Paul's letter to the Galatians that I had not anticipated before I set out to read the text closely: circumcision and the gendered nature of election both emerge as key concepts at a plain-sense, surface reading of the letter. I now close with a few expanded observations on underlying issues that have also emerged from an attempt to read the letter closely. Correlates of the first two observations are linked to two biblical aspects of covenant election: infrasession and typology. I now turn to these matters.

Covenant Election: The Universal and Particular

Because Paul understands the content of the Lord's covenant promise to Abraham to be Christ (Gal. 3:16), and because the messianic promise is made prior to the rite of circumcision long before the law (3:18), the promise precedes the covenant of election. Because Abraham's faith in the promise precedes the statute of circumcision, the Galatians' conversion to Christ does not require observance of the covenant rite. Gentile Christians are not to take on the rite of circumcision before becoming Christians. Even the Jerusalem church, the center of the Jewish mission, agrees.[1]

The Universal and Particular Covenants

While Paul does not use the terms "universal" and "particular" covenants as he interprets the Abraham stories in Galatians, he builds on an implicit

1. Gal. 2 and Acts 15 both indicate this.

understanding of two macro-covenants in the Hebrew Bible.[2] For Paul, these covenants illustrate the fit between the doctrines of creation and election; they are key to his messianic logic.[3] Because the Lord freely elects to covenant with Abraham, the patriarch himself is at the fulcrum of these two covenants; Paul therefore turns specifically to the character of Abraham in Gal. 3 and 4.

Traced to the beginning of Genesis and moving toward its apex with the story of Noah, the universal covenant is God's promise to all humanity prior to the election of Israel. Paul understands Abram's story to be told in essentially two sets of episodes of promise. In the universal covenant, (1) God calls Abram out of Ur, promising land and progeny, blessing the world through him (Gen. 12); (2) God reckons him righteous, again promising progeny and land (Gen. 15). In the particular covenant another set of episodes of the promise follows: (1) God gives Abram a new name (Abraham) and the rite of the covenant, circumcision (Gen. 17); (2) the Lord gives the law at Sinai (Exod. 20).

For Paul, the fact that God's covenant comes in these sequential episodes is key: the beginning of Abraham's story is located properly in the universal covenant. Abram, the future patriarch, is like the Galatians: a Gentile. The subsequent episodes are key for Paul because this is where the Gentile Abram enters the particular covenant (Gal. 3:15–22). This is not simply a Christian imposition on a Jewish frame; the division of the particular into the two "episodes," circumcision and law, is not even especially Pauline.[4] The linking of these two macro-covenants, according to Jonathan Sacks, is "Judaism's most singular feature: its *distinction between the universality of God as Creator and Sovereign of the universe, and the particularity of the covenant, first with Abraham, then with Moses and the Israelites*."[5] In Galatians Paul relies on this underlying narrative logic of the Hebrew Bible: the one God of Israel is canonically introduced first as creator and only then as covenant elector and law giver.

---

2. I do not follow F. C. Baur's use of the terms "universal" and "particular." He says: "Jewish particularism . . . is but a stage, a stepping stone to the universalism of Christianity, in which all nations should be embraced." Baur, *Paul, the Apostle of Jesus Christ*, 1:309. But for Paul, the universal and particular covenants do not correspond to the covenants God makes with Israel and with the church, because for Paul both dwell within the narrative sweep of the Hebrew Bible itself. For the effect that Baur's proposal has had on contemporary christologies, see Bockmuehl, "The Trouble with the Inclusive Jesus." I borrow and adapt Rabbi Jonathan Sacks's use of these terms in his *Not in God's Name*. Sacks is closer to Paul than is Baur on this issue.

3. For the logic of the fit between the doctrines of creation and election, see Novak, *Election of Israel*, 115–38.

4. See Greenberg, "Judaism and Christianity."

5. Sacks, *Not in God's Name*, 189, 195–99.

This logic of the relationship between the universal and particular covenants within the Hebrew Bible itself implicitly shapes how Paul speaks of the relationship between Abraham's promise and Christ (Gal. 3:16). Even though the particular covenant arrives second in the order of the biblical narrative, it takes theological priority; while in the biblical plot the universal precedes the particular, it is secondary to it. The particular covenant conceptually grounds the universal: there would be no universal covenant without the particular covenant.[6] It is only as Abram steps out of the universal and into the particular that both come into being together.

The universal covenant is tied to the figure of Noah, the righteous Gentile whom God chooses as servant in the renewal of creation after the flood (Gen. 6:8, 18; 9:9–17).[7] In the allegory of Hagar and Sarah in Gal. 4, the universal covenant is hinged to the particular covenant specifically through Gentile flesh; Hagar's womb gestates Abram's firstborn son. Ishmael is born to the father who receives the promise, but is not himself the promised son because he is not born of the promised womb.[8] Ishmael does not replace Isaac, nor does Hagar replace Sarah.[9] As mother of Abram's first son, Hagar herself links the Gentiles to the promise and its fulfillment in Isaac, who for Paul is a type of Christ. Because in the narrative Hagar is and remains a Gentile, she cannot serve as a replacement for Sarah, the mother of the promise.

Infrasession

The fact that the promise to Abraham is given before the covenant rite of circumcision is key to Paul's discussion throughout Galatians, not only in 3:16. This chronological givenness of the biblical narrative has profound implications for how Paul understands the relationship between law and gospel: just

---

6. This is analogous to Barth's understanding of creation as the external basis of the covenant and the covenant as the internal basis of creation. Barth, *CD* III/1, 94–329.

7. This is sometimes called the Noahide covenant. The theological import of Noah for the universal covenant and for Paul's mission to the Gentiles entered my comments explicitly in 2:10.

8. Jonathan Sacks makes an analogous comment about Hagar's role as a hinge figure in Abraham's story; see *Not in God's Name*, 107–24. The fact that Sacks points to the eschatological element of hope even in the potentially disastrous rupture in Sarah's infertility and Hagar's ability to conceive is an example of the fact that not all eschatological readings are messianic, much less Christian.

9. On the "pattern of reversal," see my comments at 4:22, 24, 30. The classic example is Jacob and Esau, but the pattern echoes throughout the Hebrew Bible. Robert Alter uses the term "deflection of primogeniture" (*Art of Biblical Narrative*, 180); Sacks uses the term "displacement narrative" (*Not in God's Name*, 109).

as Christ stands "inside" the particular covenant, so also the gospel embraces
and enfolds the law. Paul tells the Gentile Christians in Galatia that the reality of Christ is sacramentally present within the Lord's covenant with Israel
precisely as the seed promised to Abraham. Paul's preaching in Galatians is in
Christian theology a source for replacement theology only by a misreading.[10]
Nothing can replace God's election of the people of Israel, because they are
elect precisely in Christ. This has a hermeneutical corollary: the claim to the
theological relationship of the two testaments of Christian scripture is grounded
on christological confession. There is no other justification or basis for a Christian reading of the Hebrew Bible as sacred scripture.

Replacement theology is based on a caricature of Paul and assumes an entirely undifferentiated intimacy in the relationship between the covenants. The
intimacy is proper to Christian theology, but nondifferentiation is invalidated
by the rule of faith, itself tightly woven within the logic of Christian theology,
arguably until the modern era.[11] Paul's understanding of the relationship between promise and fulfillment embraces a theological intimacy that fits properly
within the bounds of the rule of faith. But when misconstrued, it promotes a
sense of undifferentiated unity that allows for the errors of replacement theolo-
gies. This is just one of the many reasons that careful and faithful Christian
biblical interpretation is a responsibility not to be taken lightly.

I suggest the term "infrasession" to describe more appropriately Paul's held
view of christological intimacy within the covenant promise. For Paul, the gospel is within (hence *infra*) the law; the gospel does not replace the law, because
it is "inside" it from eternity.[12] This framing of the relationship between gospel
and law distinguishes the covenants one from the other while maintaining the
christological hermeneutic proper to Paul and the Great Tradition. For Paul,

10. For a definition of replacement theology, also called supersessionism, see Kaminsky and
Reasoner: "Any Christian reading of the Hebrew Scriptures is likely to involve some form of supersessionism, by which we mean that the early Christians came to believe that their reading of Israel's
scriptures superseded other earlier and contemporary readings by other Jewish readers and that God's
acting through Jesus's death and resurrection had ushered in the beginning of the eschaton, thus opening a path for gentiles to participate in God's promises to Israel." Kaminsky and Reasoner, "Meaning
and Telos of Israel's Election," 422n2. This particular view of supersessionism is common, although
it bears the reverse caricature, for example, in its effective prohibition of Christian reading of more
than half of Christian scripture. This may simply be an instance of the asymmetry of the relationship
between Judaism and Christianity. See also Lindbeck, "What of the Future?," 359.

11. I find this to be implicit in the overall thesis of Frei's *Eclipse of Biblical Narrative*.

12. R. Kendall Soulen comes close to describing what I am calling infrasession: "The Lord's history
with Israel and the nations does not *prepare* for the gospel but *surrounds* the gospel and is its constant
horizon, context, and goal." Soulen, *God of Israel*, 176.

because Abraham is elect in his trust in the promise of Christ, the promise itself is not an ex post facto correction of course, a change of tack, or a redefinition of election such that Abraham would be replaced.[13]

Because election is cast precisely in christological terms for Paul, a doctrine of progressive revelation cannot be credited to him. Paul tells the Galatians that they are elect in the same promise that Abraham received and trusted: the seed, Jesus Christ. This intimacy embraces, therefore, not only the doctrine of election but also the doctrine of ecclesiology; the Gentile Christians in Galatia have joined the body of Christ, the church, the Israel of God.[14] They are "like Isaac."

Typology and Multivalence

The hermeneutical correlate of this christological intimacy is classically represented under the rubric of figural or typological reading. Recent decades have seen a renewed interest in theological uses of typology, especially among those who have found the genre of narrative to be useful in biblical interpretation. This trend can be traced in part to the late twentieth-century North American theologian Hans Frei.[15] In his groundbreaking *The Eclipse of Biblical Narrative*, Frei observes that before the Enlightenment the Christian tradition of interpretation tended to read the Bible much like a "realistic novel" whose plot had a beginning, middle, and end, and thus depicted a followable world.[16] He also suggested that in this way of reading, typological interpretation is linked closely to literal interpretation (what he called "plain sense").[17] Tied to Frei's observation that premodern Christian interpretation of scripture finds in the canon a realistic narrative plot, I would add two convictions that undergird it, certainly

13. *Pace* N. T. Wright, for whom election is "redefined, then, around the Messiah—especially his cross—and the spirit." Wright, *Paul and the Faithfulness of God*, 2:1137.

14. For an ecclesiocentric interpretation different from my own, see Hays, *Echoes of Scripture*, 84–121.

15. Lest I mislead my reader or misrepresent Frei, I clarify that he did not consider himself originally a theologian per se, but an intellectual historian of Christianity. For an autobiographical account of his intellectual and religious development, see Hans Frei, interview by Laurel Vlock, "Hans F. Holocaust Testimony," Fortunoff Video Archive for Holocaust Testimonies, https://fortunoff.aviaryplatform.com/collections/5/collection_resources/241/transcript.

16. For "realistic narrative," see the introduction to Frei, *Eclipse of Biblical Narrative*, esp. 10–16. Much of what I say about biblical interpretation is implied by but not made explicit in Frei's observations.

17. Frei called his observation of this link of figural and literal sense a "family resemblance" in the Christian theological tradition. See Frei, *Eclipse of Biblical Narrative*, 6–7, 27.

for Paul and arguably for the tradition that follows him: (1) in a fundamental but unspecifiable way the text is divinely authored;[18] and (2) the divine author of the story is also a character within its plot but is unconstrained by the trajectory of the plot. Because the divine author is not limited by the plotline, the action of the divine author within the sequence of the plot is extralinear. While Abraham's life story is "realistic" and moves in one chronological direction, the author of the story can interact with characters from within different episodes regardless of chronology. So Christ meets Abraham long before the Lord's birth in Bethlehem. It is the nature of the divine author (as opposed to the nature of the text) that determines the text's multivalence. These assumptions about the text's divinely determined multivalence are for Paul not add-ons but are linked to the prior (indeed primary) christological reality.[19]

For example, Paul shows that in the sending of the Son, the episode of Sinai is not relegated to the past: Christ sums up the law and saves through the law even as its own curse (Gal. 3:13; 4:4; 5:13–14; 6:2). Dying to the law is grounded in the cross and resurrection, a present christological reality (2:19–20). Bearing the wounds of Christ is just one of the ways Paul preaches on his own body the gospel to the Galatians (3:1; 6:17).

This characteristic of the plot's extralinearity is a defining assumption of typological interpretation. Typology for Paul is not solely an application of exegetical technique (although it is that, especially in Gal. 3 and 4) but is fundamentally grounded in God's being and act in creation and redemption. This extralinearity itself is not simply a Christian imposition on scriptural texts; rabbinic interpretation itself also operates under the assumption that the biblical texts have power to speak on more than one level. Even though for the rabbis this is not necessarily linked to messianic assumptions, it is linked to a doctrine of God. "Typological exegesis is thus not a disclosure of the *sensus plenior* of the text, in the manner of other forms of inner-biblical exegesis. It is rather a disclosure of the plenitude and mysterious workings of divine activity in history."[20] Grounded in the doctrine of providence, typology points not only

18. While divine authorship is a traditional conviction regarding the biblical text, prescribing the precise mechanics of it was not a *status confessionis* in Christian thought before the rise of twentieth-century American fundamentalism.

19. This is clear implicitly in (at least) Gal. 1:12, 16; 2:20; 5:6, 14, 21, 24; 6:2, 15, 17 and explicitly throughout chapters 3 and 4. The pastoral consequences become clear in chapters 5 and 6.

20. Fishbane, *Biblical Interpretation*, 352. Fishbane also points to the correspondence of the "spiritual-historical continuities" implied in the typologies of the patterning in the patriarchal narratives in the rabbinic tradition (383).

to the plotted nature of the biblical narrative but fundamentally to the divine action in the patterning of time.

The term "typology" can therefore be used in a number of ways. At the very least, it can refer to (1) what a writer employs (a device), (2) what a text bears (a trope), (3) what a reader crafts (an interpretation), and (4) what the divine author communicates (an intention). I use the term in all of these ways, but I have learned from Paul to understand typology less as a literary trope (1–3) and more as a theological reality (4). As I have shown, Paul uses the term "allegory" to introduce his interpretation of Sarah and Hagar in chapter 4, implicitly relying on the structures of correspondence basic to typology: a type and its antitype.[21] A type is often (although not always) prior in the plot to its antitype. One classical example of this is Noah's ark (as a type) and the church (as its antitype).[22] Another example is the Levitical sacrifices (as types) and Christ's sacrifice on the cross (as their antitype).[23] In Galatians, Isaac as the promised son of Abraham is a type of Christ; Sarah is a type of the heavenly Jerusalem and therefore a type of the church.[24]

While types often function to link the Testaments as in the above examples, they sometimes function in intratestamental correspondence, linking two or more episodes within one of the testaments. We find this within the New Testament itself: the mark of election cut onto Jesus as his parents observe the rite for their son's circumcision (Luke 2:21; Gal. 4:4); the wounds carved into Jesus's flesh on the cross; and the marks cut onto Paul's body (Gal. 2:20; 3:1; 6:14, 17).[25]

But Paul never knew the earthly Jesus. The apostle to the Gentiles inhabits the post-crucifixion world, so Christ's wounds chronologically precede Paul's own. We might think therefore that Paul's wounds are antitypes of Jesus's wounds. If divinely ordered types were purely chronological, this would be the case. But Paul's wounds are types, not antitypes, of Christ's wounds. This is no small point. The antitype is ontologically, even sacramentally, present within

21. Frances M. Young calls typology a "modern construct," adding that ancient exegetes did not distinguish between it and allegory. Young, *Biblical Exegesis*, 152, 161.
22. The beginnings of this typology are in Heb. 11:7; 1 Pet. 3:20; 2 Pet. 2:5.
23. Jesus is the paschal lamb of John 19:36 that the author says fulfills prophecy, pointing to Exod. 12:46; Num. 9:12. The church sees these texts also as a type in the sacrifice of the Mass.
24. See my comments at 4:20 on the exegetical methods based on John Cassian's observations about the two cities of Jerusalem in Paul's allegory. For a rich set of reflections on the medieval fourfold interpretative strategy, see Froehlich and Burrows, *Sensing the Scriptures*.
25. For some examples of Paul's implicit use of typology in Galatians, and of typological readings of his own words, see my comments at Gal. 3:1, 13, 16, 27–28.

the type; antitypes are fundamentally sacramental. Jesus Christ is never a type of something or someone else; he is the ultimate antitype.[26] This christological hermeneutic governs Paul's proclamation to Galatians.[27]

The plotted movement of the gospel story is essentially at the heart of the last things: eschatology. And yet the claim to the typological nature of the gospel story does not deny the concreteness of lived human reality in the limits of the sundown and sunup of days.[28] But these limits of this concreteness of time itself are contested even within the first story of the Bible; the patterning of days in Gen. 1:5, 8, 13, 19, 23, 31 is ruptured at Gen. 2:2 as the mention of evening and morning retreats from the text. This points prophetically to the eschatological feature of Sabbath perfection. Time as a creation of God is itself typological, and as such it anticipates promise and fulfillment.

Remaining Questions

Unfortunately, there are many questions that my close reading of Galatians has raised but not addressed. First, because I think that the Galatian community is composed of Gentiles alone, I find that Paul uses the term "law" differently in Galatians than in Romans. The socioreligious contexts in these communities differ from one another. While no Jews are present in the churches of Galatia, the church in Rome is composed of both Gentiles and Jews. In Galatians, the phrase "works of the law" refers primarily to circumcision and secondarily to the law of Sinai, whereas in Romans the law refers not only to Sinai but to cosmic and psychic powers as well. Paul's appraisal of the law in each letter is different. What are we to make of this difference?

Another question left unaddressed is how best to refer to the largest portion of the Christian Bible, traditionally referred to as the Old Testament. Many have found the term pejorative, as though implying that the texts were

26. Although I doubt that Frei would have intended his remark to be used in this way, I do not think he would have objected: at the heart of his comments about the logical incoherence of the concept of Christ figures is this claim to the singular christological antitype. If Jesus is essentially a type of another person (e.g., myself) or another reality (e.g., self-acceptance), he is no longer the Jesus of the Gospels. Frei, "'Literal Reading' of Biblical Narrative," 72; see also Frei, *Identity of Jesus Christ*, 59, 63. Paul is not a Christ figure.

27. This logic underlies the suggestion that the gospel moves from "solution to plight" rather than vice versa. Sanders, *Paul, the Law, and the Jewish People*, 68; Sanders, *Paul and Palestinian Judaism*, 442–47, 474–511.

28. At creation, the sun sets before it rises: "And there was evening and there was morning, the first day" (Gen. 1:5).

outdated or even of inferior sacramental value. On a purely historical level the term Old Testament was first applied to the Septuagint by Melito of Sardis in a late second-century discussion of the number and ordering of its canonical books—that is, in authorizing and conferring honor rather than denigrating.[29] The term therefore was not first used in supersession, as though the new sublimated the old. Substitutions have been suggested for the term Old Testament: Hebrew Bible, Hebrew Scriptures, Jewish Scriptures, First Testament, Elder Testament, and so on. But the problem remains with us no matter which term we choose. Van Buren's question as to whether Christian use of the Old Testament is fundamentally "reading someone else's mail" remains a challenge.[30] To respond to this question in the affirmative is simply to misapprehend, or maybe to apprehend but be overcome by shame. In either case, one may have to relinquish a christological hermeneutic. The problem itself of how to refer to the first two-thirds of the Christian Bible is mired in the caricature ushered in when a christological hermeneutic is ruled out. What this means on a pastoral, ecclesial, and interreligious scene are separate questions that demand a further project.

Another important matter that my reading of Galatians has only briefly touched on is the question of a Christian understanding of Israel as theological elder sibling.[31] The concepts of typology and infrasession both assume a unity in differentiation between gospel and law. This can have positive ethical implications. Take, for example, the innerbiblical interpretation of the destruction of the temple and exile as punishment for the people's sin (Ezra 5:11–12). Where the church has understood Israel to be fundamentally other than herself, the danger becomes that Israel's sin is perceived as fundamentally other than the church's own. But where Christ "infrasedes" Israel, the church should understand Israel's failings to be hers also to confess and repent of, including her own of the additional two millennia.

Another question raised but not addressed here is how to understand Jewish Christianity in its contemporary forms in a predominantly Gentile church; this is the inverse of the situation in most of Paul's churches. I think here especially of Messianic Judaism, a phenomenon that, while near extinction, is vibrant where it does live.[32] Regarding Galatians, the question is reflected

29. Trobisch, *First Edition*, 44.
30. Van Buren, "On Reading Someone Else's Mail."
31. See Jonathan Sacks's understanding of "sibling rivalry" as the root cause of interreligious violence among the Abrahamic faiths. Sacks, *Not in God's Name*, 87–176.
32. On Jewish Christianity in the patristic period, see Simon, *Verus Israel*, 237–70. For a modern proposal, see Kinzer, *Postmissionary Messianic Judaism*.

in Paul's relationship with Peter. If it is true, as I suggest, that there were no Jews in Galatia, and Paul's remarks about circumcision applied only to Gentile circumcision, another question emerges: what is the theological status of circumcision for Jewish Christian male infants today? The first generation of Christians were Jews, and all of the first Christian males would have already been circumcised on the eighth day. This question would not have even entered Paul's mind.[33] While Paul does not address the problem, should we? If so, how?

Additionally, my reading of Paul teaches us nothing about the theological status of non-Christian Jews in our own day.[34] The least, and most, that I can say about this here is that in Galatians Paul is not engaged in Christian-against-Jewish rhetoric.[35] But this is not sufficient for our time. Likewise, given this close reading of Galatians, what might be an adequate Christian understanding of Abraham's promise of the land in specific? What is to be the church's relation to the land and state of Israel?[36] I regret that a commentary of this length and scope has not allowed me to address these important matters. I hope others after me will continue the conversation.

---

33. Wyschogrod, "Christianity and Mosaic Law," 456; →5:2.

34. See Commission for Religious Relations with the Jews, "The Gifts and the Calling of God Are Irrevocable (Rom. 11:29)," Catholic Culture, December 10, 2015, https://www.catholicculture.org/culture/library/view.cfm?recnum=11101.

35. Martyn, *Galatians*, 41n75.

36. This question is brought up in the context of the relationship between anti-Zionism and anti-Semitism in "The Jerusalem Declaration on Antisemitism," March 25, 2021, available at https://jerusalemdeclaration.org.

BIBLIOGRAPHY

Abasciano, Brian J. "Diamonds in the Rough: A Reply to Christopher Stanley Concerning the Reader Competency of Paul's Original Audiences." *Novum Testamentum* 9 (2007): 153–83.

Alter, Robert. *The Art of Biblical Narrative*. New York: Basic Books, 1981.

Anderson, Gary A. *Charity: The Place of the Poor in Biblical Tradition*. New Haven: Yale University Press, 2013.

Augustine. *Augustine's Commentary on Galatians*. Translated by Eric Plumer. Oxford: Oxford University Press, 2003.

———. *Sermons*. Translated by Edmund Hill. Edited by John E. Rotelle. Works of Saint Augustine III/8. Hyde Park, NY: New City, 1994.

Barclay, John M. G. *Paul and the Gift*. Grand Rapids: Eerdmans, 2015.

Barrett, C. K. "The Allegory of Abraham, Sarah, and Hagar in the Argument of Galatians." In *Essays on Paul*, 154–69. Philadelphia: Westminster, 1976.

———. *On Paul: Essays on His Life, Work, and Influence in the Early Church*. London: T&T Clark, 2003.

Bauckham, Richard. "James, Peter, and the Gentiles." In *The Missions of James, Peter, and Paul: Tensions in Early Christianity*, edited by Bruce Chilton and Craig Evans, 91–142. Boston: Brill, 2005.

———. *Jesus and the Eyewitnesses: The Gospels as Eyewitness Testimony*. Grand Rapids: Eerdmans, 2017.

———. *Jesus and the God of Israel: God Crucified and Other Studies on the New Testament's Christology of Divine Identity*. Grand Rapids: Eerdmans, 2009.

———. *The Jewish World around the New Testament*. Grand Rapids: Baker Academic, 2008.

Baur, F. C. *Paul, the Apostle of Jesus Christ*. 2 vols. London: Williams & Norgate, 1876.

Becker, Adam H., and Annette Yoshiko Reed, eds. *The Ways That Never Parted: Jews and Christians in Late Antiquity and the Early Middle Ages*. Minneapolis: Fortress, 2007.

Bedford, Nancy Elizabeth. *Galatians*. Belief: A Theological Commentary on the Bible. Louisville: Westminster John Knox, 2016.

Betz, Hans Dieter. *Galatians: A Commentary on Paul's Letter to the Churches in Galatia.* Hermeneia. Philadelphia: Fortress, 1979.

Blowers, Paul M. "The Regula Fidei and the Narrative Character of Early Christian Faith." *Pro Ecclesia* 6, no. 2 (1999): 199–228.

Bochet, Isabelle, and Michel Fédou, eds. *L'exégèse patristique de l'épître aux Galates.* Collection des Études augustiniennes. Paris: Institut d'Études Augustiniennes, 2014.

Bockmuehl, Markus. "God's Life as a Jew: Remembering the Son of God as Son of David." In *Seeking the Identity of Jesus: A Pilgrimage,* edited by Richard B. Hays and Beverly Roberts Gaventa, 60–78. Grand Rapids: Eerdmans, 2008.

———. *Jewish Law in Gentile Churches: Halakhah and the Beginning of Christian Public Ethics.* Grand Rapids: Baker, 2000.

———. *Simon Peter in Scripture and Memory: The New Testament Apostle in the Early Church.* Grand Rapids: Baker Academic, 2012.

———. "The Trouble with the Inclusive Jesus." *Horizons in Biblical Theology* 33 (2011): 9–23.

The Book of Common Prayer and Administration of the Sacraments and Other Rites and Ceremonies of the Church, according to the Use of the Episcopal Church. Oxford: Oxford University Press, 1979.

Boyarin, Daniel. *A Radical Jew: Paul and the Politics of Identity.* Contraversions. Berkeley: University of California Press, 1997.

Bray, Gerald L., ed. *Galatians, Ephesians.* Reformation Commentary on Scripture, New Testament 10. Downers Grove, IL: IVP Academic, 2009.

Brock, Rita Nakashima. *Journeys by Heart: A Christology of Erotic Power.* New York: Crossroad, 1988.

Bruce, F. F. *Paul: Apostle of the Heart Set Free.* Grand Rapids: Eerdmans, 2000.

Bunyan, John. *Grace Abounding to the Chief of Sinners.* 1666. Reprint, Cambridge: Cambridge University Press, 1907.

Byrskog, Samuel. *Story as History, History as Story: The Gospel Tradition in the Context of Ancient Oral History.* Wissenschaftliche Untersuchungen zum Neuen Testament 123. Tübingen: Mohr Siebeck, 2000.

Calvin, John. *The Epistles of Paul the Apostle to the Galatians, Ephesians, Philippians and Colossians.* Translated by T. H. L. Parker. Edited by David W. Torrance and Thomas F. Torrance. Calvin's Commentaries. Grand Rapids: Eerdmans, 1965.

———. *The Institutes of the Christian Religion.* Translated by John T. McNeil. Philadelphia: Westminster, 1960.

Catechism of the Catholic Church. Liguori, MO: Liguori, 1994.

Cohen, Shaye J. D. *The Beginnings of Jewishness: Boundaries, Varieties, Uncertainties.* Berkeley: University of California Press, 1999.

———. "The Origins of the Matrilineal Principle in Rabbinic Law." *AJS Review* 10 (1985): 19–53.

———. *Why Aren't Jewish Women Circumcised? Gender and Covenant in Judaism.* Berkeley: University of California Press, 2005.

Cohn-Sherbok, Dan, ed. *Holocaust Theology: A Reader.* New York: New York University Press, 2002.

Cone, James H. *The Cross and the Lynching Tree*. New York: Orbis Books, 2011.

Cooper, Stephen Andrew. *Marius Victorinus's Commentary on Galatians: Introduction, Translation, and Notes*. Oxford: Oxford University Press, 2005.

de Boer, M. C. "The Meaning of the Phrase τα στοιχεια του κοσμου in Galatians." *New Testament Studies* 53 (2007): 204–24.

DiMattei, Steven. "Biblical Narratives." In *As It Is Written: Studying Paul's Use of Scripture*, edited by Stanley E. Porter and Christopher D. Stanley, 59–93. Atlanta: Society of Biblical Literature, 2008.

———. "Paul's Allegory of the Two Covenants (Gal. 4:21–31) in Light of First-Century Hellenistic Rhetoric and Jewish Hermeneutics." *New Testament Studies* 52 (2006): 102–22.

Diogenes Laertius. *Lives of Eminent Philosophers*. Translated by R. D. Hicks. Cambridge, MA: Harvard University Press, 1966.

Dodd, C. H. *The Apostolic Preaching and Its Developments*. London: Hodder & Stoughton, 1944.

Downs, David J., and Benjamin J. Lappenga. *The Faithfulness of the Risen Christ: Pistis and the Exalted Lord in the Pauline Letters*. Waco: Baylor University Press, 2019.

Dunn, James D. G. *The Epistle to the Galatians*. Black's New Testament Commentaries. London: Black, 1993.

———. "The Incident at Antioch (Gal. 2:11–18)." In *The Galatians Debate*, edited by Mark D. Nanos, 199–234. Peabody, MA: Hendrickson, 2002.

———. *Jesus, the Law, and the Jewish People*. Louisville: Westminster John Knox, 1990.

———. *Jews and Christians: The Parting of the Ways, AD 70–135*. Grand Rapids: Eerdmans, 1992.

———. *The New Perspective on Paul: Collected Essays*. Grand Rapids: Eerdmans, 2008.

Eastman, Susan Grove. "Israel and the Mercy of God: A Re-reading of Galatians 6.16 and Romans 9–11." *New Testament Studies* 56 (2016): 367–95.

Edwards, Mark J., ed. *Galatians, Ephesians, Philippians*. Ancient Christian Commentary on Scripture, New Testament 8. Downers Grove, IL: InterVarsity, 2005.

Episcopal Church. *The Hymnal 1982*. New York: Church Pension Fund, 1985.

Epstein, Isidore, trans. *The Babylonian Talmud: Seder Kodashim*. London: Soncino, 1948.

Eusebius. *The Ecclesiastical History*. Translated by Kirsopp Lake. Loeb Classical Library 153. Cambridge, MA: Harvard University Press, 1980.

Farmer, William R., and Roch Kereszty. *Peter and Paul in the Church of Rome: The Ecumenical Potential of a Forgotten Perspective*. Theological Inquiries. New York: Paulist Press, 1990.

Fishbane, Michael. *Biblical Interpretation in Ancient Israel*. Oxford: Oxford University Press, 1985.

———. "Introduction." In *The JPS Bible Commentary: Haftarot*. Philadelphia: Jewish Publication Society, 2002.

Fitzmyer, Joseph A. *The Acts of the Apostles: A New Translation with Introduction and Commentary*. Anchor Bible 31. New Haven: Yale University Press, 1998.

Fredriksen, Paula. "Gods and the One God." Lecture presented at Yale Divinity School, Shaffer Lecture Series, February 17, 2020. Available at https://youtu.be/dTSR4bNlNT0.

————. "Judaism, the Circumcision of the Gentiles, and Apocalyptic Hope: Another Look at Galatians 1 and 2." In *The Galatians Debate*, edited by Mark D. Nanos, 235–60. Peabody, MA: Hendrickson, 2002.

Frei, Hans W. *The Eclipse of Biblical Narrative: A Study in Eighteenth and Nineteenth Century Hermeneutics*. New Haven: Yale University Press, 1974.

————. *The Identity of Jesus Christ: The Hermeneutical Bases of Dogmatic Theology*. Philadelphia: Fortress, 1975.

————. "The 'Literal Reading' of Biblical Narrative in the Christian Tradition: Does It Stretch or Will It Break?" In *The Bible and the Narrative Tradition*, edited by Frank McConnell, 36–77. Oxford: Oxford University Press, 1986.

Froehlich, Karlfried. "Fallibility Instead of Infallibility? A Brief History of the Interpretation of Galatians 2:11–14." In *Teaching Authority and Infallibility in the Church*, edited by Paul C. Empie, T. Austin Murphy, and Joseph A. Burgess, 259–69, 351–57. Lutherans and Catholics in Dialogue 6. Minneapolis: Augsburg, 1980.

Froehlich, Karlfried, with Mark S. Burrows. *Sensing the Scriptures: Aminadab's Chariot and the Predicament of Biblical Interpretation*. Grand Rapids: Eerdmans, 2014.

Gaventa, Beverly R. "Galatians 1 and 2: Autobiography as Paradigm." *Novum Testamentum* 28, no. 4 (1986): 309–26.

————. "The Maternity of St Paul: An Exegetical Study of Galatians 4:19." In *The Conversation Continues: Studies on St Paul and John in Honor of J. Louis Martyn*, edited by Robert T. Fortna and Beverly R. Gaventa, 189–201. Nashville: Abingdon, 1990.

Gerhardsson, Birger, and Eric J. Sharpe, trans. *Memory and Manuscript: Oral Tradition and Written Transmission in Rabbinic Judaism and Early Christianity*. Biblical Resource Series. Lund: Gleerup, 1961.

Ginzberg, Louis. *Legends of the Jews*. 7 vols. Philadelphia: Jewish Publication Society, 1909–1938.

Goodrich, John K. "Until the Fulness of the Gentiles Comes In: A Critical Review of Recent Scholarship on the Salvation of 'All Israel' (Romans 11:26)." *Journal for the Study of Paul and His Letters* 6, no. 1 (2016): 5–32.

Greenberg, Irving. "Judaism and Christianity: Covenants of Redemption." In *Christianity in Jewish Terms*, edited by Tikva Frymer-Kensky, David Novak, Peter Ochs, David Fox Sandmel, and Michael A. Signer, 141–58. Boulder: Westview, 2000.

Harink, Douglas. *Paul among the Postliberals: Pauline Theology beyond Christendom and Modernity*. Grand Rapids: Brazos, 2003.

Harker, Christina. *The Colonizers' Idols: Paul, Galatia, and Empire in New Testament Studies*. Tübingen: Mohr Siebeck, 2018.

Harmon, Matthew S. *She Must and Shall Go Free: Paul's Isaianic Gospel in Galatians*. Beihefte zur Zeitschrift für die neutestamentliche Wissenschaft. Berlin: de Gruyter, 2010.

HarperCollins Study Bible: New Revised Standard Version, with the Apocryphal/Deuterocanonical Books. Edited by Wayne A. Meeks. New York: HarperCollins, 1993.

Harrisville, Roy A., III. "*Pistis Christou*: Witness of the Fathers." *Novum Testamentum* 36 (1994): 233–41.

Hays, Richard B. *Echoes of Scripture in the Letters of Paul*. New Haven: Yale University Press, 1989.

————. *The Faith of Jesus Christ: The Narrative Substructure of Galatians 3:1–4:11*. Grand Rapids: Eerdmans, 2002.

Hengel, Martin, and Anna Maria Schwemer. *Paul between Damascus and Antioch: The Unknown Years*. Louisville: Westminster John Knox, 1997.

Herron, Thomas J. *Clement and the Early Church of Rome: On the Dating of Clement's First Epistle to the Corinthians*. Steubenville, OH: Emmaus Road, 2008.

Hertz, J. H. *The Authorised Daily Prayer Book*. New York: Bloch, 1948.

Hiestermann, Heinz. *Paul and the Synoptic Jesus Tradition*. Leipzig: Evangelische Verlag, 2017.

Hill, Robert Charles, trans. *Theodoret of Cyrus: Commentaries on the Letters of St. Paul*. 2 vols. Brookline, MA: Holy Cross Orthodox Press, 2001.

Hill, Wesley. *Paul and the Trinity: Persons, Relations, and the Pauline Letters*. Grand Rapids: Eerdmans, 2015.

Howard, George E. "Faith of Christ." In *Anchor Bible Dictionary*, edited by David Noel Freedman, 758–60. Vol. 2. New Haven: Yale University Press, 1992.

Hunsinger, George. *Philippians*. Brazos Theological Commentary on the Bible. Grand Rapids: Brazos, 2020.

Ignatius. *Letter to the Romans*. In *The Apostolic Fathers*. Vol. 1. Translated by Kirsopp Lake. Loeb Classical Library 24. Cambridge, MA: Harvard University Press, 1985.

Jerome. *Commentary on Galatians*. Translated by Adam Cain. Fathers of the Church. Washington, DC: Catholic University of America Press, 2010.

————. *St. Jerome's Commentaries on Galatians, Titus, and Philemon*. Translated by Thomas P. Scheck. Notre Dame, IN: University of Notre Dame Press, 2010.

Jovanović, Zdravko. "St. Irenaeus, *Regula Fidei*, and the Ecclesiological Context of Interpretation." *Philotheos* 13 (2013): 134–40.

Kahl, Brigitte. *Galatians Re-imagined: Reading with the Eyes of the Vanquished*. Minneapolis: Fortress, 2010.

Kähler, Martin. *The So-Called Historical Jesus and the Historic Biblical Christ*. Translated by Carl Braaten. Minneapolis: Fortress, 1988.

Kaminsky, Joel, and Mark Reasoner. "The Meaning and Telos of Israel's Election: An Interfaith Response to N. T. Wright's Reading of Paul." *Harvard Theological Review* 112 (2019): 421–46.

Keener, Craig S. *Galatians: A Commentary*. Grand Rapids: Baker Academic, 2019.

Kinzer, Mark S. *Postmissionary Messianic Judaism: Redefining Christian Engagement with the Jewish People*. Grand Rapids: Brazos, 2005.

Kittel, Gerhard, and Gerhard Friedrich, eds. *Theological Dictionary of the New Testament*. Translated by Geoffrey W. Bromiley. 10 vols. Grand Rapids: Eerdmans, 1964–1976.

Klausner, Joseph. *From Jesus to Paul*. Translated by William F. Stinespring. New York: Macmillan, 1943.

Klein, Charlotte. *Anti-Judaism in Christian Theology*. London: SPCK, 1978.

Kugel, James L., and Rowan A. Greer. *Early Biblical Interpretation*. Library of Early Christianity 3. Philadelphia: Westminster, 1986.

Leith, John H., ed. *Creeds of the Churches: A Reader in Christian Doctrine, from the Bible to the Present*. Atlanta: John Knox, 1982.

Lessing, Gotthold Ephraim. *Lessing's Theological Writings*. Translated by Henry Chadwick. Library of Modern Religious Thought. Stanford, CA: Stanford University Press, 1957.

Levine, Amy-Jill, and Marc Zvi Brettler, eds. *The Jewish Annotated New Testament*. Oxford: Oxford University Press, 2011.

Levy, Ian Christopher, trans. and ed. *The Letter to the Galatians*. Bible in Medieval Tradition. Grand Rapids: Eerdmans, 2011.

Lewis, C. S. *Reflections on the Psalms*. New York: Harcourt, Brace, 1958.

Lightfoot, J. B. *The Epistle of St. Paul to the Galatians: With Introductions, Notes, and Dissertations*. 1865. Reprint, Grand Rapids: Zondervan, 1957.

Lindbeck, George A. "What of the Future? A Christian Response." In *Christianity in Jewish Terms*, edited by Tikva Frymer-Kensky, David Novak, Peter Ochs, David Fox Sandmel, and Michael A. Signer, 357–66. Boulder: Westview, 2000.

Longenecker, Bruce W. *Remember the Poor: Paul, Poverty, and the Greco-Roman World*. Grand Rapids: Eerdmans, 2010.

Luedemann, Gerd. *Paul, the Founder of Christianity*. Amherst, NY: Prometheus, 2002.

Luther, Martin. *Lectures on Galatians 1535, Chapters 1–4*. Vol. 26 of *Luther's Works*. Translated and edited by Jaroslav Pelikan and Walter A. Hansen. St. Louis: Concordia, 1963.

———. *Lectures on Galatians 1535, Chapters 5–6; Lectures on Galatians 1519, Chapters 1–6*. Vol. 27 of *Luther's Works*. Translated and edited by Jaroslav Pelikan and Walter A. Hansen. St. Louis: Concordia, 1964.

Martyn, J. Louis. *Galatians: A New Translation with Introduction and Commentary*. Anchor Bible 33A. New York: Doubleday, 1997.

———. "A Law-Observant Mission to the Gentiles." In *The Galatians Debate*, edited by Mark D. Nanos, 348–61. Peabody, MA: Hendrickson, 2002.

Mason, Steve. "Jews, Judaeans, Judaizing, Judaism: Problems of Categorization in Ancient History." *Journal for the Study of Judaism in the Persian, Hellenistic, and Roman Periods* 38, no. 4 (2007): 457–512.

Matera, Frank J. *Galatians*. Edited by Daniel J. Harrington. Sacra Pagina. Collegeville, MN: Liturgical Press, 1992.

McDonald, Lee Martin. *Formation of the Bible: The Story of the Church's Canon*. Peabody, MA: Hendrickson, 2012.

Meeks, Wayne A. "The Image of the Androgyne: Some Uses of a Symbol in Early Christianity." *History of Religions* 13, no. 3 (1974): 165–208.

———. *The Origins of Christian Morality: The First Two Centuries*. New Haven: Yale University Press, 1993.

Millar, Fergus. *The Roman New East 31 BC–AD 337*. Cambridge, MA: Harvard University Press, 1993.

Millard, Matthias. "Die rabbinischen noachidischen Gebote und das biblische Gebot Gottes an Noah: Ein Beitrag zur Methodendiskusion." *Wort und Dienst* 23 (1995): 71–90.

Müller, Klaus. *Tora für die Völker: Die noachidischen Gebote und Ansätze zu ihrer Rezeption im Christentum*. 2nd ed. Studien zu jüdischen Volk und christlicher Gemeinde 15. Berlin: Institut Kirche und Judentum, 1998.

Nanos, Mark D. *The Galatians Debate*. Peabody, MA: Hendrickson, 2002.

Neusner, Jacob, and Richard S. Sarason, eds. *The Tosefta: First Division, Zeraim*. Hoboken, NJ: Ktav, 1986.

Niebuhr, H. Richard. *The Meaning of Revelation*. New York: Macmillan, 1946.

Novak, David. *The Election of Israel: The Idea of the Chosen People*. Cambridge: Cambridge University Press, 1995.

————. *The Image of the Non-Jew in Judaism: The Idea of Noahide Law*. Edited by Matthew Lagrone. Portland, OR: Litman Library of Jewish Civilization, 2011.

————. "Supersessionism Hard and Soft." *First Things* 290 (February 2019): 27–31. https://www.firstthings.com/article/2019/02/supersessionism-hard-and-soft.

Novenson, Matthew V. "Paul's Former Occupation in *Ioudaismos*." In *Galatians in Christian Theology*, edited by Mark W. Elliott, Scott J. Hafemann, N. T. Wright, and John Frederick, 24–39. Grand Rapids: Baker Academic, 2014.

Oakes, Peter. *Galatians*. Paideia. Grand Rapids: Baker Academic, 2015.

Pauck, Wilhelm, trans. *Melanchthon and Bucer*. Library of Christian Classics. Philadelphia: Westminster, 1969.

Perkins, William. *A Commentary on Galatians*. Edited by Gerald T. Sheppard. Pilgrim Classic Commentaries. New York: Pilgrim, 1989.

Pitre, Brant. *Jesus and the Jewish Roots of Mary: Unveiling the Mother of the Messiah*. New York: Image, 2018.

Ramsay, W. M. *A Historical Commentary on St Paul's Epistle to the Galatians*. New York: Putnam, 1900.

Richards, E. Randolph. *Paul and First-Century Letter Writing: Secretaries, Composition, and Collection*. Downers Grove, IL: InterVarsity, 2004.

Riches, John. *Galatians through the Centuries*. Blackwell Bible Commentaries. Malden, MA: Blackwell, 2008.

Robinson, Thomas A. *Ignatius of Antioch and the Parting of the Ways: Early Jewish-Christian Relations*. Peabody, MA: Hendrickson, 2009.

Roetzel, Calvin J. *The Letters of Paul: Conversations in Context*. Louisville: Westminster John Knox, 2015.

Rowe, Kavin. "Biblical Pressure and Trinitarian Hermeneutics." *Pro Ecclesia* 11, no. 3 (2002): 295–312.

Ruether, Rosemary Radford. *Faith and Fratricide: The Theological Roots of Anti-Semitism*. New York: Seabury, 1974.

Sacks, Jonathan. *Not in God's Name: Confronting Religious Violence*. New York: Schocken Books, 2015.

Sanders, E. P. *Paul, the Law, and the Jewish People*. Philadelphia: Fortress, 1983.

————. *Paul and Palestinian Judaism: A Comparison of Patterns of Religion*. Philadelphia: Fortress, 1977.

Sandmel, Samuel. *A Jewish Understanding of the New Testament*. New York: University Publishers, 1960.

Sanneh, Lamin. *Translating the Message: The Missionary Impact on Culture.* American Society of Missiology Series 42. Maryknoll, NY: Orbis Books, 2009.

Schiffman, Lawrence. "The Early History of Public Reading of the Torah." In *Jews, Christians, and Polytheists in the Ancient Synagogue,* edited by Steven Fine, 44–55. New York: Routledge, 1999.

Schoeps, Hans Joachim. *Paul: The Theology of the Apostle in the Light of Jewish Religious History.* Philadelphia: Westminster, 1961.

Schwartz, Seth. "How Many Judaisms Were There?" *Journal of Ancient Judaism* 2 (2011): 208–38.

Schweitzer, Albert. *The Mysticism of Paul the Apostle.* Translated by B. D. Montgomery William. New York: Seabury, 1968.

Schweizer, Eduard. "What Do We Really Mean When We Say 'God Sent His Son'?" In *Faith and History: Essays in Honor of Paul W. Meyer,* edited by John T. Carroll and Charles H. Cosgrove, 298–312. Atlanta: Scholars Press, 1990.

Scroggs, Robin. "Paul and the Eschatological Woman." *Journal of the American Academy of Religion* 40, no. 3 (1972): 283–303.

Senn, Frank C. *Christian Liturgy: Catholic and Evangelical.* Minneapolis: Fortress, 1997.

Silva, Moisés. "The Text of Galatians: Evidence from the Earliest Greek Manuscripts." In *Scribes and Scriptures: Essays in Honor of J. Harold Greenlee,* edited by David Alan Bloch, 17–25. Winona Lake, IN: Eisenbrauns, 1992.

Simon, Marcel. "The Apostolic Decree and Its Setting in the Ancient Church." *Bulletin of the John Rylands Library, Manchester University* 52, no. 2 (1970): 437–60.

———. *Verus Israel: A Study of the Relations between Christians and Jews in the Roman Empire AD 135–425.* Translated by H. McKeating. London: Littman Library of Jewish Civilization, 1986.

Sonderegger, Katherine. "The Doctrine of Justification and the Cure of Souls." In *Disruptive Grace: Studies in the Theology of Karl Barth,* edited by George Hunsinger, 167–81. Grand Rapids: Eerdmans, 2000.

Soulen, R. Kendall. *The God of Israel and Christian Theology.* Minneapolis: Fortress, 1996.

Stendahl, Krister. *Paul among Jews and Gentiles, and Other Essays.* Philadelphia: Fortress, 1976.

Stern, David H. *Jewish New Testament Commentary.* Clarksville, MD: Jewish New Testament Publications, 1992.

Sullivan, Ruth. "Saints Peter and Paul: Some Ironic Aspects of Their Imaging." *Art History* 17, no. 1 (March 1994): 59–80.

Swain, Scott R. "Heirs through God: Galatians 4:4–7 and the Doctrine of the Trinity." In *Galatians and Christian Theology: Justification, the Gospel, and Ethics in Paul's Letter,* edited by Mark W. Elliott, 258–70. Grand Rapids: Eerdmans, 2014.

Sweeney, Marvin. *Reading the Hebrew Bible after the Shoah: Engaging Holocaust Theology.* Minneapolis: Fortress, 2008.

Theodoret of Cyrus. *Commentary on the Letters of St. Paul.* 2 vols. Translated by Robert Charles Hill. Brookline, MA: Holy Cross Orthodox Press, 2001.

Thiessen, Matthew. *Paul and the Gentile Problem.* Oxford: Oxford University Press, 2016.

Trobisch, David. "The Council of Jerusalem in Acts 15 and Paul's Letter to the Galatians." In *Theological Exegesis: Essays in Honor of Brevard S. Childs*. Edited by Kathryn Greene-McCreight and Christopher Seitz. Grand Rapids: Eerdmans, 1999.

———. *The First Edition of the New Testament*. Oxford: Oxford University Press, 2000.

Updike, John. "Seven Stanzas at Easter." In *John Updike: Selected Poems*, edited by Christopher Carduff, 15. New York: Alfred A. Knopf, 1960.

van Buren, Paul M. "On Reading Someone Else's Mail: The Church and Israel's Scripture." In *Die Hebräische Bibel und ihre zweifäche Nachgeschichte*, edited by Erhard Blum, 595–606. Neukirchen-Vluyn: Neukirchener Verlag, 1990.

———. *A Theology of the Jewish-Christian Reality*. San Francisco: Harper & Row, 1980–1988.

von Campenhausen, Hans. *The Formation of the Christian Bible*. Translated by J. A. Baker. Philadelphia: Fortress, 1972.

von Rad, Gerhard. *Old Testament Theology*. 2 vols. San Francisco: HarperSanFrancisco, 1962.

Wallis, Ian G. *The Faith of Jesus Christ in Early Christian Traditions*. Society for New Testament Studies Monograph Series. Cambridge: Cambridge University Press, 1995.

Westerholm, Stephen. *Perspectives Old and New on Paul: The "Lutheran" Paul and His Critics*. Grand Rapids: Eerdmans, 2004.

Wheeler, Sondra Ely. *Wealth as Peril and Obligation: The New Testament on Possessions*. Grand Rapids: Eerdmans, 1995.

White, Carolinne. *The Correspondence (394–419) between Jerome and Augustine of Hippo*. Lewiston, NY: Mellen, 1990.

Wiley, Tatha. *Paul and the Gentile Women: Reframing Galatians*. New York: Continuum, 2005.

Wilken, Robert Louis. "*Fides Caritate Formata*: Faith Formed by Love." *Nova et Vetera*, English Edition 9 (2011): 1089–1100.

Williamson, Clark. *A Guest in the House of Israel*. Louisville: Westminster John Knox, 1993.

Witherington, Ben, III. *Grace in Galatia: A Commentary on St. Paul's Letter to the Galatians*. Grand Rapids: Eerdmans, 1998.

Wright, N. T. *The Climax of the Covenant: Christ and the Law in Pauline Theology*. Minneapolis: Fortress, 1992.

———. *Galatians*. Commentaries for Christian Formation. Grand Rapids: Eerdmans, 2021.

———. *Paul and the Faithfulness of God*. Christian Origins and the Question of God 4. Minneapolis: Fortress, 2013.

———. *Pauline Perspectives: Essays on Paul, 1978–2013*. Minneapolis: Fortress, 2013.

Wyschogrod, Michael. *The Body of Faith: Judaism as Corporeal Election*. New York: Seabury, 1983.

———. "Christianity and Mosaic Law." *Pro Ecclesia* 2, no. 4 (1993): 451–59.

Yeago, David S. "The New Testament and Nicene Dogma: A Contribution to the Recovery of Theological Exegesis." *Pro Ecclesia* 3, no. 2 (1994): 152–64.

Young, Frances M. *Biblical Exegesis and the Formation of Christian Culture*. Cambridge: Cambridge University Press, 1997.

Zucker, David J. "Sarah: The View of the Classical Rabbis." In *Perspectives on Our Father Abraham: Essays in Honor of Marvin R. Wilson*, edited by Steven A. Hunt, 221–52. Grand Rapids: Eerdmans, 2010.

SCRIPTURE INDEX

197

SUBJECT INDEX

abba, 109–10, 112
Abraham
  and circumcision, 68–69, 71
  covenant with, 5, 67, 71,
    76–77, 83, 105, 163
  as covenantal name, 82
  election of, 51
  faith of, 66–72, 78
  as interpretive key to Gentile
    inclusion, 67–73, 76, 83
  offspring of, 77–78
Abram
  covenant with, 63
  election of, 81
  as Gentile, 68, 80
  name change of, 82
Acts of Paul and Thecla, 47
adoption, 89, 109
allegory of the two mothers,
  118–30
  as ecclesiological, 121–23
  and election, 116, 121, 123
  128
  and prophecy of Isaiah,
    126–27
  relationship of brothers in,
    127–28
  and universal covenant, 177
Ambrosiaster, 25, 112
Antioch, controversy at, 40–43
Arabia, 20–21, 26
atonement, doctrine of, 9,
  58–59

Augustine
  on Antioch controversy, 43
  on Christ as mediator of the
    law, 86
  deer analogy of, 159–60
  on faith working through
    love, 139
  on the law, 88–89
  on Peter and Paul, 47–48
Augustine of Dacia, 121

baptism
  clothing imagery of, 90
  in early Christian art, 90
  and identity in Christ, 93–94
  typology of, 90
  gender differences and,
    95–96
Barnabas, 30–32
Barth, Karl, 76
Bauer, F. C., 176n2
burdens, bearing of, 158–61,
  164, 170

Cassian, John
  on allegory of the two
    mothers, 121
  on senses of scripture, 121
  on two Jerusalems, 125–26
Christ
  as antitype of the law, 105
  as content of the law, 86–87
  crucifixion with, 56–57

and curse of the cross, 70–74
  identity in, 90–95
  preexistence of, 103
  as seed of Abraham, 79,
    96–97
  See also Jesus of Nazareth
Christology, Chalcedonian,
  5, 53, 76
churches, Galatian. *See* Galatian churches
circumcision, 2–3, 16, 35, 45,
  134–39, 143–44, 168–69
  and adoption, 89
  and controversy at Antioch,
    41–42
  as denial of the gospel, 115
  and election, 3–4, 18, 49,
    70, 82–83, 116
  as sign of covenant, 4, 34,
    50–51, 71
circumcision faction, 41–42,
  44–45
Clement, 47
Commandments, Ten, 147–49
Constantinople, Second
  Council of, 13, 25
covenant, 93, 106, 119
  with Abraham, 5, 67, 71,
    76–77
  chronology of, 82, 84, 100,
    138, 176–77
  circumcision as sign of, 4,
    34, 50–51, 71

201